Past, Present, and Future

A READING-WRITING COURSE 4TH EDITION

JOAN YOUNG GREGG
New York City Technical College
of the City University of New York

JOAN RUSSELL
New York City Technical College
of the City University of New York

HEINLE & HEINLE PUBLISHERS
An International Thomson Publishing Company I(T)P
Boston, Massachusetts 02116

To our parents:
Mollie Silverman
Sylvia and Harry Young

The publication of *Past, Present, & Future*, Fourth Edition was directed by the members of the Newbury House Publishing Team at Heinle & Heinle:

Erik Gundersen, Editorial Director
John F. McHugh, Market Development Director
Kristin Thalheimer, Production Services Coordinator

Also participating in the publication of this program were:
Publisher: Stanley J. Galek
Director of Production: Elizabeth Holthaus
Project Manager: Mary Reed, Imageset Design
Senior Assistant Editor: Ken Pratt
Production Editor: Maryellen Eschmann
Production Assistant: Lisa Winkler
Manufacturing Coodinator: Mary Beth Hennebury
Photo/Video Specialist: Jonathan Stark
Photo Researcher: Philippe Heckly
Interior Designer and Compositor: Imageset Design
Illustrator: Charles Martin
Cover Artist: Gina Petti, Rotunda Design

Art /Photo Credits:: pp. 1, 32, 104, 164, 195, 227, 270 Joan Gregg; pp. 2, 5, 9, 32 Richard Kenefick; pp. 2, 51 The Province of British Columbia; pp. 2, 24, 28 Joan Russell; p. 16 Tony Gahanle; p. 32 Catherine Clark-Nelson; p. 32 Audrey Cody; p. 32 King Kong; p. 32 Heather McLean; p. 32 Elayne Rinn; p. 32 Evelyn Feliz; p. 32; pp. 32, 90, 98, 168 United Nations; p. 37 UN photo/Shelly Rotner; pp. 42, 144, 265 Superstock; pp. 46, 82, 170 Charles Martin; pp. 55, 57, 178 NY Public Library; p. 61 NASA; pp. 64, 70, 164, 216, 219 John Gregg; pp. 65, 243 Serena Nanda; pp. 83, 85 International Business Machines Corporation; pp. 89, 161, 237, 269, 272 Jonathan Stark; p. 90 NY Public Library/Gunther Holtorf; p. 111 Southhampton University, England; p. 116 Pierpont Morgan Library/Art Resource; p. 118 Gallaudet College; p. 121 Deena Burton; p. 131 The National Archives; p. 140 Rhoden Studios; p. 147 Joseph Tenga p. 164 Tom Monaster/Guide Dog Foundation for the Blind; p. 173 Brooklyn Friends School; p. 174 Chicago Historical Society; p. 32 Vasser College; p. 205 Nebraska Historical Society; p. 213 Bob Dammich; p. 222 Eliza Pacheco; p. 227 Pamela Harrison; p. 240 Jeffry W. Myers Photos.

Printed in the United States of America

Library of Congress Cataloging-in-Publication Data

Gregg, Joan Young.
    Past, present, and future: a reading-writing course / Joan Young Gregg, Joan Russell.—4th ed.
        p. cm.
    ISBN 0-8384-5282-5
        1. English language—Textbooks for foreign speakers. I. Russell, Joan, 1929– . II. Title.
PE 1128.G66 1996   95-45910
428.2'4—dc20   CIP

0-8384-5282-5
10 9 8 7 6 5 4 3 2

CONTENTS

Chapter Two
The Diversity of North America   32

Native Americans, settlers of the past, and recent immigrants make for a fascinating diversity in Canada and the United States.

Chapter Three
Steps to the Future   61

If we want to preserve our unspoiled wilderness lands and the green spaces in our cities, we cannot continue the irresponsible activities that are destroying our environment.

Unit II   Our World of Language

Chapter Four
Echoes of the Past   90

*From gestures to hieroglyphics, picture writing to our modern
alphabet, this reading traces some important developments in the
history of written language.*

Unit III Our Social World

Chapter Seven
Women of the American Past   **174**

PREFACE

Past, Present, & Future, Fourth Edition, is a reading and writing program designed for intermediate level of English as a second or foreign language (ESL/EFL). Through extensive writing and composing exercises, students will develop competence in expressing their ideas, describing their environment, and narrating personal events using basic English structures and sentence patterns.

For advanced level students, consider *Communication & Culture* by Joan Young Gregg. Modeled after the approach taken with *Past, Present, & Future, Communication & Culture* reviews and expands upon the lessons learned at the intermediate level with the former text.

The readings in *Past, Present, & Future* are thematically related within each of the three units. The themes of the reading selections are also the subject of the accompanying writing and composition assignments. Vocabulary is recycled throughout the units, and students are provided with an academically oriented information base for oral and written work.

This revision has a number of significant changes from the previous edition. Several new readings replace earlier ones; others have been revised to include current information. In response to reviewer suggestions, an additional adapted short story has been included. The text has been streamlined in a number of ways. First, the grammar targets in the Writing Exercise sections of several chapters have been reduced in order to sharpen the focus of these chapters. Instruction in pronouns, for example, was duplicated in the Reading and Writing Exercise sections of the previous edition. In this revision, the pronoun chart has been removed to the appendix, where it can serve as a reference for students, and drill on pronouns is limited to the appearance of this target in the Reading section. Instruction on article use has been brought together from various chapters into one, utilizing revised material formerly in the appendix. Second, the number of exercises for several of the grammar targets has been reduced to bring the proportion of sentence level practice into a better balance with the composing work and to eliminate certain items which the reviewers found less useful than others. The number of items in selected reading and grammar exercises has been shortened where reviewer comments suggested that this would be appropriate. Third, the Additional Readings are limited to reading and vocabulary exercises to retain the emphasis of these sections on reading skills development, which was their original purpose. Discussion and Information questions have also been revised and reformatted for greater clarity.

THE ORGANIZATION OF THE TEXT

As evidenced in the table of contents, *Past, Present, & Future* is divided into three units. Each unit contains three chapters, whose main reading passages are loosely related to the past, the present, and the future. Additional readings, with their own condensed apparatus, follow the main section of each chapter. Each main section is arranged in the following way.

Prereading

Varied cognitive activities engage the student with the theme of the chapter and provide motivation for the reading passage and the comprehension exercises.

Free Write

A free-write assignment allows the student to write for discovery on some aspect of the chapter's theme or serves as a warmup to composition. Free writing encourages the student to compose freely without worrying about sentence level correctness or specific types of organization.

Vocabulary in Context

This preliminary vocabulary exercise directs attention to the words that comprise the New Word list and are the basis of the Vocabulary exercises. Here the student is encouraged to find meanings by using context clues.

Reading Passage

The focus of the reading passages is some subject or issue that relates to the overall theme of the unit. The level of the reading passages is, in general, more difficult than the writing exercises because our experience and the professional literature suggests that most viable college ESL students are able to read at a higher level of proficiency than they are able to write. Each reading passage is followed by a comprehension exercise of a cumulative type, such as summarizing.

Reacting to the Reading

Following each reading passage are questions for discussion that tap both the student's own experience and the information presented in the passage. These questions are usually more conceptually challenging than the level of the material presented in the writing exercises because many ESL college students are mature adults with a wide variety of life experiences and an ability to express complex ideas, albeit in imperfect English. The principles of fluency and communication rather than that of correctness underlie these questions. Although instructors may wish to use the material from the

oral discussions as a basis for essay writing, it is not necessary nor always appropriate to do so. The discussion questions are valuable in and of
themselves as a base for student interaction and as a simulation of mainstream academic settings.

Reading Comprehension

In this section, students practice both literal and inferential reading skills. They learn to recognize paragraph topics, central ideas, significant details, and supporting examples, as well as understand the more basic paragraph patterns such as development by time order, spatial arrangement, and enumeration of reasons. Several chapters include more general academic study skills such as outlining or summarizing. Students are encouraged to apply the skills learned in the reading comprehension exercises to their composing processes as well.

Vocabulary

A New Word list directs attention to selected words in the reading passage and provides a number of exercises for their receptive and productive use. It is helpful for the instructor to pronounce these words aloud with the students and encourage them to use them in their own writing. Both dictionary work and contextual and semantic strategies are incorporated in the various vocabulary exercises. Each vocabulary section offers a special word family activity for broader vocabulary enrichment.

Language Focus

The structures comprising this section reflect current consensus about those items that form the foundation of ESL writing or the first half of an ESL "grammar" course. Emphasis is on basic tenses; sentence boundaries, components, and word order; and signal expressions and clause markers necessary for coherence at this introductory level. Although many exercises in this section operate at the sentence level, they compel the student to apply linguistic principles, make choices, and master sentence-level correctness as a prelude to writing longer connected discourse. Review of such items as articles, pronouns, and prepositions is included throughout, but the material is not intended to be comprehensive because most college ESL students have studied these items before.

Composing Process

There is increased emphasis in this edition on brainstorming and clustering as prewriting activities, and students are encouraged to see writing as a multidrafting process, with editing for correctness the last of several steps. As any instructor who incorporates process approaches in his or her teaching recognizes, however, it is almost a paradox to speak of encapsulating process writing within the covers of a text. Because ESL students at this level often come from educational systems where composing is not part of the English curriculum, we have tried to provide some guidance and structure in the activities that comprise this section. Instructors will be the best judges of the degree to which their students will benefit from the topic frameworks provided by the text.

Brainstorming, the process of generating subtopics and details for an essay by jotting down the ideas that come to mind in regard to a given topic, may be done by students individually or by the class as a whole, with all the items listed in the chalkboard.

Clustering, the step following brainstorming, groups items together in some logical organization (depending on the assignment) to serve as an informal outline or basis for the essay. Because clustering is probably a new activity for many ESL students, and one that taps cognitive skills that may not be developed to the same degree, this activity is best done, at least for the first few essays, as a class, with the instructor using the chalkboard to display the students' responses.

Appendices

Appendix A contains a basic terminology for English-language study and a list of principal parts of irregular verbs.

Appendix B contains the paragraph corrections symbols sheet. Instructors may wish to mark the symbols from the paragraph corrections symbol sheet in the margin or body of the student's essay, or they may simply circle or underline the points at which the error occurs and direct the student to the paragraph corrections symbols sheet to determine the nature of the error and the means of correcting it. Students should spend at least a short period immediately following the return of their papers making the corrections as a prelude to rewriting. This process can be done in pairs so that students can help each other before turning to the instructor as a last resort for corrections. This pair-correction process adds an oral/aural dimension to composition correction and reinforces the idea that writing is communication with another.

ACKNOWLEDGMENTS

It gives us great pleasure to acknowledge the contributions of our colleagues at New York City Technical College who have provided us with valuable insights in language skills instruction. We would also like to acknowledge our colleagues in TESOL, who have been so generous in sharing their ideas at conferences and in publications.

We are especially grateful to Margaret Maron for her contribution to the reading, "Witching for Water," and to Serena Nanda, Paisley Gregg, and Richard Kenefick for their contributions to other reading selections in this revision.

Reviewers to whom we are thankful for their constructive suggestions are:
    Judith García, Miami-Dade Community College
    Jan Thoele, Monterey Peninsula College
    Richard Nitshe, Monterey Peninsula College
    Carolyn DuPaquier, California State University, Fullerton
    John Avery, Pacific Lutheran University
    Phillip Winfield, New York City Technical College
    Brad Stocker, Miami-Dade Community College
    Allan Jacobson, Los Angeles Harbor College
    Elsa Luciano, University of Puerto Rico at Arecibo

UNIT I

Our
Diverse World

CHAPTER ONE

UNCOVERING THE PAST

I PREREADING

Class Discussion.   These pictures show things from earlier times. How are they similar to things that we have today? How are they different? What are some ways we can find out about the past?

FREE WRITE

A museum visit can be an enjoyable experience. Write about a museum you have explored. Tell what kind of museum it is. Describe the objects you enjoyed looking at, and explain why they impressed you.

Vocabulary in Context. The words in this exercise will appear in the reading passage. Circle the word(s) in the second sentence that mean the same as the italicized word in the first sentence. The first one is done for you.

1. How do we show *respect* for the people of the past? Museums pay (honor) to their memory by displaying their art.

2. *Recently,* a show of African art opened in Chicago. The objects were created not too long ago by Nigerian artists.

3. Some people prefer to see *ancient* art and objects. They can go to a museum of archeology where the works of the distant past are shown.

4. The Archeological Museum in Mexico City tells the history of Mexico's Indian *ancestors.* All Mexicans are proud of the creations of their forebears.

5. New York's Museum of Natural History is an *extraordinary* place. Visitors can see the remarkable display of dinosaur skeletons and other creations from the world of nature.

6. The objects of the past can *reveal* the life of the past. Human and animal bones can tell us something about life before written records.

7. The museums of New York are often *crowded.* During the week they are packed with schoolchildren.

8. Museum visitors like to *examine* the objects carefully. But it is often difficult to look closely at them when the exhibit is crowded.

9. Loud talking in museums *disturbs* some people. It interferes with their concentration on the displays.

10. Museums *preserve* art and the physical remains of life. Museums save the creations of people and of nature so that we can better understand our world.

II   READING

Archeology: Making the Bones Speak

[1]   Have you ever seen an Egyptian mummy or the skeleton of an ancient human being in a museum? Archeologists and other researchers all over the world have discovered these remains and brought them to museums to study. When ancient human skeletons are carefully examined, they reveal information about how people of the past lived and died. Archeologists believe that as people of the present and the future should learn about the dead in order to understand the culture of the past.

[2]   Archeologists "make the bones speak." They use measurements, X-rays, and chemical tests to get answers to their questions: Which are males, and which are females? How many are children? How old were the people when they died? What foods did they eat? What diseases did they have? For example, did they suffer from arthritis or tooth decay? What medicines did the people use? Did they die in a war or of natural causes? Did they live well, or did they live poor, hardworking lives? With the answers to these questions, archeologists can give us a picture of a whole society of ancestors.

[3]   Some groups of people, however, are against the study of their ancestors' remains. One such group is the Native Americans* of the United States. Museums all over the United States hold great numbers of Native American human remains. For example, the Smithsonian Institution in Washington, D.C., has about 18,500 human bones in its collection. Many Native Americans now want the museums to return the bones of their ancestors for reburial. They believe that when museum researchers study these bones, they disturb their ancestors' spirits. As long as the spirits are suffering, the living will suffer too. To Native Americans, digging, collecting, and studying ancient bones are acts of disrespect. Archeologists believe that ancient bones belong to the whole human race, but Native Americans feel that the bones of their ancestors belong only to them. Now museum directors must decide the right thing to do about these collections.

[4]   African-Americans have also faced this problem concerning *their* ancestors. Recently, an extraordinary discovery was made beneath the crowded streets of lower Manhattan in New York City. When a street was cleared to construct a new building, archeologists uncovered the African Burial Ground. This was a cemetery for African slaves that was used during the 1700s. The cemetery covers a large area under many city streets. Here in one section of it archeologists unearthed the graves of over 400 Africans. Some skeletons lay with coins in their hands or over their eyes, perhaps to pay for the journey to the next life. One had a seashell next to the head. Perhaps this relates to the traditional saying: "By the sea we came, and by the sea we shall go." One body was found with the gold buttons of a uniform. Perhaps this man was a soldier in the

*Formerly called American Indians

A view of the African Burial Ground as imagined by school-children today.

Revolutionary War. In the area around the African Burial Ground, archeologists discovered thousands of objects of daily life, including pottery, glassware, tools, children's toys, and even some food. These objects and the human remains from the graves can help us understand how some slaves lived and died in this neighborhood over 200 years ago.

[5]   Before the graves were closed to the public, hundreds of people visited the African Burial Ground to pay their respects to the dead. Many of them, especially African-American people, had mixed feelings about seeing the skeletons. Noel Pointer, a jazz musician, cried when he saw them. He explained, "You hear about these archeological and scientific terms and you say to yourself, 'This is very interesting.' But until you get down there and you see what the bodies look like—you see the skeletons of the children lying there in the earth—then you realize that these are people." Dr. Howard Dobson is the chief of the Schomburg Center for Research for Black Culture in Harlem. He said that when he saw the open graves, the scientist part of him wanted to learn more about the past from the bones. But, as a person of African ancestry, he felt, "You're not supposed to mess with the dead." These statements help us understand the similar feelings of Native Americans about the bones of their ancestors.

[6]   Unlike the Native Americans, however, the African-American community has agreed to the study of its ancestors' bones. The history of the black people of New York in the eighteenth century is not written down. It is the story of several thousand people. Many of them may still lie undisturbed in the earth beneath the city's skyscrapers. The study of the 400 skeletons that were unearthed will "open a window" into the lives of this whole community.

Researchers already know from the number of skeletons of children that about 50% of these black people died at birth or in the first few years of life. Scientists doing further research at Howard University in Washington, D.C., are using modern tools to study the remains from the African Burial Ground. They are looking for signs that reveal where in Africa these people were born, where they lived before they came to New York—possibly Brazil or the Caribbean—what their life was like in New York, and how they died. Professor Michael Blakey, director of this project, says, "To learn from archeology is another form of respect for our ancestors." At the end of the six-year project, the ancestors will be reburied in the cemetery in New York and a monument will be built to preserve their memory. Finally, they will have respect and peace.

Summary Completion.   Fill in each blank space with the correct word from the reading passage.

Archeologists study ancient human (1)_____ to learn how people of

the past lived and died. They use measurements and chemical (2)_____

of the bones to get answers to their questions. The answers can give us a picture of a

whole (3)_____ of ancestors. The Native American people are

(4)_____ the study of their ancestors' bones. They want

(5)_____ to return the bones to them. They believe it is an act of

(6)_____ to keep these bones for study. African-Americans have also

faced this (7)_____ concerning their ancestors' bones. In New York City,

archeologists discovered the African Burial Ground, a (8)_____ for

African slaves in the 1700s. When people visited the graves in the African Burial

Ground, many of them had (9)_____ feelings about seeing the skeletons

and using them for the purpose of study. But the African-American community

(10)_____ to the study of these bones. The study will "open a window"

into the (11)_____ of the African people in eighteenth-century New

York. When the study is over, the African ancestors will be (12)_____

in New York and a monument will preserve their memory.

Reacting to the Reading

Archeologists study human remains to find out how people of the past lived and died.

   a. Is it important to know about the people and culture of the past? Explain your answer.

   b. Do you believe that human remains should be studied to advance our knowledge of the past?

   c. What information would you be interested in concerning your ancestors' lives? Which century would you like to know about?

Reading Comprehension

1. Understanding the Text.   Choose the correct answer, or follow the directions.

   a. In Paragraph [1], Sentence 2, the words *these remains* refer to
     (1) archeologists and other researchers.
     (2) people of the present and the future.
     (3) ancient human skeletons.

   b. Most of the sentences in Paragraph [2] are questions. These questions
     (1) are basic to the study of ancient human bones.
     (2) refer to the tools archeologists use in their studies.
     (3) are answered in the paragraph.

   c. Write an expression that explains the meaning of *make the bones speak* in the first sentence of Paragraph [2].

   _____

   d. Native Americans believe that
     (1) archeological work is disrespectful to their ancestors.
     (2) studying ancient bones is a good way to learn about ancestors.
     (3) ancient human remains belong to the whole human race.

   e. According to the information in Paragraph [4], we can say that the bodies in the African Burial Ground were
     (1) buried together in one mass grave.
     (2) buried with household objects such as pottery and tools.
     (3) carefully buried in separate graves.

f. In Paragraph [4] the word *perhaps* is used three times. This word is used to introduce
   (1) definite facts.
   (2) guesses or opinions.
   (3) unimportant details.

g. We can infer from the information in Paragraph [4] that lower Manhattan was
   (1) entirely a burial ground in the 1700s.
   (2) a poor neighborhood in the 1700s.
   (3) the center of business in the 1700s as it is today.

h. In paragraph [5] both Noel Pointer and Dr. Howard Dobson express
   (1) their sadness at seeing the dead in the African Burial Ground.
   (2) completely different points of view about the remains.
   (3) mixed feelings about seeing the skeletons.

i. Dr. Dobson's comment: "You're not supposed to mess with the dead" is expressed as
   (1) an emotional or perhaps religious point of view.
   (2) a scientific point of view.
   (3) the official view of the Schomburg Center researchers.

j. Another expression for the words *mess with* in Dr. Dobson's comment is

   _____ .

k. The first words in Paragraph [6], *Unlike the Native Americans,* refer to information in
   (1) Paragraph [2].
   (2) Paragraph [3].
   (3) Paragraph [4].

l. According to the information in Paragraph [6],
   (1) fifty percent of the skeletons in the African Burial Ground have been dug up.
   (2) a study will be made of the 400 unearthed skeletons.
   (3) archeologists will dig for more skeletons in the African Burial Ground.

m. Write an expression that means the same as the words *open a window* in

   Paragraph [6], Sentence 5. _____

In the 1700s people lived and worked in the area of the African Burial Ground.

2. Answering Information Questions.   Answer the following questions in complete sentences.

   a. What scientific tools do archeologists use to get answers to their questions about human bones?

   b. What specific group of people is against the study of its ancestors' remains?

   c. How many human bones does the Smithsonian Institution have in its collection?

   d. Where was the recent discovery of the African Burial Ground made?

   e. What objects of daily life did archeologists discover in the area of the African Burial Ground?

   f. Did the African-American community agree to or disapprove of the study of its ancestors' bones?

   g. What does Professor Michael Blakey say about the archeological study of the remains?

Ⅲ THE READING PROCESS

General and Specific Words; Topics. A general word is a word used for a large group or class of things. A specific word is used to give us a special detail or example of a more general word.

General word: people	General word: student
Specific words: Native Americans	Specific words: archeology student

a. For each set of words, mark *G* next to the more *general* word(s) and *S* next to the more *specific* word(s). The first one is done for you.

(1) tool _G_
    hammer _S_

(2) city ____
    New York ____

(3) notebook ____
    book ____

(4) ball ____
    doll ____
    toy ____

(5) chair ____
    furniture ____

(6) scientific tool ____
    X-ray ____

(7) tooth decay ____
    arthritis ____
    disease ____

(8) occupation ____
    farming ____
    teaching ____

(9) silver ____
    metal ____
    gold ____

b. In the blank space, write a general word that names the group of specific words. The first one is done for you.

(1) picks   spades   shovels _____*tools*_____

(2) Mexico   China   Nigeria   Italy _____

(3) farmers   schoolchildren   soldiers   scientists _____

(4) chairs   desks   beds   bookcases _____

(5) ring   bracelet   necklace   beads _____

(6) jars   pots   dishes _____

(7) dress   hat   shirt _____

(8) statues   paintings   drawings _____

(9) piano   guitar   violin   harp _____

(10) guns   spears   bombs _____.

SUB did these on 9/2/92

c. The topic of a paragraph or a passage is the general idea or general subject. We use general words to talk about topics. Read the following paragraph. Look for the sentence that tells the topic, or the general subject of the paragraph.

> Extraordinary discoveries have been made in ancient tombs. Recently, Dr. Walter Alva found a tomb of the Moche people of Peru. It contained the bones of a ruler, three other men, and two women, possibly the ruler's wives. The objects included face masks, beads shaped like peanuts, and knives, all made of gold. In the 1920s, Sir Leonard Woolley uncovered the grave of Shub-ad, the queen of Ur in ancient Iraq. Such items as jewelry, furniture, vases, statues, musical instruments, and weapons, all made of the most expensive materials, filled the grave. There were also wagons, carts, and a special carriage for the queen. Shub-ad, like the Moche ruler, was buried with members of her household.

Circle the item that tells the topic, or general subject of the paragraph.

(1) human remains in ancient tombs

(2) the archeologists Alva and Woolley

(3) the Moche people of ancient Peru

(4) ancient jewelry from Peru and Iraq

(5) extraordinary discoveries in ancient tombs

(6) art objects from the tomb of Shub-ad

The correct choice from the list is item (5). Item (5) is the most general idea of the paragraph. The other items are specifics, or details that support the topic.

Circle the correct answer for the following items about the reading passage "Archeology: Making the Bones Speak."

(1) The topic of Paragraph [2] is

    a. scientific tools for the study of bones.

    b. questions archeologists ask about bones.

    c. bone diseases of the past.

(2) The topic of Paragraph [3] is

    a. the collection of Native American bones in the Smithsonian.

    b. the spirits of Native American ancestors.

    c. the Native Americans' disagreement with archeologists.

(3) The topic of Paragraph [4] is

  a.   the discovery of the African Burial Ground in New York.

  b.   objects found around the African Burial Ground.

  c.   life in New York in the 1700s.

(4) The topic of Paragraph [5] is

  a.   Noel Pointer's visit to the African Burial Ground.

  b.   the skeletons of children in the African Burial Ground.

  c.   mixed feelings about seeing the bones of the African ancestors.

(5) The topic of Paragraph [6] is

  a.   learning about the African ancestors from the study of bones.

  b.   Howard University's modern laboratory for bone study.

  c.   finding out where New York's African population came from.

IV VOCABULARY

1. New Words.   Pronounce the words, following your instructor.

Verbs	Nouns	Adjectives	Adverbs
preserve	(dis)respect	crowded	recently
reveal	ancestor	ancient	
examine		extraordinary	
disturb			

USING VOCABULARY. Write a complete sentence to answer each question. Use the italicized word in your answer. The first one is done to show you a possible answer.

  a. Does your friend ever *reveal* secrets to you?

   _____ *My friend never reveals secrets to me.* _____

  b. Do you ever *reveal* your secrets to a friend?

  c. Where do people go to see *ancient* objects?

  d. Why is a giraffe an *extraordinary* animal?

  e. What kind of noise *disturbs* you?

f. Which street in your neighborhood is usually *crowded* with shoppers?

g. What movie did you see *recently*?

h. What is a good way to *preserve* family photographs?

i. How can you find out more about your *ancestors*?

j. Where do archeologists *examine* the objects they find?

k. What qualities should a politician have to earn your *respect*?

2. Word Families.   Study the following lists:

Type of Work	Person Who Does That Type of Work
archeology	archeologist
art	artist
science	scientist
chemistry	chemist
writing	writer
teaching	teacher
photography	photographer
research	researcher
history	historian
music	musician

SENTENCE COMPLETION.   Choose the correct word in parentheses to fill in the blank space in each sentence.

a. (archeology, archeologist) An _____ digs in the earth to find hidden

objects. We learn about the people of the past through _____ .

b. (art, artist) Pablo Picasso was a famous Spanish _____ .

His _____ is in museum collections all over the world.

c. (farming, farmers) In the past, _____ was the usual type of work.

Ancient _____ probably made their own tools.

d. (history, historian) Edith Hamilton was a professor of ancient _____ .

Many books about ancient society were written by this famous _____ .

e. (photography, photographer) A good _____ always takes interesting pictures. In _____ , it is important to know how to compose a picture.

f. (writing, writer) Composing a mental picture is the job of a _____ . Think about composing a clear, interesting picture in your own _____ .

g. (science, scientist) Geology is the branch of _____ that deals with the rocks that compose the earth. Dr. Mary Landers is a well-known _____ in the field of geology.

h. (teaching, teacher) Does your _____ enjoy _____ this class?

i. (psychology, psychologist) A _____ studies the human mind. Teachers of young children often take courses in child _____ .

j. (astronomy, astronomer) One of the most difficult subjects is _____ , the study of the planets and stars. An _____ spends long hours looking through a telescope.

Now fill in the blank spaces in the following sentences with information about yourself.

I want to be a (an) _____ . I am taking courses in _____ .

V LANGUAGE FOCUS

Sentence Kernels

1. Verbs. The verb is the heart of the English sentence. There cannot be an English sentence without a complete main verb. The main verb is the word that tells us the state of being, the feeling, or the action of a person, place, or thing.

> An archeologist *digs* in the ground

RECOGNIZING VERBS. Underline the verbs in the following sentences:

    a. The earth holds many secrets about the past.

    b. An archeologist looks for remains of the past.

    c. Archeologists examine the remains in a laboratory.

    d. They never keep objects for themselves.

    e. We learn about the past from ancient objects.

2. Subjects. The subject of a sentence answers this question: *Who* or *what* is doing the verb action?

> An *archeologist* **digs** in the ground. (Who digs?)

RECOGNIZING SUBJECTS. Go back to sentences *a, b, c, d,* and *e.* Circle the subject of each underlined verb.

3. Identifying Verbs and Subjects.

    a. Read the following paragraph carefully. Find the complete main verb in each sentence. Put each verb in the Verb column of the chart that follows. Then find the subject of each verb. Put the subject in the Subject column. The first one is done for you.

> (1) Professor Ortiz teaches archeology in Mexico City. (2) He has permission to dig in certain areas of the city. (3) His students help him in the field. (4) They follow his instructions carefully. (5) They receive course credit for their work. (6) The professor writes a report about their discoveries at the end of the dig.

	Subject	Verb
1	Professor Ortiz	teaches
2	He	has
3	His students	help
4	They	follow
5	They	receive
6	The professor	write

Now respond to the following questions orally, in short answers. The first set of answers is given to you.

Sentence (1): What does Professor Ortiz teach? *Archeology*. Where? *In Mexico City.*

Sentence (2): What does he have permission to do? Where?

Sentence (3): Where do his students help him?

Sentence (4): What do they follow? How?

Sentence (5): What do they receive? For what?

Sentence (6): What does the professor write? About what? When?

Now place the chart of subjects and verbs on the board. With your books closed, reconstruct as closely as possible the paragraph about Professor Ortiz and his students.

b. Write a short paragraph about someone you know who has an interesting job. Check each sentence for a subject and a verb.

Simple Present Tense

The simple present tense is used to tell a fact or describe something that is generally true without a limit of time. It is used to tell about things that people usually do (not what they are doing right now). All the verbs in your Verb column are in the simple present tense.

Archeologists sometimes find the bones of people who died long ago.

> Archeologists *dig* in the ground. (This is something they usually do.)

Study the following simple present tense forms.

	Singular	**Plural**
First Person	I dig	An archeologist and I dig We dig
Second Person	You dig	You dig
Third Person	An archeologist digs He/She/It digs	Archeologists dig They dig

Notice that only the third person singular form has the extra *s* at the end. For verbs ending in *y* preceded by a consonant, the third person singular form is *ies*: *reply, replies.*

1. Sentence Completion. In the blank space, write the correct verb form from the pair in parentheses. First you must find the subject. Is the subject singular or plural? Choose the verb that agrees in number with its subject.

Dr. Diana Warren is a famous archeologist. She (work, works)

(1)____works____ in Italy during the summer. Many archeologists (dig, digs)

(2)____dig____ with her. They (bring, brings) (3)____bring____ the

past to life. But Dr. Warren also (discover, discovers) (4)____discovers____ the past

of New York City, where she (live, lives) (5)____lives____. She sometimes (dig,

digs) (6)____digs____ on Staten Island or in lower Manhattan. She (look,

looks) (7)____looks____ for objects from the Dutch or English periods. Her

discoveries (give, gives) (8)____give____ us an interesting picture of daily life

in those times. Many secrets of New York (lie, lies) (9)____lie____ beneath

the city streets. As Dr. Warren (say, says) (10)____says____ "Every day we

(walk, walks) (11)____walk____ on top of our history."

2. Scrambled Sentences. The words in each of the following items form a complete English sentence, but they are out of order. Rewrite the words in the correct order so they form a correct sentence. Punctuate the sentence. Remember to look for the verb first. Then find its subject. See the example on page 18.

ground   .   archeologists   maps   the   draw   of

Archeologists draw maps of the ground.

a. us . tell archeologists a lot the past about

b. find sometimes and archeologists . bones tools

s. arch. find b. & tools.

c. of the past . discover also written records they

They also discover writt records. of the past.

d. museums bring to . all the objects archeologists to study

Arch. bring all the obj. to museums to study.

e. carefully these . the museums objects preserve ancient

The museums. carefully preserve these ancient objet

Plurals

An *archeologist* is one person. *Archeologist* is singular. *Archeologists* refers to more than one person. *Archeologists* is plural.

1. Regular Plurals. Most regular plural nouns are formed by adding *s* to the singular form.

Singular	Plural
a place	places
a toy	toys

Regular plurals of nouns ending in *y* preceded by a consonant are formed by changing the *y* to *i* and adding *es*.

Singular	Plural
a discovery	discoveries

Regular plurals of nouns ending in *sh*, *s*, or *x* are formed by adding *es* to the singular form.

Singular	Plural
a class	classes
a wish	wishes
a tax	taxes

Regular plurals of nouns ending in *f* or *fe* are formed by changing the *f* or *fe* to *v* and adding *es*.

Singular	Plural
a knife	knives

Note that the plural of the nouns *belief, chief,* and *roof* are formed by adding *s* only.

LIST COMPLETION.   Fill in the blank spaces with the correct singular or plural form.

Singular	Plural
an action	_____
a bone	_____
_____	communities
a body	_____
a piece	_____
_____	objects
a boy	_____
a country	_____
_____	boxes
_____	games
a dish	_____
a story	_____
a brush	_____
_____	lives

When a singular noun is not specific, we use the indefinite article *a* or *an* in front of it. When we write plural nouns, we do not use *a* or *an*.

2. Irregular Plurals. Irregular plurals do not follow one pattern. Study the following list of irregular plurals.

Singular	Plural
a man	men
a woman	women
a child	children
a mouse	mice
a tooth	teeth
a foot	feet

SENTENCE COMPLETION. Choose the correct word in parentheses to fill in the blank space in each sentence.

a. (place, places) Archeologists go to many _____ to dig in the earth.

b. (plan, plans) Archeologists make careful _____ of the areas before they dig.

c. (Child, Children) _____ like to dig in the sand at the beach.

d. (object, objects) An archeologist is always happy to find a gold _____ in the earth.

e. (bone, bones) Archeologists sometimes find animal _____ when they dig.

f. (tooth, teeth) You can see the _____ and bones of extinct animals on display in museums.

g. (woman, women) A _____ of the past usually made her own clothing.

h. (man, men) Most _____ a thousand years ago were farmers.

i. (story, stories) Do you like to read _____ about men and women of the past?

Prepositions

Prepositions are short but important words in English. They show the relationships among things, people, and places. The words *in, on, to, from, at, between,* and *next to* are just a few of the many prepositions. Some prepositions indicate direction, some indicate a place, and some indicate a time.

> Archeologists take the objects *from* the field *to* the laboratory. (direction)
> I keep my books *on* the desk. I sit *at* the desk to study. (place)
> I get up *at* 7:00 A.M. I usually work until late *at* night. (time)

1. Prepositional Phrases of Direction.   A prepositional phrase is a group of words that begins with a preposition and includes a noun or pronoun that names a person, place, or thing. The prepositions *to* and *from* will begin a phrase that includes a noun.

> She comes *from New York*. She goes *to Turkey* in the summer.

ANSWERING QUESTIONS WITH PREPOSITIONAL PHRASES.   Write the answers to the following questions in complete sentences. Use a phrase with *to* or *from* in each sentence. Underline the prepositional phrases of direction in your sentences.

   a. What country do you come from?

   b. Where do you often go on a warm day?

   c. Do you walk to school, or do you take a bus or train?

   d. Is the plane ride from New York to London one hour or six hours?

   e. Do you go home from school by yourself or with friends?

2. Prepositional Phrases of Place.   A prepositional phrase of place will include a preposition and a noun. The phrase will tell *where* someone or something is located.

> She sits *next to her friend*. She keeps her books *under the chair*.

   a. Study the following list of some common prepositions of place. Then read an archeologist's description of an ancient Roman house. Underline the prepositional phrases of place. The first one is done for you.

at, at the back of	around	on, on the side of
under	beside	behind
next to	inside	among
by	in, in the center of	

The entrance of a Roman house was a simple doorway <u>next to the shops</u> on the street. Inside the doorway there was a courtyard. The roof of the courtyard had an opening in the center, and under the opening there was a basin on the ground to collect the rainwater. Around the courtyard were a few small bed-rooms. At the back of the courtyard was another room that the Romans used for eating or studying. A large open garden was located behind that room. Here the Roman family sat by the fishpond or among the fruit trees and enjoyed their free time. Sometimes they ate in a dining room on the side of the garden. The plan of an ancient Roman house was simple, and it gave the family a lot of privacy.

b. Think of the place where you live. Describe some features of the place and your activities there. Include appropriate prepositional phrases. Use the preceding paragraph as a model.

c. Write a complete sentence, using a prepositional phrase of place.
   (1) Where is the best place for a telephone in the home?
   (2) When they are not in the closet, where do you sometimes find your shoes?
   (3) Where is the light switch in your kitchen?
   (4) Where does a house cat like to sleep to keep warm?
   (5) Where do you like to sit in a movie theater?
   (6) In what city does your best friend live?
   (7) Where is the best place for a reading lamp?

3. Prepositional Phrases of Time.   Study the list of prepositional phrases that answer the question *when?*

in the morning/afternoon/ evening	on July Fourth	at 6 A.M./P.M./o'clock
in the summer/winter	on holidays	at lunch time
in May/August	on the weekend	at night/noon/midnight
in the past	on Friday/Sunday	at the end/beginning of the day/semester

SENTENCE COMPLETION. Fill in the blank spaces with *at, in,* or *on* to complete the prepositional phrase of time.

a. We always talk about the day's events _____ dinnertime.

b. _____ weekends I usually go to bed _____ midnight.

c. _____ the beginning of the semester I'll buy my new textbooks.

d. I'll take a trip to Boston _____ Easter or _____ the summer.

e. My parents pay all their bills _____ the beginning of every month.

f. My friend from Colorado will visit me _____ July.

g. I usually go shopping _____ Saturday afternoons.

h. Americans celebrate Independence Day _____ July Fourth.

i. I attend school _____ night because I work _____ the morning and afternoon.

j. I get home _____ 11:00 P.M. I'm very tired _____ the end of the day.

Punctuation and Capitalization

In English, every new sentence begins with a capital letter. Every complete sentence ends with a period, exclamation point, or question mark. The names of countries, states, cities, and other specific places are capitalized. Punctuate and capitalize the following paragraph.

> my friend robert is a field worker for the museum of natural history in new york every summer he goes out west to montana he looks for the remains of ancient life in the rocks what does he find he usually discovers animal bones sometimes he finds the remains of plant life he never finds human bones in that part of the united states next summer i am going to montana i want to see robert at work in the field

Only one English pronoun is always capitalized. It is capitalized at the beginning of a sentence and within the sentence. Do you know which pronoun this is? Can you find it in the paragraph? Did you capitalize it?

This Turkish potter is working with the same materials potters used in ancient times.

VI THE COMPOSING PROCESS

1. Sentence Combining to Form a Paragraph. In some areas of the world today, as in ancient times, the potter is an important member of a village community. The following sentences describe the potter in the photograph. The second and third sentences in a set contain a prepositional phrase of place. Combine each set into one complete sentence. Leave out unnecessary words. Write your new sentences in the form of a paragraph. The first combination is done for you.

(1) The potter works everyday. He is in his shop. The shop is next to his house.

    The potter works every day in his shop next to his house.

(2) He keeps the clay. The clay is in a tub. The tub is in a corner of the shop.

(3) There is a potter's wheel. It is near the window. The window is on the other side of the shop.

(4) To make a pitcher, the potter throws a lump of clay. The clay is on the wheel.

(5) The clay spins around by means of a pedal. The pedal is under the wheel.

(6) The potter moves his hands. His hands are over the clay to form a beautiful shape.

(7) He uses his fingers. His fingers are around the neck of the pitcher to create an interesting design.

(8) Sometimes he paints a design. The design is around the body of the pitcher. Or sometimes it is just on the neck.

(9) He dries his pitchers. They are outside the workshop. They are in the sun.

2. Developing a Central Topic.   The topic of a paragraph is its main subject matter. Once you have a topic for writing, you can develop a paragraph by noting specific information to support the topic.

a. Read the following paragraph. Then, with your classmates, discuss the questions.

> Archeologists usually have a busy day. They eat breakfast at 6:00 A.M. Then they go to work in the field. They dig until 11:00 A.M. They have an early lunch and take a rest in the afternoon. After that, they return to the field and work until sundown. In the evening, after dinner, they write their reports or work in the laboratory. Sometimes they have free time to relax or read a book. They usually go to bed late.

What is the topic of this paragraph?
In which sentence does the topic appear?
How is the topic developed?
Is there a logical order to the sentences? What kind of order?
Do all the specific sentences support the topic?

b. Choose one of the following topics to develop a paragraph similar to the one about archeologists: My Busiest Day; My Best Day; My Worst Day. Before you write, make a list of specific activities. Then arrange your items in time order, from earliest to latest.

Begin your paragraph by telling your reader about your topic. Use your list of activities to write your first version. Exchange papers with a classmate. Does your partner understand your schedule? Can he or she suggest ways to make your writing clearer? Rewrite your paragraph, making necessary changes. Check for correct use of the present tense, pronouns, and prepositional phrases.

3. Composing a Paragraph.   Read the following description of the steps archeologists follow when they work in the field.

> Archeologists spend long hours preparing an area for digging. First they take photographs of the surface so they have a record of how the place originally looked. Then they clear the area of any large rocks or vegetation. They measure the area and draw an accurate plan of the ground. After that, they divide the area into sections with rope. Then the field workers are assigned to specific sections. They are ready to dig.

Use this description as a model to compose a paragraph based on the topic. *Preparing for a Party*. Some items are listed for you. Add others after you discuss the topic with your classmates. Begin your paragraph with a sentence that introduces the reader to your topic. Develop the paragraph in time order.

prepare special foods   get dressed   clean the house

Paragraph Topics

1. Write a paragraph telling what you do on a typical summer day when you are free. Tell where you like to go and with whom you usually go. Include the different activities in which you take part on such a day. Begin with an appropriate topic sentence.

2. Compose a paragraph that describes the steps you take to do a certain activity. Here are some suggestions for topics: washing a car, dressing a baby, taking a photograph, making a sandwich. You and a classmate may want to brainstorm and collaborate on the paragraph. Begin with a sentence that introduces your topic.

ADDITIONAL READING

A Hero's Life

Ancient people wrote stories on clay tablets. The Sumerians, a group of people who lived in the Middle East 3,000 years ago, wrote the story of their hero Gilgamesh in this way. Gilgamesh wanted to uncover mysteries and gain knowledge. He wanted to understand the meaning of life and death. The legend of Gilgamesh is 3,000 years old, but it reveals something about the joys and sorrows of life at any time and in any place.

When his tale begins,* Gilgamesh is the young king of Uruk, a city in the land of Sumer. He rules his people with a strong hand, but he is restless and ambitious. He wants to do great deeds and become famous throughout the world. His people want to be left in peace, so they pray to the sky god Anu for help. "O Great Anu," they cry, "create a companion for Gilgamesh, someone who is equal to him in strength and courage. Then they can go away together on adventures, and we will be left in peace."

In response, the god creates Enkidu to be Gilgamesh's best friend. At last, Gilgamesh has someone he loves and trusts, a comrade who will join him in great deeds.

---

* *Stories about the past are often told in the simple present tense to make them more real to the reader or listener.*

Together, Gilgamesh and Enkidu set out to find fame and wealth. They travel to the faraway land of the Cedar Forest. They want to cut down the trees and bring the wood back to build temples for all the gods of the land. This is a dangerous task. The giant Humbaba guards the forest against all enemies. Humbaba has great powers. He hears everything, he breathes fire, and he never sleeps. As the two companions come near the home of this giant, they begin to feel afraid and weak. They wait a little to overcome their fear. Then they attack. Humbaba fights for his life but knows that the two together are stronger than he is. "Let me go free, and the trees will be yours," the giant begs.

Gilgamesh and Enkidu must decide if their enemy should live or die. It is a difficult choice, but they decide to kill him. When Humbaba is dead, they cut down the trees and return to Uruk with the wood. Then Gilgamesh builds his temples for all the gods.

Now Gilgamesh is a hero in his city and famous throughout the land. Immediately, the goddess Ishtar falls in love with him. "Take me as your bride," she says, and offers him all kinds of splendid gifts.

Gilgamesh refuses her. "You are cruel to those you love. You never remain faithful to those who love you," he responds.

Ishtar becomes very angry and calls on Anu for help. "Father Anu, send down to earth the Bull of Heaven to punish Gilgamesh for this insult," she demands.

Anu agrees, and the bull falls on the land of Sumer. It kills hundreds of people. Then it attacks Enkidu. To save his friend, Gilgamesh stabs the bull in the neck. With the death of the bull, the people are free from fear.

Everyone in the land is joyful, but sadness soon follows. The gods decide that Enkidu must die as punishment for the death of the bull. He falls sick. Day after day he suffers, and Gilgamesh cries for him. Finally, Enkidu's life ends, and Gilgamesh loses a dear friend, a brother. He waits for the body to return to life, but he soon understands the meaning of death: "I too will die someday and lie in the earth forever."

Gilgamesh cannot rest or be at peace. He is afraid of death. He wants to discover the secret of everlasting life. He leaves Uruk to find the Far-Away, the only man who has everlasting life. It is a long and difficult trip to the home of this wise man, down an unknown road. Along the way he meets a mysterious woman and tells her of his wish. "Accept death," she tells him. "Eat and dance, marry and have children, for these things make men happy."

Gilgamesh cannot accept her advice. In pain and sorrow, he continues on the dark road. At last, after many hardships, he arrives at the Far-Away's home. "Oh, Far-Away, I wish to question you about the living and the dead. How can I find everlasting life as you did?" he asks.

"Everything changes," explains the Far-Away. "No one lives forever. I am free of death as a special gift from the gods. No one else can have that gift."

The Sumerians were very respectful of their gods and goddesses and built many temples to honor them. Here is a statue of a worshipper found in a temple in Sumer.

Then the Far-Away tells the story of the mysterious ways of the gods. At the end he says, "You, Gilgamesh, must return to Uruk and live the way all men live." He gives his guest new clothes for the journey home. Gilgamesh leaves with understanding in his heart.

Old and tired, he arrives home. He is worn out from his difficult travels and his suffering. But he is proud of his city of Uruk, the beautiful towers and temples, the high walls of brick, and the rich fields of grain for his people. Gilgamesh is wise now, not sad. He accepts death and life. His people shout, "O Lord Gilgamesh, greatly we praise you." They say that they will write his story, a hero's life, for others to read in the future.

Reacting to the Reading

Gilgamesh is a hero to his people.

a. Describe his deeds, and explain why his people are so proud of him.

b. Discuss the deeds of a leader whom you think of as a hero.

c. Do you think of any entertainer or sports figure as a hero? What heroic qualities does that person have?

Reading Comprehension

Understanding the Text. Choose the correct answer, or follow the directions.

1. When the tale begins, Gilgamesh

    (a) is not happy just being the ruler of Uruk.

    (b) prays to the gods for a companion.

    (c) wants to be left in peace.

2. Gilgamesh and Enkidu leave their city

    (a) to guard the Cedar Forest.

    (b) to find fame and wealth.

    (c) to find everlasting life.

3. Write the sentence from the tale that best describes the powers of Humbaba:

    _____

4. In this tale, we learn that a great hero

    (a) never needs the help of a friend.

    (b) can sometimes feel afraid and weak.

    (c) is always brave and strong.

5. Gilgamesh and Enkidu seem to feel sorry for their enemy Humbaba when they face him. Which expression from the story shows this?

    (a) Humbaba has great powers.

    (b) It is a difficult choice.

    (c) This is a dangerous task.

6. Gilgamesh doesn't want to marry Ishtar because

    (a) he is afraid of her father Anu.

    (b) he isn't in love with her.

    (c) he doesn't trust her love for him.

7. After the Bull of Heaven is killed, the story states: *Everyone in the land is joyful, but sadness soon follows.* Write the part of this sentence that is important for the next part of the story.

    _____

8. Gilgamesh travels far and wide

    (a) to ask the advice of a mysterious woman.

    (b) so he can forget the death of his best friend.

    (c) because he wants to be saved from death.

9. The mysterious woman
   (a) gives him some practical advice.
   (b) wants to marry him.
   (c) gives him directions to the Far-Away.

10. At the home of the Far-Away, Gilgamesh
    (a) asks the gods for the special gift of everlasting life.
    (b) finds out how everyone can live forever.
    (c) learns that his wish for everlasting life is hopeless.

11. When Gilgamesh returns to Uruk, his people
    (a) are sad to see him.
    (b) welcome him with great respect.
    (c) refuse to hear his story.

12. In the following list, mark G for the *general* item and S for the *specific* items.

    beautiful gardens and temples ____

    rich fields of grain for the people ____

    the proud features of Uruk ____

    high walls of brick ____

13. In the following list, circle the sentences that show that Gilgamesh is a very real human being in this story.

    (a) He kills a giant. (b) A goddess falls in love with him. (c) He has a good

    friend. (d) He accepts death and life. (e) He kills the Bull of Heaven.

    (f) He suffers over the death of a friend. (g) He cuts down a whole forest.

    (h) He is proud of his city. (i) He sometimes feels weak and afraid.

    (j) He is worn out from his travels.

14. Choose the sentence that best expresses the meaning of this tale.
    (a) The love of one's city is the most important kind of love.
    (b) It is better to have good friends than to be married.
    (c) The struggle for wisdom and self-knowledge will bring us peace.

Vocabulary

Expanding Vocabulary.   Choose the word(s) that have the same meaning as the italicized word(s) in the sentence. Use your dictionary only if necessary.

a.   Gilgamesh is *restless*; ruling his people isn't enough for him.

(1) patient   (2) inactive   (3) unsettled

b.   Gilgamesh wants to be famous throughout the world; he *is ambitious.*

(1) wants to succeed   (2) feels lazy   (3) is trustful

c.   Gilgamesh and Enkidu are good *companions*. Together, the *comrades* set out on an adventure.

(1) heroes   (2) warriors   (3) friends

d.   They *travel* to the faraway land of the Cedar Forest.

(1) hurry   (2) go on a journey   (3) move their home

e.   A giant guards the forest, so cutting down the trees is a dangerous *task.*

(1) discovery   (2) object   (3) job

f.   Ishtar wants to marry Gilgamesh, but he *refuses* to be her husband.

(1) doesn't agree   (2) expects   3) would like

g.   Ishtar is *insulted* by Gilgamesh's reply and becomes angry.

(1) offended   (2) destroyed   (3) frightened

h.   Enkidu falls sick; day after day he *suffers.*

(1) feels angry   (2) is in pain   (3) gets better

i.   Gilgamesh cannot *accept* the advice of the mysterious woman; he refuses to be an ordinary man.

(1) understand   (2) reveal   (3) take or agree with

CHAPTER TWO

NORTH AMERICA: A CONTINENT OF MANY CULTURES

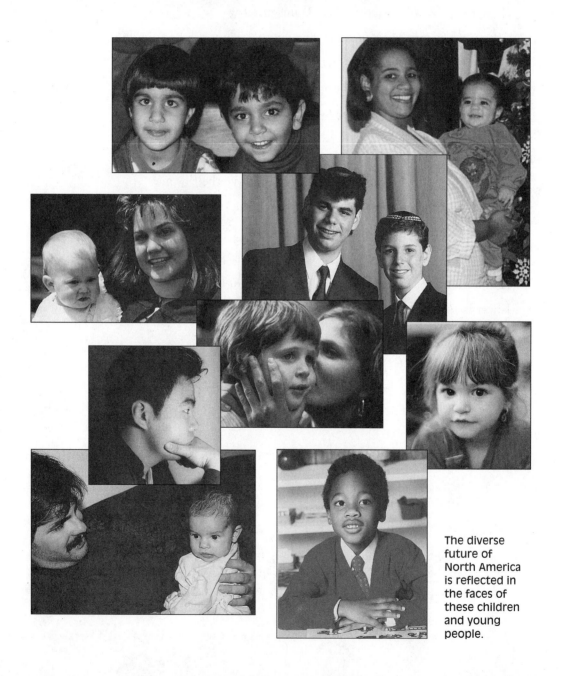

The diverse future of North America is reflected in the faces of these children and young people.

Ⅰ PREREADING

Class Activity.   The people of North America come from many different cultural backgrounds. The photographs on the opposite page represent different ethnic groups in North America.

Choose a partner in your class. Interview the person to find out the information on the list. Fill in the line with that information.

Name of student _____

Native country _____

Native language(s) _____

Important holidays in native country _____

_____

Favorite holiday (explain why) _____

_____

Basic foods of native country _____

Favorite food(s) _____

Favorite American/Canadian city (explain why) _____

_____

Is the person from the same background as yours or from a different background? _____

Is any of the information the same as yours? If so, list the information that is the same. _____

_____

FREE WRITE

Immigrants face many problems when they first come to the United States or Canada. Write about your first experiences (or those of your relatives or friends) with language, housing, food, social customs, or other issues.

Vocabulary in Context.   The words in this exercise will appear in the reading passage. Circle the word(s) that mean the same as the italicized word in each sentence.

1. People like to *celebrate* important events in their lives such as birthdays, weddings, and graduations.

    a. examine

    b. honor

    c. ignore

2. An *occasion* like a wedding usually has a *ceremony* in a place of worship, with many people attending.

    a. event   a. chance

    b. area   b. crowd of people

    c. occupation   c. formal observance

3. When *immigrants* first come to North America, they usually feel more at home when they practice their *native* customs.

    a. foreign products   a. original

    b. people from other homelands b. accurate

    c. citizens of the United States c. new

4. All over North America, people enjoy eating *delicious* meals prepared according to national customs.

    a. ancient

    b. heavy

    c. flavorful

5. Everyone enjoys going to street fairs and festivals to see people of different nationalities *perform* folk dances in native dress or to watch other activities.

    a. do

    b. reveal

    c. preserve

6. Sometimes the dances and the music *represent* something important in the history of the people who perform.

    a. communicate

    b. contrast with

    c. hide

7. The *inhabitants* of large cities are used to a fast pace of life.

   a. people who work in a certain place

   b. people who live in a certain place

   c. people who immigrate to a certain place

8. Some people think that toy *weapons* create violent feelings in children.

   a. athletic equipment

   b. things to fight with

   c. cars and trucks

9. Immigrants from farming areas must sometimes *settle* in cities in order to find jobs.

   a. educate themselves

   b. make their homes

   c. save their money

Ⅱ READING

Canada and the United States: Two Nations of Many Cultures

[1]   The North American continent stretches east to west for over three thousand miles from the Atlantic to the Pacific Ocean. In the north of the continent are the extremely cold areas of Alaska and Canada. In the south of the continent are some tropical regions, such as the American states of Florida and Louisiana. The two nations of Canada and the United States occupy most of the North American continent. There are many similarities between these two countries. For example, English is the primary language of both countries, although French is also an official language in Canada. Both countries have many immigrants who speak their own native languages, but most newspapers, books, films, and television programs are in English. However, in both Canada and the United States there are also many publications, films, and radio and television programs in other languages.

[2]   Most people in Canada, as in the United States, are of European origin. However, unlike the United States, Canada was never a slaveholding society. Therefore, it does not have a large African-American population as the United States does. However, many people of African descent from the Caribbean area have come to settle there. In particular, Haitian immigrants, who speak French, feel comfortable in Canadian cities such as Montreal, where French is widely

used. Canada and the United States both have large populations of Chinese and Japanese origin. Some of these Asian people are the descendants of immigrants who came to North America many years ago. Some other Asians, from the Indian subcontinent, are more recent immigrants. In both Canada and the United States there are also small populations of Native Americans (formerly called Indians) and Inuits (formerly called Eskimos). These people were the original inhabitants of the North American continent.

[3]   The French were the first Europeans to settle Canada in large numbers. They settled along the eastern coast of Canada. Some of them also settled in the northeastern part of the United States, and in the 1700s many of these French Canadians traveled south to Louisiana. Therefore, the French language and culture are important in both countries. For example, the American city of New Orleans has kept many French traditions in food, architecture, and religion. In Canada, Montreal and Quebec, the two largest cities in the province of Quebec, have the atmosphere of French cities. People speak French everywhere, and the children learn French in school. There are cafes and restaurants that prepare delicious food in the French style. French films, television programs, publications, artistic exhibits, and entertainment are very popular. The motto, or proverb, of Quebec province, *Je me souviens,* means "I remember." It suggests that French Canadians will always remember their French background.

[4]   While the French settlers made their homes mostly in the eastern parts of North America, members of other European groups settled farther west on the continent. For instance, many people from Finland settled in the American states of Wisconsin and Montana. In Canada, in the early 1900s, a group of Finnish people started a settlement in the western province of British Columbia. These Finns wanted to escape their hard life as coal miners in Finland and start a new life based on farming, fishing, and logging. They called their new Canadian community "Sointula," which means "harmony," or people getting along well together. Unfortunately, this new Finnish community had several problems. A fire killed some of the immigrants, there were not enough houses for all the families, and businesses did not succeed. Finally, only about 100 Finnish people remained in Sointula. Today, the descendants of these Finnish pioneers still live in the area around Sointula. In this region some people still speak Finnish, and the telephone book contains many Finnish names.

[5]   Like the Finns, many immigrants of Asian, African, and Latin American descent came to Canada and the United States to make a better life for themselves and particularly for their children. There are large Japanese and Chinese communities in the Canadian provinces of British Columbia and Alberta and on the West Coast of the United States. Some of these Asian immigrants are farmers, while others operate various businesses in the towns and cities. Several generations ago, Sikh people from India settled in western Canada and in California, and today their descendants live throughout North America. Most of the newer immigrants from the Indian subcontinent live in the larger cities of

The Inuit people make their own clothing to protect them from the cold.

Canada and the United States, where they work in scientific and technical industries or in their own shops, restaurants, or trading companies.

[6]   Recently, a young man of Indian background named Srinivas Krishna made a film about the Indian immigrants to Canada. His film is named *Marsala*, which means "blended spices." The title suggests the movie's main idea. The film shows some of the problems of Indian people trying to make a new life in Canada. Some of these problems are treated with humor. For example, the grandmother in the film likes to cook in her traditional Indian style. Some funny scenes in the movie show her in the modern kitchen of her son's home using appliances such as the food processor. However, other problems of the Indian immigrants are more serious. Some Canadians discriminate against these new immigrants and attack them violently. Some of the young Indian people have disagreements with their parents' ideas about work and marriage. These same problems are common in various immigrant groups, so this film has meaning for many people throughout Canada and the United States.

[7]   In both Canada and the United States there are small, traditional groups of people who live quite differently from the majority of their neighbors. For example, the Inuit (Eskimo) people of northern Canada and the American state of Alaska are neither farmers nor city people. They earn their living primarily by fishing and hunting. Most of their food, clothing, oil, tools, and weapons come from sea mammals such as seals or from the caribou, which is a large deer. In the winter the Inuit people live in huts made of earth, wood, or stone; the

snow igloo that most of us have seen in pictures is rarely used. In summer, the Inuit make tents from caribou skins. The Inuit people live in small groups, and most of their property is held by the community rather than by private persons. The Inuit have not mixed into Canadian or Alaskan society a great deal, and they still speak their own language.

[8]   The Inuit people have a rich tradition of arts and crafts. They carve small, useful objects such as weapons and tools out of soapstone, ivory, and bone. They carve statues, animals, and masks that represent figures from their religion or their everyday life as hunters and fishers. The Inuit people also make much of their own clothing from animal skins and fur, and decorate these items with their own designs. Useful and beautiful items such as fur hats, parkas, and waterproof moccasins have been part of the Inuit tradition for 2,000 years. When the European settlers first arrived in the northern part of North America, they used many articles of Inuit clothing to protect them from the cold. Today, tourists from all over the world buy Inuit art and crafts for their usefulness and beauty.

[9]   The diversity of people living in North America makes this a rich and inter-esting continent. Canada and the United States share some similar problems and are searching for useful solutions to them. Perhaps this is what makes them such good neighbors.

Summary Completion.   To test your comprehension of the reading passage, fill in each blank space with an appropriate word or phrase from the text.

Canada and the United States, the two countries of the (1)_____

continent, have many similarities. People in these two nations speak many different

languages, but the primary language in both countries is (2)_____ .

The Native American and Inuit people were the (3)_____ inhabitants of

the continent, but today there are many (4)_____ from Europe, Asia, and

the Caribbean. French-speaking Canadians continue many of the (5)_____

of their ancestors; that is why their motto is (6)_____ . The first Finnish

settlement in Canada (7)_____ , but people of Finnish descent still live in

the midwestern and western parts of the continent. Many Asian immigrants from coun-

tries such as (8)_____ live both on farms and in the cities of North America.

A recent Canadian film shows some of the (9)_____ that these immigrants

face in their new home. Small, traditional populations such as the Inuit people have a

life-style that is (10)_____ from the majority of their neighbors.

Reacting to the Reading

The French, (East) Indian, Chinese, and many other immigrant groups in Canada and the United States try to keep their native language alive in the younger members of their groups.

    a. How important do you think it is for an immigrant group to keep its own language? What are some ways in which immigrants can pass their language down to their children? What are some problems that might occur in this situation?

    b. Can people keep their culture alive without their own language? What are some ways that they can do this?

Reading Comprehension

1. Understanding the Text.   Choose the correct answer, or follow the directions.

    a. What is the main point that Paragraph [1] makes about the language of both Canada and the United States?

    b. Refer back to Paragraph [1], Sentence 6, which uses the word *although*. This word indicates that

       (1) two pieces of information contrast with each other.

       (2) one piece of information describes the other.

       (3) a result is following a reason.

There are two other words in the paragraph that have the same meaning as *although*. List them. _____

    c. According to Paragraph [2], why doesn't Canada have a large African-American population? _____

    d. Which European group was the first to settle in Canada?

    _____

    e. Next to each paragraph number, write the name of the cultural group that is the subject of that paragraph.

Paragraph [3] _____   Paragraph [5] _____

Paragraph [4] _____   Paragraph [7] _____

f. Paragraph [4] implies that people immigrate to a new country
   (1) to improve the difficult conditions of their lives.
   (2) to earn a living as farmers and fishers.
   (3) to learn a new language.

g. The introductory phrase of Paragraph [5], *Like the Finns*, suggests that
   (1) the Asian immigrants like and respect the Finns.
   (2) the Asian immigrants are similar to the Finns in some way.
   (3) the Asian immigrants will probably succeed in their new lives.

h. According to Paragraph [6], what is the main purpose of Srinivas Krishna's film *Marsala*? _____

   _____

i. Various signal expressions in Paragraph [6] help the reader follow the relationships between pieces of information. Which word(s) in that paragraph show
   (1) a time period? _____
   (2) a contrast? _____
   (3) an example? _____

j. According to Paragraph [6], the film *Marsala*
   (1) is of interest only to Indian immigrants.
   (2) is a comedy about older people.
   (3) presents problems common to many immigrant groups.

k. Paragraphs [7] and [8] primarily describe
   (1) the similarities between the Inuit and other Canadians.
   (2) the special features of Inuit life.
   (3) the benefits that Europeans received from the Inuit.

l. The Inuit people are skilled in making items that are
   (1) beautiful but not useful in everyday life.
   (2) not useful for themselves but popular with Europeans.
   (3) useful for daily needs and beautiful in design.

2. Answering Information Questions.   Answer the following questions in complete sentences.

a. What are some similarities between Canada and the United States?

b. In which areas of Canada and the United States do people follow French traditions?

c. Why did the first Finnish settlers come to Canada?

d. From which countries in Asia did immigrants come to Canada and the United States?

e. What is the film *Marsala* about?

f. How is the Inuit life-style different from the life-styles of most other North Americans?

Ⅲ THE READING PROCESS

Identifying Main Ideas.   A main idea states the topic or subject of a passage. It also tells something important about the topic. A main idea is a *general* statement. It helps the reader understand the writer's *basic* idea or opinion. It does not give specific details, facts, or examples. Look for the main idea sentence in the following paragraph.

> Gatineau Park is a splendid recreation center near the city of Ottawa. Although the park is close to a large city, it contains forests, wildflowers, wildlife such as deer, fox, and beaver, and a thousand species of birds. There are lakes for canoeing and swimming, and forest trails for hiking and jogging. There is also an interesting old house that belonged to a prime minister of Canada almost one hundred years ago.

Underline the first sentence, which tells you the main idea of this paragraph. It states the topic: *Gatineau Park*. It tells something important about the topic: Gatineau Park is a *splendid recreation center*. The first sentence is the most general statement in this paragraph.

a. Read the following paragraphs. Then write the topic of the paragraph and the main idea of the paragraph on the lines provided.

> (1) Montreal's Winter Festival celebrates the winter season. The festival's symbol is *Boule de Neige*, a jolly snowman who watches over the city at this time. There are winter activities for every age and interest during this two-week festival. Clowns and makeup artists stroll the city's parks to entertain people. There are skiing and ice skating events for beginners and experts

Ice skating and cross-country skiing are favorite sports of the people in the colder parts of North America.

alike. Specialists in ice carving create huge sculptures that represent the life of the people of Canada. There are more than 125 special events available to all by public transportation.

Topic: _____

Main Idea: _____

(2) Dinesh Mehta's parents immigrated to Canada from the Indian city of Bombay. Jane Hoffer's parents are the descendants of European Jews. Eleanor Omoto's grandparents were from Japan. They first settled in Winnipeg; then they moved to Vancouver on Canada's west coast. Pierre Mondesire was born in Montreal. His parents originally came from Haiti. In Canada, there are many people like these whose ancestors came from different cultures.

Topic: _____

Main Idea: _____

b. Choose three paragraphs from the reading passage. Write the topic of each paragraph, and copy the sentence that expresses the paragraph's main idea.

Ⅳ VOCABULARY

1. New Words.   Pronounce the words, following your instructor.

Verbs	Nouns	Adjectives
celebrate	ceremony	native
perform	immigrant	delicious
represent	occasion	
settle	inhabitants	
	weapons	

EXPANDING VOCABULARY.   Fill in each blank space with a word from the New Word list.

(1) In the United States we _____ Independence Day on July 4.
It is always a happy _____ .

(2) An _____ to Canada can learn to speak English by attending classes. Many foreign students are bilingual; they speak English and
their _____ language.

(3) The _____ of extremely cold areas must wear clothing that
protects them from the weather.

(4) In today's world we have much to fear from the spread of nuclear
_____ that could destroy whole countries.

(5) Traditionally, a Western bride wears white to _____ purity.

(6) At many festivals the people _____ their native dances and
sell _____ and unusual native foods.

(7) Some immigrants like to _____ in large cities because there
are more job opportunities.

USING VOCABULARY.   Write a complete sentence in answer to each of the following questions. Use the italicized word in your statement.

(1) In your opinion, what kinds of fruit are *delicious*?

(2) Where do you like to go to *celebrate* your birthday?

(3) Is Thanksgiving Day a special *occasion* in your family?

(4) What holiday is important in your *native* country?

(5) Who usually *performs* a wedding *ceremony* in your place of worship?

(6) Do most *immigrants* have an easy time or a difficult time when they first come to their new homeland?

(7) What does the $ sign *represent*?

(8) How many *inhabitants* are there in the city where you live?

2. Word Families: Adjectives Versus Noun Forms.   A noun is the name of a person, place, or thing. An adjective describes a noun. An adjective usually goes before the noun.

He is from *Canada*.
          (noun)
Some *Canadian men* are *excellent* hockey *players*.
    (adjective)(noun)   (adjective)   (noun)
(What kind of men? Canadian. What kind of hockey players? Excellent.)

In English, some adjectives and nouns are related to each other in meaning, but they have different forms. Study the following lists.

Noun	Adjective
Canada	Canadian
Alaska	Alaskan
America	American
Mexico	Mexican
India	Indian
(the) east	eastern
(the) west	western
richness	rich
tradition	traditional
culture	cultural

SENTENCE COMPLETION. Choose the correct word in parentheses to fill in the blank space in each sentence.

a. (west, western) The Yukon is a _____ province of Canada.

b. (culture, cultural) French settlers in Canada introduced and preserved the music from their own _____ .

c. (America, American) There are fifty stars on the _____ flag, one for every state.

d. (tradition, traditional) The Winter Festival is a _____ that takes place in Quebec every January.

e. (ancestor, ancestral) Many Americans and Canadians save money to take a trip to their _____ homeland.

f. (kindness, kind) Visitors to Canada find _____ and friendly people to welcome them.

g. (rich, richness) Farming in North America is successful because of the _____ of the soil.

h. (Mexico, Mexican) There aren't many people from _____ in Canada.

 ## V LANGUAGE FOCUS

Simple Present Tense of *To Be*

The simple present tense of *to be* connects the subject with the rest of the sentence to show the existence of a person, place, or thing. It also describes or gives information about a person, place, or thing.

	Singular Subjects	**Plural Subjects**
First Person	I am (I'm)	The teacher and I are We are (we're)
Second Person	You are (You're)	You are (You're)
Third Person	The teacher is He is (He's) She is (She's) It is (It's)	Teachers are They are (They're)

The negative forms are *am not (I'm not), are not (aren't)*, and *is not (isn't)*.

> The teacher *is* a Canadian.
> Teachers *are not* usually late to class.

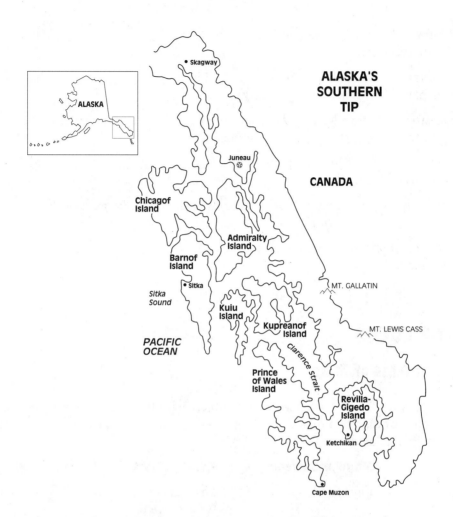

Answering Questions with Simple Present of *To Be*. Write complete sentences to answer the following questions. Look at the map of Alaska for your answers.

    a. In what ocean are the Alaskan islands?

    b. Which is the smallest island on this map?

    c. Which country is on the border of Alaska?

    d. Are Mt. Gallatin and Mt. Lewis Cass on an island?

    e. Which city is the capital of Alaska?

    f. Is the capital on the Alaskan mainland or on an island?

    g. On which island is the city of Ketchikan?

    h. What body of water is between the mainland and Prince of Wales Island?

    i. Are Chichagof Island and Admiralty Island in the southern part of Alaska?

There Is or *There Isn't* and *There Are* or *There Aren't*

When the subject of the verb *to be* is not a specific person or thing, we usually use the expression *there is* or *there are* + a noun. The negative forms are *there isn't* and *there aren't*.

	Verb	Subject	Rest of sentence
There	is	a festival	in Quebec in January.
There	isn't	much snow	in Louisiana.
There	are	many beaches	on the Canadian coasts.
There	aren't	any roads	in some parts of Alaska.

The subject is not *there*. The subject comes after the verb. When the subject is plural, the verb must be plural.

1. Choosing the Correct Form: *Is/Are* or *There Is/There Are*.   Fill in the blank spaces with the correct verb or verb phrase. Use negatives as indicated.

Holidays (1) _____ usually happy occasions. Thanksgiving Day (negative) (2) _____ celebrated in Canada, but it (3) _____ an especially happy occasion in the United States. In some cities (4) _____ special events such as ball games or parades. In New York City (5) _____ an extraordinary parade with balloon figures of Mickey Mouse, Superman, and other cartoon characters. If you don't arrive early, (negative) (6) _____ much chance to see the parade because the streets (7) _____ always crowded with children and their parents. In most American homes (8) _____ a traditional Thanksgiving feast with turkey, pumpkin pie, and other delicious foods. Thanksgiving (9) _____ a time for fun and relaxation. It (negative) (10) _____ a time to think about diets.

2. Sentence Composing.   Write the answers to the following questions in complete sentences. Use *there is*, *there isn't*, *there are*, and *there aren't* in your answers. The first one is done for you.

    a. How many states are there in the United States?

       There are fifty states in the United States.

    b. Where can I find a map of Alaska?

    c. Why can't people live on the moon?

d. How many verbs are there in this sentence?

e. What is one problem with your neighborhood?

f. Are there any rivers in your city?

g. Where can I find a good restaurant around the college?

To Be + Adjective + Noun

Study the sentences in the chart.

Subject	Verb	Article	Adjective	Noun
An archeologist	is	an	active	person.
Japan	isn't	a	large	country.
Dogs and cats	aren't		extraordinary	animals.

Adjectives don't change for plural nouns. Adjectives never add an *s* for plural nouns. Do we use the article *a* or *an* for plurals?

1. Sentence Building.

a. Draw a line from the subject on the left to an appropriate adjective-noun phrase on the right.

	Subject	Adjective-Noun
(1)	Japanese	difficult subject
(2)	a lion	Asian language
(3)	gold	Canadian city
(4)	igloo	wild animal
(5)	trout	expensive metal
(6)	Montreal	delicious fish
(7)	chemistry	Inuit word

Now write a complete sentence with the simple present tense of the verb *to be*, using your matched items.

Japanese is an Asian language.

b. Now rewrite each sentence from Part A by using the following plural subjects.

(1) Japanese and Chinese

(2) lions and tigers

(3) gold and silver

(4) igloo and umiak

(5) trout and bass

(6) Montreal and Ottawa

(7) chemistry and astronomy

Japanese and Chinese are Asian languages.

Remember that the article *a* or *an* is not used with plurals.

2. Sentence Completion.   Write an appropriate subject and the correct form of the verb *to be* for the given adjective-noun combinations. Use the positive or negative form of the verb as appropriate for your meaning.

_____ *Boxing is a* _____ dangerous sport.

_____ *We aren't* _____ native speakers of English.

---

a. _____ exciting city.

b. _____ Asian countries.

c. _____ cold area of the world.

d. _____ my best friend.

e. _____ deep bodies of water.

f. _____ interesting subject.

g. _____ useful tools.

h. _____ my native language.

i. _____ extraordinary animal.

j. _____ convenient forms of transportation.

3. Sentence Combining.   The first sentence in each group states the subject. The second sentence states the adjective. The third sentence states the place *where* or the time *when*. Place the adjective in the correct order, and add the prepositional phrase to make one complete sentence. Leave out any unnecessary words. See the examples on page 50.

---

(1) Toronto is a city. (2) The city is important. (3) The city is in Canada.
_____*Toronto is an important city in Canada.*_____

(1) There is a restaurant. (2) The restaurant is Chinese. (3) The restaurant is in my neighborhood.
_____*There is a Chinese restaurant in my neighborhood.*_____

---

a. (1) Anticosti is an island. (2) The island is beautiful. (3) The island is in the St. Lawrence River.

b. (1) There are animals. (2) The animals are wild. (3) The animals are in some of the Canadian Forests.

c. (1) There are beaches. (2) The beaches are splendid. (3) The beaches are along the coast.

d. (1) There are seashells. (2) The seashells are interesting. (3) The seashells are on the beach.

e. (1) There are lots of activities. (2) The activities are cultural. (3) The activities are during the summer.

f. (1) There are workers. (2) The workers are skillful. (3) The workers are in my native country.

VI   THE COMPOSING PROCESS

1. Sentence Combining to Form a Paragraph.   Combine each set of sentences into longer, more interesting statements to form a paragraph about a festival in New Orleans. Leave out all unnecessary words. Place adjectives before nouns to combine sentences. Use the word *and* to combine sentences where appropriate. Write your complete paragraph on a separate sheet of paper.

a. (1) New Orleans is a city.
   (2) It is in Louisiana.

b. (1) There is a festival there.
   (2) It is exciting.
   (3) It is in the winter.
   (4) It is called Mardi Gras.

c. (1) During Mardi Gras there are parades.
   (2) They are throughout the city.

d. (1) There are marching bands.

   (2) There are floats with people in costumes.

   (3) The costumes are extraordinary.

e. (1) The people on floats toss out trinkets.

   (2) They toss out candy.

   (3) This is for the children watching the parades.

f. (1) People dance in the streets.

   (2) They dance all day and night.

g. (1) They wear masks.

   (2) The masks are interesting.

   (3) The masks cover their faces. (Use *to cover*.)

h. (1) Everyone enjoys eating the food.

   (2) The food is delicious.

   (3) The food is French-Creole.

   (4) They eat outdoors or in restaurants.

i. (1) There are other carnivals such as this.

   (2) They are in different parts of the country.

j. (1) But New Orleans has the largest celebration.

   (2) It has the most colorful celebration.

   (3) The celebration is in the United States.

k. (1) It is a place to visit.

   (2) It is wonderful at Mardi Gras time.

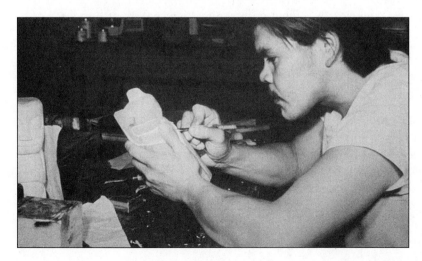

Many Native
Americans continue
to work at their
traditional crafts.

2. Developing a Unified Paragraph.   A unified paragraph is a group of sentences about one topic. A unified paragraph contains a main idea sentence that states the topic and gives the writer's opinion or point of view about the topic. Students learning to write paragraphs should place the main idea statement first in the paragraph.

a. In the following exercise, each set of sentences has a single topic. One of the sentences contains the main idea statement. Other sentences contain details about the topic. One sentence does not relate to the main idea. Rearrange each set of sentences so that the main idea comes first and the details follow in logical order. Omit the unrelated sentence. Rewrite the complete paragraph on a separate sheet of paper.

> In some Inuit workshops, people also make fur gloves and hoods. Other workers carve beautiful bowls and statues of wood. The Inuit people are skilled workers in arts and crafts. For example, some Inuit are skillful at carving in soapstone and ivory. The Inuit live primarily by hunting and fishing. There are excellent workers who create useful articles of bone and stone.

b. In this set you must arrange the sentences in logical order. Use words such as *then*, *after*, or other signals to guide you in arranging the correct order. There are prepositional phrases of time and other phrases to help you find the correct sentence order.

(1) In May, the pathways along the canal in Ottawa are bordered by a beautiful display of tulips during the Spring Festival.

(2) There are other summer celebrations, too, such as the Jazz Festival.

(3) All summer long, the National Capital Region of Canada is alive with the color and music of festivals.

(4) Then August brings an international bicycling festival to Hull-Ottawa.

(5) After that, later in July, there is an international sailboat and motorboat regatta.

(6) On July 1, the whole country celebrates Canada Day.

(7) At that time, the skies are filled with the brilliant colors of hundreds of balloons.

(8) In September, the town of Gatineau hosts a hot-air balloon festival.

(9) People from all over the world come to see this splendid spectacle on the Outaouais River.

3. Composing a Paragraph.   Write a paragraph describing a holiday, festival, or special occasion that is celebrated in your native culture. Include details about the significance of each aspect of the celebration. Begin by filling in the topic and the main idea sentence on the lines provided. Then use the sentences in the list to guide you in writing your paragraph. Write your paragraph on a separate piece of paper, and use correct paragraph form.

Topic:_____

Main Idea: _____

Your main idea statement should tell the name of the holiday, your opinion about the holiday (important, enjoyable), and the name of the country in which it is celebrated. Your main idea statement will be the first sentence of your paragraph.

(1) State the reason for the celebration. Tell when it was first celebrated. (Is it ancient or more recent?)

(2) Tell when it takes place. Explain why it is celebrated at this time.

(3) Describe what special costumes the people wear. Explain the significance of any unusual clothing.

(4) Tell what the people carry or use (flags, statues, paper animals) in the celebration. What is the meaning of these items?

(5) Describe any performances (dancing, music, shows, or other entertainment) that take place. Explain how these performances relate to the occasion.

(6) Tell what special food or drink is prepared. What is the reason for these special preparations?

(7) Describe other activities during the day or night in which people participate. (Perhaps there are sports events, games, or fireworks displays.) What meaning do these events have for the occasion?

(8) Explain how the people feel during the celebration. Are they proud, serious, sad, joyful, enthusiastic? Tell why the people feel as they do at this time.

(9) Tell how you in particular feel about this celebration.

Paragraph Topics

1. In North America, immigrants from all over the world still practice some of their native customs and traditions. What are some customs or traditions that you or your family members maintain? Write a composition in which you describe one or more customs. Describe the custom or tradition, and tell who participates in it, and when and how it is observed. Begin each new paragraph with a main idea sentence that states the topic of the paragraph and expresses something important about the topic.

2. In many countries people wear traditional clothes only on special occasions. Describe some traditional clothes in your native country. Write about the different occasions when you might wear these clothes.

Ⓥ️ ADDITIONAL READING

Witching for Water

[1]   People who live in cities rarely think about their water supply. When they are thirsty or need water to cook or bathe, they simply turn on the tap. Their water usually comes from a reservoir outside the city. A reservoir fills up with rainwater and melted snow from mountains, and the water flows through pipes to the city. In rural areas, however, there aren't any reservoirs to supply farmhouses with water. People who live in the countryside obtain their water from an underground spring, and so they must dig a well. When a well goes dry, they must dig another in a different place. It is an important and difficult task to find the right place for a good supply of well water.

[2]   How do people make a choice about where to dig a well? There is no scientific method of detecting underground water, but there is a traditional "magic" way. It is called water witching, or dowsing. Some farmers in the United States practice this ancient folk custom. They use a divining rod, a switch from a tree, as their tool. Of course, they must have a special ability too; not everyone can be a dowser. Dowsers think that they have a reliable method of searching for hidden springs of water. Margaret Maron, a writer of mystery stories, agrees with them.

[3]   Mrs. Maron was born and raised on a farm in North Carolina but moved to New York when she got married. Then in 1968 her mother gave her three acres of land at the edge of the family farm to build a vacation house, which later became her permanent home. Mrs. Maron and her husband went back to North Carolina to make all the arrangements. Here is Mrs. Maron's account of "witching for water":

[4]   This particular lot had been the site of my grandparents' house, a pinewood farmhouse that was built in the 1880s and burned to the ground in 1954. During those seventy-five years, at least three wells had been dug on the grounds. They provided fresh water for humans and animals and then went dry. My mother reminded us of this and I jokingly said, "Perhaps we should bring in a dowser to witch us a well." Mother laughed and said, "If you want, we can ask Mr. Randall Woodall. He's a dowser."

I knew that Mr. Randall was a tobacco farmer, the same age as my grandfather, but I didn't know that he had the mysterious powers of a dowser. My husband and I were thrilled with the idea of folk magic, so mother asked him and he agreed to come.

Mr. Randall arrived on our property a few days later. He was a tall man with white hair and a weather-worn face. He was dressed in a neat blue shirt, faded overalls, and high-top shoes. He was a little shy as we showed him around the property, but as soon as he started to work, he seemed quite sure of himself.

Some farmers in the United States practice the ancient folk custom of dowsing for water. A farmer in Maine is holding a divining rod that is pointing down to a strong spot in the ground.

He began by cutting a switch from a hickory tree. He picked a young green shoot. "A green shoot is full of water, and like calls to like," he explained. The switch was slightly thicker than his thumb and about four feet long. He held one end of the stick in each hand, elbows at his side, forearms parallel to the ground, and palms down. He held the hickory stick so tightly that his knuckles turned white and the stick bent out in front of him like a half-loop.

We told Mr. Randall where we wanted to build our house, so he began to walk back and forth over that general area. Occasionally the tip of the stick began to shake slightly, but Mr. Randall paid no attention. "They don't mean much of nothing. Jest little streamlets. We're looking for something stronger," he explained.

After he had walked for about twenty minutes, the hickory loop suddenly made a strong downward movement. Mr. Randall slowed his steps and swept over the area with the stick more thoroughly. As he moved away from the "strong spot," the loop would swing back up until it was parallel with the ground. But, as he returned to that area, we watched in fascination as the end of the loop bent downward again with great force. It seemed as if something in the earth were pulling it.

"Dig here," he told us. "Hit's 'bout as strong a sprang as I've ever felt."

So we hired a man to come out and dig the well in that spot. He went down sixty feet and found thirty feet of water. That was over twenty years ago. About two years ago there was a terrible dry spell, and all our neighbors' wells were going dry. My husband and I went out and took the cap off our well and measured the depth of the water. It had only gone down eighteen inches!

Mr. Randall promised us "hit won't never run dry," and I for one believe him.

[5]   People in many parts of the world have a folk-magic tradition. Folk magic helps people make a choice when they do not have all the information they need to solve a problem. A dowser helped Mrs. Maron make a difficult choice. In her case, the "magic" worked well.

[6]   What do scientists think of dowsing? They say there is no connection between the use of a divining rod and the discovery of water. They believe that the downward motion occurs because the dowser, without knowing it, stops squeezing the rod and relaxes his muscles. It is just accidental, a matter of chance, that water is later discovered in places where the movement occurred. Perhaps you would agree with the scientists, but you might still want to take a chance with a dowser.

Reacting to the Reading

1. This story shows a situation in which someone makes a choice without clear-cut scientific information.

    a. Would you take a chance on a dowser? Explain why or why not.

    b. Tossing a coin is one way of making a choice. How would you choose a sports team or a racehorse to win? Is your way a "reasonable" decision, or is it just taking a chance?

2. Scientists don't believe in "folk" methods of finding water.

    a. Do you have a "folk" or family tradition for curing a cold? If so, what do you use? What cures have you heard about but haven't tried?

    b. What "folk" customs are practiced in your native country that may be of interest to your classmates and teacher?

Reading Comprehension

1. Understanding the Text.   Choose the correct answer, or follow the directions.

Divining rods are used to detect metals, oil, and other minerals in the ground. This drawing from 1556 shows divining rods in use for finding metals.

a. Which statement is true according to Paragraph [1]?

  (1) It is just as easy for rural people to obtain water as it is for city people.

  (2) Reservoirs supply farmhouses with a steady stream of fresh water.

  (3) In rural areas, people use well water for their daily needs.

b. According to the information in Paragraph [2],

  (1) scientists have their own method of detecting hidden springs.

  (2) some farmers practice a form of folk magic to detect hidden springs.

  (3) dowsers use a scientific method of detecting hidden springs.

c. What was the situation on Mrs. Maron's property?

  (1) There was a good well, but it was in the wrong place for the house.

  (2) There was a house, but no well.

  (3) There was no well for the house that she was going to build.

d. When Mrs. Maron first spoke to her mother about a dowser,

  (1) she said it in a joking way.

  (2) she was really serious about calling one in.

  (3) her mother did not approve of the idea.

e. Mrs. Maron decided to have Mr. Randall come to her property because

(1) her mother told her to do it.

(2) she and her husband were excited about seeing some folk magic.

(3) she knew Mr. Randall and wanted to see him again after so many years.

f. Write the sentence from Mrs. Maron's account that describes how Mr. Randall looked.

_____

g. Write the sentence that describes Mr. Randall's clothes.

_____

h. Mark *T* for *true*, *F* for *false*, or *N.I.* for *no information* about Mr. Randall in this story.

(1) He was a full-time dowser _____

(2) He was a young man. _____

(3) He sometimes spoke English ungrammatically. _____

(4) He had found water many times in the past. _____

(5) He came dressed in work clothes. _____

(6) He was a well digger. _____

(7) He earned his living as a tobacco farmer. _____

(8) He didn't take payment for his dowsing service. _____

i. Mr. Randall chose a green shoot from a hickory tree because it was full of water and *"like calls to like."* This expression means that

(1) the water in the shoot will attract water in the ground.

(2) Mr. Randall likes water.

(3) the young shoot looks like the hickory tree from which it came.

j. Mrs. Maron wrote her account using some of Mr. Randall's exact words and pronunciation. In the following items the italicized words are either used incorrectly or are spelled incorrectly. Write the correct form of the word.

(1) They don't mean much of *nothing*. _____

(2) *Jest* little streamlets. _____

(3) *Hit's 'bout* as strong a *sprang* as I've ever felt. _____

_____ _____

(4) *Hit* won't *never* run dry. _____ _____

k. Mrs. Maron believes in the mysterious powers of dowsers because

  (1) she is a writer of mystery stories.

  (2) her well has been full of water for over twenty years.

  (3) Mr. Randall was a mysterious man.

2. Sequencing Events in Time Order.   Time order is important in relating an event. Recalling activities in sequence helps the reader to reconstruct the event correctly.

  a. The following items are about Mrs. Maron's property. Number the sentences in correct order according to the time the event takes place. Number 1 will be the first thing that happened. Number 5 will be the last.

  (1) The farmhouse burned down. ____

  (2) Mrs. Maron lives there now. ____

  (3) Mrs. Maron's grandparents lived in that house. ____

  (4) Mrs. Maron built a house on the property. ____

  (5) A pinewood farmhouse had been built on the property. ____

  b. When the following sentences are put in correct time order, they will make a paragraph about the steps Mr. Randall took to dowse for water. Arrange the sentences correctly, and write them in a paragraph.

  (1) In some places the stick would shake slightly.

  (2) He told Mrs. Maron to dig there.

  (3) First he cut a switch from a hickory tree.

  (4) Then he began to walk back and forth over the property.

  (5) But he paid no attention to those spots.

  (6) He held the stick with both hands so that it formed a loop.

  (7) Then he found a strong spot.

  (8) He walked around some more.

Vocabulary

Expanding Vocabulary.   Choose the word(s) that mean(s) the same as the italicized word in each sentence. Use a dictionary only if necessary.

  a. People who live in cities *obtain* their water from reservoirs located outside the city.

  (1) drink   (2) keep   (3) get

b. People who live in *rural* areas usually obtain their water from a well.

(1) crowded   (2) tropical   (3) agricultural

c. Farmers depend on underground springs to *supply* them with water for drinking, bathing, and cooking.

(1) provide   (2) measure   (3) show

d. It is impossible to *detect* an underground spring without digging in the earth, or perhaps asking a dowser to help you.

(1) destroy   (2) discover   (3) hide

e. Dowsers think that their way of searching for water is *reliable*.

(1) dependable   (2) silly   (3) delicious

f. Mrs. Maron was *thrilled* with the idea of seeing a dowser at work.

(1) annoyed   (2) bored   (3) excited

g. Mr. Randall kept his forearms *parallel to* the ground as he held the dowsing stick.

(1) away from   (2) in the opposite direction from

(3) extending in the same direction as

h. When he found a strong spot, he went over the area more *thoroughly* to make sure it was the right place to dig.

(1) quickly   (2) frequently   (3) completely

i. There is no scientific *method* of detecting underground springs, so dowsing may be as good as any other *method* of finding water.

(1) technique   (2) problem   (3) discovery

C H A P T E R   T H R E E

STEPS TO THE FUTURE

I PREREADING

Class Discussion.   Study the following entries from The Newbury House Dictionary of American English:

> **predict** / pri' dikt / *v.* to say what will happen in the future, foretell: *Scientists are not able to predict earthquakes very well.*

> **prediction** / pri' dikʃan / *n.* a statement about what will happen in the future, forecast: *The meteorologist's prediction that it would rain today was correct.*

What does the dictionary tell you about the entry words? What do the abbreviations mean?

FREE WRITE
What are your predictions of the future? What will the world be like when the next generation of children is grown?

Apollo II astronaut Edwin E. Aldrin, Jr., leaves his footprints on the surface of the moon. What predictions can you make about living on the moon in the future?

Vocabulary in Context. The words in this exercise will appear in the reading passage. Circle the word that means the same as the italicized word in each sentence.

1. Scientists can *observe* the stars through a telescope.

   a. watch closely   b. hear clearly   c. instruct

2. They also send spacecraft to *explore* the planets.

   a. explain about   b. record   c. go over closely

3. Nine planets *revolve* around the sun.

   a. shine   b. remain   c. turn

4. The air around the Earth *protects* it against the sun's dangerous rays.

   a. attacks   b. guards   c. provides

5. The Earth has air and water *necessary* for life.

   a. needed   b. traditional   c. unimportant

6. Without the Earth's special *environment*, there would be no life.

   a. planet   b. surroundings   c. rays

7. There are many *varieties* of plants and animals on Earth.

   a. kinds   b. areas   c. millions

8. If we don't take care of our planet, we may *destroy* some of the life on it.

   a. save   b. disturb   c. ruin

9. There must be a *balance* of all kinds of life forms to have a good life on Earth.

   a. harmony   b. culture   c. responsibility

10. If you enjoy the beach, it would be *irresponsible* of you to leave your trash in the sand.

    a. very kind   b. expected   c. totally careless

Ⅱ READING

Improving Our Environment Is Everybody's Job

[1]   In the past, many people liked to think that life existed on other planets in our solar system. It was an exciting thought. Perhaps we had friendly neighbors out there. Perhaps we had enemies. Today we know that we have no neighbors in our solar system. All the planets have been explored by space robots.

According to the scientific information, no planet but Earth has the air, water, and vegetation necessary for life.

[2]   Earth has the best position among the nine planets that revolve around the sun. Neither too near nor too far from the sun, it receives the necessary amount of heat and light. High up in the air, the ozone layer protects us from the sun's dangerous rays. As Earth revolves, the seasons change. Winds blow rain clouds over the land, and our fields are green with vegetation. Without this special environment, there would be no life on Earth. If we change this environment, we may destroy some of life's treasures.

[3]   Earth was formed over 4 billion years ago. At first it was a dead object of rock, like the moon now, without air or water. It took millions of years to develop into a world of life. Now Earth is the home of over 13 million different plant and animal species. All the varieties of living things depend on the sun, on air and water, and on each other. The sun will shine for millions of years. Will we be able to keep Earth a special place in the solar system?

[4]   The future doesn't look bright. Environmental problems have harmful effects on our health and on all of nature. We may observe these problems at home with our drinking water, at the beach where garbage floats in the ocean, in our polluted rivers and streams where fish can no longer live, and on our farmlands and woodlands where acid rain falls. Scientists warn us that our problems will get worse. In some parts of the world, whole forests are being cut down. As a result, wildlife species become homeless and may even die out. Moreover, scientists predict that, without our forests, Earth's climate will change. They say that the continued use of fuels such as coal and oil will add to the climate problem. These fuels and other chemicals pollute the air and slowly destroy the ozone layer that protects us from the sun's dangerous rays. This will result in higher temperatures, droughts, and severe storms all across the globe.

[5]   Can we live on our land without spoiling the environment? In the United States the federal government owns large areas of wilderness. This land is managed by the National Park and Forest Service to provide recreation for the public without upsetting the balance of nature. To keep these areas unspoiled, the Service limits the number of people and cars in the parklands. Park attendants patrol the forests to clear out firewood left by campers because deadwood makes the soil poor. They try to prevent fires by watching closely for danger signals. They control noise and air pollution from boats on the lakes and rivers. They have strict rules to protect the animals in the forest from harm by visitors, and to protect the visitors too.

[6]   The National Forest Service also manages Echo Lake, a vacation community in the Sierra Nevada Mountains of California. There are only 125 cabins on the lake because the Service wants to prevent overcrowding. Cabin owners cannot have electricity or flush toilets. They cannot chop down trees for firewood, and they cannot dig up rocks to add space to their cabins. They cannot burn or bury their garbage. They must carry their garbage out by boat. To protect the

This ideal environment at Echo Lake could be spoiled easily by the use of large power boats, electricity, or flush toilets.

lake from pollution, the Service forbids powerboats; residents must use sailboats, rowboats, or canoes for transportation.

[7]   Chemicals in soaps and detergents can also pollute the lake, so the cabin owners must have a special drainage system for wastewater. One owner was letting her soapy sink water drain into the lake. When this was reported, the Service directed her to dig a dry well, a huge hole under her cabin. The hole is filled with rocks and sand. The dry well filters the dirty water through the rocks and sand. Then the water flows cleanly into the lake. When the woman completed the job, the Service was satisfied that she had followed the rules. Cabin owners on Echo Lake must take great care of everything in their daily lives, but they also enjoy a healthful, pleasant environment.

[8]   Echo Lake is a vacation community, and, unfortunately, most of us can't take part in it. However, in our crowded cities, in our industrial world, in the lands of wild vegetation and animals, we cannot go on with irresponsible activities that will lead to the further destruction of nature. No one wants the Earth to become like the planet Venus—a world of carbon dioxide, acid rain, and 900° temperatures!

[9]   Stories about the future—in books and in movies—show people living on other planets, on the moon, or in space. But Earth is our real home, our only home. "How strange and wonderful is our home, our earth, with its swirling atmosphere, its flowing and frozen rivers, its climbing creatures, the things with wings that hang on rocks and soar through fog, the furry grass, the scaly seas . . . how utterly rich and wild. . . ." With these words, the writer Edward Abbey

expressed his love of nature. All of us, governments, private companies, and we as individuals must act responsibly in our home. We must work to make it safer for a brighter future.

Summary Completion.   Fill in each blank space with the correct word from the reading passage.

Earth is the only (1)_____ with the necessities of life. Our environment supports a great variety of plant and animal (2)_____ . But we are in danger of losing our treasures because of environmental (3)_____ . Chemicals are polluting our water and (4)_____ . Scientists predict that our (5)_____ will change because we are destroying the ozone layer. In the United States the National Park and Forest Service provides (6)_____ in wilderness areas without (7)_____ the balance of nature. At Echo Lake, for example, cabin owners enjoy a (8)_____ , pleasant environment because they follow the Service's strict (9)_____ . In the rest of the world we cannot continue our irresponsible (10)_____ that lead to further destruction. Earth is our only (11)_____ , and we must plan well for a better future.

Health problems are caused by smoke from cars, factories, and homes. Describe the quality of the air, water, and other features of your environment.

Reacting to the Reading

1. Environmental problems exist everywhere, and scientists predict worse conditions to come.

   a. What kinds of pollution do you notice in your neighborhood? Discuss such things as noise, garbage, gasoline fumes, and smoke from chimneys.

   b. What can ordinary people do about these problems? Which of the problems are the government's responsibility?

   c. Which environmental problem bothers you the most? How would you solve this problem if you had the authority?

2. Stories about the future describe people living on other planets, on the moon, or in space.

   a. Do you agree with people who predict this possibility? Explain why or why not.

   b. If it were possible to live somewhere other than Earth, what reasons might there be for doing so?

Reading Comprehension

1. Understanding the Text. Choose the correct answer, or follow the directions.

   a. According to Paragraph [1], all the planets in our solar system
      (1) have been visited by human astronauts.
      (2) have not yet been explored.
      (3) have been explored by unmanned spacecraft.

   b. The topic of Paragraph [2] is
      (1) the sun's dangerous rays.
      (2) Earth's special environment.
      (3) our changing seasons.

   c. In Paragraph [3], we learn that
      (1) life always existed on Earth.
      (2) Earth was originally like the moon.
      (3) Earth was formed recently.

d. In Paragraph [4], the author

    (1) gives us a description of our environmental problems.

    (2) offers some suggestions for improving our environment.

    (3) describes our environment in positive terms.

e. The main idea of Paragraph [5] is expressed in

    (1) the second sentence.

    (2) the third sentence.

    (3) the last sentence.

f. Paragraphs [6] and [7]

    (1) are unrelated to the main idea of Paragraph [5].

    (2) describe a place where people can visit but not stay.

    (3) add information about protected areas as described in Paragraph [5].

g. The information about the dry well in Paragraph [7] is given

    (1) to explain why Echo Lake is polluted.

    (2) to show how careless cabin owners are about the environment.

    (3) as an example of the strict rules against pollution.

h. In Paragraph [8] we are told that

    (1) we can all live in places like Echo Lake.

    (2) we must change our activities to save our environment.

    (3) we have an environment like that of Venus.

i. Paragraph [8] uses the phrase *irresponsible activities*. Check (✔) the items that would be considered irresponsible actions.

    (1) dumping chemicals in rivers and lakes _____

    (2) keeping endangered species of animals in zoos _____

    (3) burning garbage _____

    (4) drilling for oil in national wildlife areas _____

    (5) hunting elephants, lions, and tigers _____

    (6) establishing fast, cheap public-transportation systems _____

    (7) recycling newspapers _____

    (8) cutting down whole forests _____

    (9) throwing garbage on the streets _____

  (10) using the sun's energy to heat homes _____

j. In Paragraph [9] the writer Edward Abbey expresses

   (1) his appreciation of all of nature.

   (2) his concerns for the future.

   (3) his love of modern society.

2. Answering Information Questions.   Answer each of the following questions in a complete sentence.

a. What protects us from the sun's dangerous rays?

b. What was the Earth like 4 billion years ago?

c. What U.S. agency manages federal wilderness areas?

d. What kind of world is the planet Venus?

e. Who wrote the words quoted in Paragraph [9]?

Ⅲ THE READING PROCESS

Identifying Specific Information.   Specific information sentences give the details or facts in a paragraph. These sentences support the main idea of a paragraph. Details and facts explain the main idea sentence by answering the questions *why, when, where, how, what, who,* and *which* about the main idea. Specific information sentences can also give examples of something or give a time order of when things happen.

a. In the following paragraph, the main idea sentence is italicized. Read the specific information sentences carefully, and answer the questions at the end of the paragraph orally with your class.

   It is the job of the United States Park and Forest Service to manage our unspoiled wilderness areas. The Service must limit the number of people and cars in the parklands because overcrowding causes damage to the environment. Park attendants patrol the areas to clear out old firewood because it makes the soil poor. They try to prevent fires by keeping watch for danger signals. They control noise and air pollution from boats on the lakes and rivers. They have strict rules to protect the animals in the forests from harm by visitors, and to protect the visitors too.

   (1) Do the specific information sentences give examples of something, or do they give a time order?

   (2) Name all the things that answer the question *where,* and underline them in the paragraph.

(3) Tell *why* the Service limits the number of cars and people in the park-lands.

(4) Tell *why* park attendants clear out old firewood. What word in the paragraph signals a reason *why*?

(5) Tell *how* they try to prevent fires.

(6) Tell *who* they protect with strict rules.

(7) Do all the specific information sentences in the paragraph support the main idea?

b. In the following exercises, you will be asked for specific information about the reading passage. Follow the directions for each item. Write your answers in brief form on the lines.

(1) Look through the reading passage to find answers to the following *how* questions.

   (a) How many planets are there in the solar system? _____

   (b) How old is Earth? _____

   (c) How many different plant and animal species exist? _____

   (d) How many cabins are there at Echo Lake? _____

(2) According to Paragraph [4]:

   (a) There are environmental problems everywhere. List the places where these problems occur.

   _____   _____   _____

   _____   _____   _____

   (b) What are the two harmful effects of cutting down our forests?

   _____ and _____

   (c) What will be the result of the destruction of the ozone layer?

   _____   _____   _____

   (d) Which fuels are given as examples of air pollutants?

   _____   _____

(3) At Echo Lake, what activities or things are not allowed?

   _____   _____   _____

   _____   _____   _____

(4) What kinds of boats are permitted at Echo Lake?

_____   _____   _____

(5) Complete the following sentences about Echo Lake. Use the signal word
      because to introduce your reason.

   (a) There are only 125 cabins at Echo Lake _____

   _____ .

   (b) Powerboats are forbidden _____

   _____ .

   (c) The residents must have a special drainage system for wastewater

   _____

   _____ .

Many species of animals like this caiman are dying out because people kill them
for their skins.

Ⅳ VOCABULARY

1. New Words. Pronounce the words, following your instructor.

Verbs	Nouns	Adjectives
explore	balance	necessary
observe	environment	(ir)responsible
revolve	variety	
protect		
destroy		

EXPANDING VOCABULARY. Choose a word from the list that correctly completes each sentence.

(1) A loving home _____ is important for children.

(2) On the Fourth of July, I always go up on the roof to _____ the fireworks.

(3) If you tell lies, you may _____ your relationship with those who trust you.

(4) It isn't _____ to copy these sentences on a separate sheet of paper.

(5) There are parts of this city I haven't been to, but I'll _____ them sometime in the future.

(6) My friend's garden is blooming with such a wonderful _____ of flowers.

(7) When you prepare a meal, you should consider a good _____ between proteins and carbohydrates.

(8) To leave a young child alone in the house is an _____ action.

(9) In many areas of the world, there are strict laws to _____ endangered species of animals.

(10) As Earth travels around the sun, it must also _____ on its own axis.

USING VOCABULARY. Write a complete sentence in answer to each question. Use the italicized word in your statement.

(1) Can people *observe* the stars best in a city or in the countryside?

(2) What kind of *environment* must a palm tree have, a warm one or a cool one?

(3) What kind of clothing is *necessary* for work in outer space?

(4) Are there many or few *varieties* of fruit available in the summer?

(5) What kind of natural disaster can *destroy* an entire city?

(6) How long does it take for the Earth to *revolve* around the sun?

(7) What area of the world would you like to *explore* someday?

(8) What kind of clothing do you wear in the winter to *protect* you from the cold?

2. Word Families: Adjective Formation with -Less.   Some English adjectives can be formed by adding the suffix -*less* to a noun. The suffix -*less* means *without*.

The moon is a world without *life*. (*Life* is a noun.)
The moon is a *lifeless* world. (*Lifeless* is an adjective.)

Study the following lists of nouns and adjectives.

Noun	Adjective
life	lifeless
air	airless
hope	hopeless
care	careless
tree	treeless
home	homeless
pain	painless
sleep	sleepless

SENTENCE COMPLETION.   Choose the correct word in parentheses to fill in the blank space in each sentence.

a. (home, homeless) Social agencies are responsible for finding suitable housing

for _____ families.

b. (sun, sunless) During the winter in North America there are many

_____ days.

c. (pain, painless) Do you usually have _____ during your visit
to the dentist?

d. (meat, meatless) People with heart trouble often eat _____
dinners.

e. (hope, hopeless) We must all have _____ that the future will
be brighter.

f. (star, starless) In the past, sailors couldn't sail their ships across the ocean

without a _____ to help them.

g. (sleep, sleepless) Astronomers spend _____ nights watching the

stars through telescopes.

h. (water, waterless) Scientists used to think there were rivers on Mars, but now

they know that the planet is _____ .

i. (tree, treeless) A traveler will see a _____ environment at the North and South Poles.

j. (care, careless) We must treat the Earth with _____ or we will destroy it.

Ⅴ LANGUAGE FOCUS

Simple Present Tense Negative Forms

The negative form of the simple present tense is the auxiliary verb *don't* + base verb for all persons, singular and plural, except the third person singular. The third person singular forms the negative by *doesn't* + base verb.

> I (You, We, They) ***don't travel*** by bus very often.
> The planet Venus ***doesn't have*** a suitable environment for life.

1. Sentence Building.   Write a complete sentence using the given items. Use the simple present tense of the verb in parentheses. Use the negative when appropriate. The first two are done for you.

a. a car (run) without gas

A car doesn't run without gas.

b. this book (have) many writing exercises

This book has many writing exercises.

c. my school library (charge) students a late fee for overdue books

_____

d. art museums (allow) people to touch the paintings

_____

e. most of my friends (go) to bed before midnight

_____

f. the moon (have) air and water necessary for life

_____

g. a salesperson (earn) as much as the company's boss

_____

h. banks (offer) interest-free loans

_____

i. traffic noise (bother) me very much

_____

j. I (consult) a doctor when I have a mild headache

_____

k. smoking (harm) a person's health

_____

l. the National Forest Service (permit) the use of electricity at Echo Lake

_____

2. Sentence Composing.   Compose a complete sentence in response to each of the following items. The first one is done for you.

a. Tell which three vegetables you don't like.

_____ *I don't like carrots, peas, or spinach.* _____

b. Tell which two fruits you don't like.

_____

c. Tell one thing you don't like about your school.

_____

d. Name two sports you don't know how to play.

_____

e. Tell which item your mother, father, or other family member doesn't have, but would like to have.

_____

f. Write which two household items you don't own, but would like to have.

_____

g. Name an item you don't need because you have one.

_____

h. Tell what your little brother, sister, cousin, or other child doesn't like to do.

_____

i. Tell what expensive article of clothing you don't have, but will buy someday.

_____

j. Name what kind of weather you don't like.

_____

k. Tell one thing your teacher doesn't want the students to do in class.

_____

Verbs + Adjectives

The verbs *be, become, feel, seem, look,* or *appear* are often used to connect a subject with an adjective.

> I *am happy* in my new job.
> Sometimes people *feel sad.*
> The students *don't appear nervous* during an exam.

1. Recognizing Verbs + Adjectives.   Listen carefully as your instructor reads the following paragraph about the moon. Underline the complete verb forms and their adjectives.

What do we know about the moon? It looks bright in the night sky, but it doesn't have its own light. The sun shines on it for half a month; the rays are strong and would be dangerous for a human without a space suit. To someone standing on the moon's surface, everything would appear gray in the sharp light. The surface isn't smooth; there are rocks everywhere. In between the small rocks, the soil is fine and dusty. Nothing moves because there is no wind. To us the moon seems like a strange world; to those people who have explored it, it is calm and peaceful. The footsteps they left behind will remain in the soft dust for millions of years.

2. Sentence Composing.   Write a complete sentence, following the directions for each item. Use a verb + adjective for each answer. The following adjectives will help you write your sentences. The first sentence is done for you.

noisy	comfortable	splendid	busy
messy	serious	tired	easy
crowded	hungry	bright	relaxed
careless	difficult	neat	careful
friendly	blue	nervous	

a. Tell us how you feel on Sunday mornings.

I feel tired on Sunday mornings.

b. Describe how the school cafeteria appears at lunchtime.

c. Tell how students seem during an exam.

d. Tell what color the sky appears to us.

e. Describe how you are when you meet a new person.

f. Explain how the exam seems when you don't know the answers.

g. Describe how your living room looks after a party.

h. Tell how the stores are at Christmastime.

i. Describe how the moon appears in the night sky.

j. Tell how the exam seems when you know all the answers.

Singular Possessives

my friend's computer (the computer belonging to my friend)
Hawaii's climate (the climate of Hawaii)
a bird's nest (the nest of a bird)
the doctor's office (the office of the doctor)

The apostrophe + s ('s) form is used to show that one person, place, or thing has or owns another noun.

1. Sentence Completion.   Choose the correct word from the following list to fill in the blank space in each sentence. Change the noun before each blank space to the singular possessive form to show the correct relationship between the two nouns. The first one is done for you.

museums   boss   brain   house   desk   health

progress   rays   jewelry   office   mistakes   laws

explanations   past

  a. My sister _'s jewelry_____ is expensive.

  b. I always get nervous sitting in the doctor _____ .

  c. The city _____ against smoking on buses are strict.

  d. Objects from the earth tell us about our country _____ .

  e. I'm going to my friend _____ for dinner.

  f. My father _____ is president of the company.

  g. The instructor _____ are quite clear.

  h. There is a typewriter on the secretary _____ .

  i. Some of the sun _____ are dangerous.

  j. Smoking is harmful to a person _____ .

  k. A father is always interested in his child _____ in school.

2. Proofreading.   Read the following paragraph about the usefulness of garbage. Circle all the forms that should be singular possessives, and insert the apostrophe in the correct position. The first one is done for you.

(1) Some people in New York help clean up the environment by reusing other people's garbage. (2) Mr. Salinas, for example, found a wooden wire holder in front of a factory building and turned it into a night table for his childs room. (3) Mrs. Conroy noticed a cooking pot on top of her neighbors garbage pile and now cheerfully uses it in her kitchen. (4) One night Mr. Minsky brought home a clay container from a trash bin to add to his wifes collection of flower pots. (5) Skip LaPlante goes through garbage cans looking for cardboard tubes, pieces of pipe, or other industrial products. (6) He uses these items to make music. (7) All of Mr. LaPlantes instruments are created from trash. (8) Going through garbage is not everyones idea of fun, but we can say that one persons garbage may be another persons treasure.

THE COMPOSING PROCESS

1. Sentence Combining to Form a Paragraph.   The following sentences are about Lake Minnewaska, a recreational area in New York state. Combine each group of sentences into one sentence. Use pronouns instead of nouns when appropriate. Use the words in parentheses to help you. Leave out unnecessary words. Write your sentences in the form of a paragraph, on a separate sheet of paper.

    a. (1) Lake Minnewaska is a nature preserve.

       (2) It is beautiful.

       (3) It is unspoiled.

       (4) It is in New York state.

    b. (1) People go there to picnic.

       (2) They picnic by the waterfalls.

       (3) The waterfalls are in the lakeside forests.

    c. (1) Nature lovers follow the trails.

       (2) The trails are through the forests.

       (3) This is to observe the variety of plants.

       (4) They observe the variety of birds.

    d. (1) Now this area is in danger.

       (2) Some hotel owners want to build cabins. (Use *because*.)

       (3) This is by the lakeside.

    e. (1) The hotel owners would like to clear some of the forest.

       (2) This is for tennis courts.

       (3) This is for a golf course.

    f. (1) Hotel owners would pave over a part of the lakeside.

       (2) This is for parking lots.

       (3) They would need to build a pumping station. (Use *and*.)

       (4) This is near the waterfall.

    g. (1) Nature lovers are trying to keep Lake Minnewaska unspoiled.

       (2) They are raising money for lawyers. (Use *by raising*.)

       (3) This is to make a case against the hotel owners.

    h. (1) It is important to preserve Lake Minnewaska.

       (2) This is for all nature lovers now.

       (3) This is for them in the future.

2. Developing a Paragraph.

OUTLINING. Making an outline of a paragraph helps the reader understand the writer's main idea and how the idea is developed with specific information details. Outlining is also important for writing your own compositions. It helps you organize your thoughts before writing.

An outline begins with the complete main idea sentence. Then specific information is written in brief note form.

a. Read the following paragraph. Fill in the main idea sentence of the paragraph on the lines that follow. Then, in the spaces following the main idea, fill in the specific information in short note form. The specific information items are *examples* of the main idea statement. Two of the details are done for you.

> Some people predict that in the near future there will be many good solutions to the world's problems. People will use sun and wind power to heat homes and run factories. Farmers will be able to grow food in very dry and cold areas of the world. There will be faster and cheaper public transportation. Cars will run on electricity rather than gasoline. Then our cities will have cleaner air for a healthier population. There will be stronger laws against the use of dangerous chemicals on farm crops. Scientists will find cures for serious illnesses such as cancer and heart disease. Life may be more pleasant in the future.

Main Idea: _____

_____

Details: _____ *sun and wind power for homes and factories* _____

_____

_____ *faster and cheaper public transportation* _____

_____

_____

_____

Now copy the main idea sentence from your outline onto a separate sheet of paper. Without looking at the paragraph, use just your outline to complete a paragraph with your own sentences.

b. What do you predict about the future of your city? What things will change for the better? In an outline like that in Exercise A, list several details to expand in a paragraph. Begin with a main idea statement that expresses your general opinion about the topic.

3. Composing a Paragraph.   Every day we are faced with environmental problems in our cities. Keep a journal for one day. Write down all the problems you notice from the time you leave your house to the time you return. For example, you may notice uncovered garbage cans, noise, and air pollution. Note where these problems occur. Also note your physical sensations when you experience these problems.

a. Review your journal notes with a group of classmates. Are your experiences similar or different?

b. Think about what bothers you most about what you experienced.

c. Choose three of your items to write about.

d. Note these in outline form.

e. Use this topic to head your outline: The Things That Bother Me Most.

f. Begin your paragraph with a sentence appropriate to the topic.

g. Develop your paragraph by being specific about the items you listed. Tell what each problem is, where it occurs, how it affects you and your city.

You may want to exchange papers with a partner for helpful suggestions. Write a second version to improve your organization and sentence structure.

Paragraph Topics

1.   How can people make their city a better place in which to live? Think of the problems you wrote about in your journal and how they can be corrected. Write about what you, your friends, shopkeepers, and others do or can do to help. You may use the following items to help you in writing your paragraph:

cover trash   sweep sidewalks   curb a dog

play radio softly   plant flowers

2.   We all appreciate people in our society who offer valuable services: sanitation workers, fire fighters, postal workers, taxi drivers, and teachers. Choose two or three occupations to write about. Describe the good that results from them. Begin your paragraph with an appropriate topic sentence. Be specific in your descriptions. Think of such question words as *who, where, when,* and *how often* to generate details about your topic.

Ⅶ ADDITIONAL READING

Smart Machines: Our Tireless Helpers

[1]   Can machines be as intelligent as human beings? There is a lot of discussion these days about artificial-intelligence machines and their relation to human intelligence. People in many different occupations are involved in this discussion. They want to know how artificial intelligence will improve their lives. They also want to know if "intelligent" machines can be harmful to them. They would like to know what scientists predict for their future.

[2]   Some computer scientists are developing machines that can be programmed to think and act in some ways like human beings. As inventors work on their projects, they are learning more about a computer's capabilities in relation to a human's. One team of experts in California is developing an artificial-intelligence research machine. It will offer services and advice like a thoughtful assistant. Imagine a zoology student in a college. She is using this computer to outline a report on certain animals. Her computer notices some key words such as *lions, tigers,* and *bears*. It will then ask the student a question: "Would you like me to do some research on lions, tigers, and bears?" If the answer is yes, the machine will communicate with another research service for related material. It will be able to tell the student which facts are more important than others for her particular report. It might even tell the student which facts it thinks are interesting and which ones are boring. With such a "smart" machine at her fingertips, this student will not be late in handing in her report to her zoology instructor.

[3]   A "smart" machine such as this one would be capable of helping people in a variety of professions. For example, it could work tirelessly to help a doctor identify a person's illness. It might summarize a reporter's news story, help a lawyer fight a court case, and even make up a quiz for an English teacher. Someday doctors, reporters, lawyers, and teachers might want to consult an artificial-intelligence psychologist for advice on their personal problems.

[4]   What happens when scientists take a "smart" machine and make it move? They get a robot. Robots are capable of performing a series of motions without stopping. Robot arms are used today in many factories, but without a "head" they aren't really "intelligent." However, some new robots are quite extraordinary.

[5]   When a team of scientists working in Antarctica wanted to explore the volcano Mount Erebus, they designed Dante to do the job. Dante is a robot. It is over nine feet long, over five feet wide, and weighs almost one thousand pounds. It looks like a giant spider with eight legs that can move in all directions at a speed of six and a half feet a minute. In the center of its body is a pole holding six video cameras, three looking forward and three looking back to give a 360° view of an area.

[6]   The scientists gave Dante instructions on how to climb down a steep slope. They taught it how to step over rocks and how to avoid dangerous objects in its path. They figured that it would take Dante twenty-four hours to complete its journey seven hundred feet down to the lake of lava at the bottom of the volcano. Once at the bottom, Dante would take temperature readings, measure the composition of the gases, and collect samples of minerals. It would send pictures back up to the control team. When its explorations were over, Dante would climb back up to safety.

[7]   Filled with the knowledge of how to do everything, Dante seemed ready for its job. Placed at the edge of the volcano, it started down. But after traveling only a few feet, Dante stopped dead. The cable connecting it to its controllers had broken. Even the smartest, most extraordinary robots, like people, can become disabled.

[8]   Dante's controllers were disappointed with their experiment, but they didn't give up. They say that they can learn from their failures, and as they get smarter, so will Dante. An improved Dante can then provide them with information never before available about the gases and minerals inside a volcano. The gases and minerals in Mount Erebus may be responsible for the hole in the ozone layer that develops over Antarctica each year. The hole allows increased rays from the sun that can cause cancer. The scientists say that Dante is an important new tool that can help solve some of our environmental problems. They also say that someday more advanced descendants of Dante will be sent to explore the planet Mars.

[9]   Some robots of the future may also do ordinary jobs. There may be robot gas-station attendants that can fill a tank without the driver leaving the car. Robot dressmakers will construct a dress to exact measurement while the woman is having a cup of coffee in the dress shop. Perhaps everyone will have a personal robot for the home. Imagine what a robot will do for you!

An artist's conception of the robot, Dante.

[10]   Can science and technology take us too far by programming intelligence into machines? Some people think there is a danger in this. They say that these machines will take over jobs and leave many people unemployed. Scientists think differently. They say that artificial-intelligence will free people from difficult, dangerous, or boring work. Then people can use their abilities and time for more creative occupations. Some people see another kind of danger. They are afraid that intelligent machines or robots will become smarter than humans and turn into evil monsters. Scientists answer this fear simply: People will always be in control of "smart" machines. The prediction is for a good working relationship between human beings and their tireless helpers.

Reacting to the Reading

1. Computers can help us in various ways.

    a. How important is it today to be computer "literate"? Have you ever used a computer in a class? How can a computer be helpful in your English class?

    b. What kind of computer can help you today in some specific way at home, in school, or at work?

The main elements of some computers are tiny microprocessor chips like these on the woman's finger. They receive and interpret signals from this electronic typewriter.

c. What dangerous, boring, or difficult work would you like a robot to do?

2.   Some people fear a future with artificial intelligence.

a. From what you have read or heard, are you afraid that machines may become too human? Give your reasons.

b. Discuss the movies you have seen that show robots. Describe their characteristics. Are they good, bad, or funny characters? Do they have feelings?

Reading Comprehension

Understanding the Text.   Choose the correct answer, or follow the directions.

a. Artificial intelligence refers to
   (1) the human brain.
   (2) ordinary computers.
   (3) special computer programs.

b. According to Paragraph [1], what are the two things people want to know about artificial intelligence?

   _____

   _____

c. The computer described in Paragraph [2] will be like a *thoughtful assistant*. This means that it
   (1) will be useful only to zoology students.
   (2) may be useful to anybody doing research.
   (3) will be helpful only to very intelligent people.

d. The statement *It might even tell the student which facts it thinks are interesting and which ones are boring* shows that the computer might
   (1) offer an opinion on a subject.
   (2) state a fact about a subject.
   (3) solve a problem in zoology.

e. The main idea of Paragraph [3] is contained in which sentence?

   _____

f. Which words in Paragraph [3] introduce the details?

   _____

Computers are used by people in many professions. In which workplaces have you seen computers such as this one?

g. The topic of Paragraph [5] is
   (1) the exploration of Mount Erebus in Antarctica.
   (2) the features of an extraordinary robot explorer.
   (3) a team of scientists controlling a giant robot.

h. We can infer that the scientists wouldn't go down Mount Erebus themselves because
   (1) it would take them longer than it would take a robot.
   (2) they wanted to try out their new robot invention.
   (3) it would be dangerous for them to go down there.

i. Complete the following sentence: When it got to the bottom of the volcano, Dante was supposed to_____ , _____ , and _____.

j. An improved Dante may provide the scientists with information that
   (1) can help solve some environmental problems.
   (2) can cure cancer.
   (3) can be used for the exploration of the moon.

k. What kind of ordinary robots are predicted for the future?

   _____

l. According to Paragraph [10], what are the two fears that people have about the use of artificial intelligence?

_____

_____

m. In Paragraph [10], scientists say that artificial intelligence
   (1) will be a danger to society.
   (2) will improve people's lives.
   (3) will be better than human intelligence.

Vocabulary

Expanding Vocabulary.   Choose the word that means the same as the italicized word in each sentence.

a. People *communicate* by telephone, telegram, and letters, as well as in person. When people *communicate*, they
   (1) use machinery.
   (2) exchange thoughts.
   (3) are lonely.

b. Chemists make different kinds of *artificial* material such as plastic and nylon. Something *artificial* is always
   (1) made by humans.
   (2) useful.
   (3) natural.

c. It is sometimes difficult to *solve* a problem. When you *solve* something, you
   (1) look in a textbook.
   (2) ask a question.
   (3) discover an answer.

d. Help is *available* for students who want to learn how to use a computer. To be *available* means
   (1) to be close at hand.
   (2) to have questions.
   (3) to advance.

e. Scientists need to *develop* better computer programs for air-traffic safety. To *develop* means to

(1) fly in an airplane.

(2) bring to an advanced state.

(3) do an experiment.

f. If you have bad stomach pains, you should *consult* a doctor. When you *consult* someone, you

(1) ask someone for advice.

(2) agree with a person.

(3) do someone a favor.

g. Many people are *involved* in community projects that help young children have a better life. To be *involved* in something means to

(1) be uninterested in it.

(2) be happy about it.

(3) be concerned about it.

h. A child's language *capabilities* must be developed in school. A person's *capabilities* are things that

(1) a person can do.

(2) a person owns.

(3) can be seen.

i. To *avoid* a parking ticket, you should always read the signs. To *avoid* something means to

(1) pay for it.

(2) be sorry about it.

(3) keep it from happening.

UNIT II

Our World of Language

CHAPTER FOUR

ECHOES OF THE PAST

❶ PREREADING

Class Discussion.   The English language is written in an alphabet of twenty-six letters. Other languages have alphabets, but they look different from the one used by English. Do you recognize the alphabetic languages shown here?

تَقَابِلَ فَخْرِی بِفِعْلِی ـ سَـلَّمَ الرَّئِیسُ الْحِصْنَ إِلَى الْمُحَاصِرِینَ.

Если вы дадите   мне эту книгу читать, я возвращу вам её скоро.

תְּמוּנוֹת יְקָרוֹת תְּלוּיוֹת עַל הַקִּירוֹת.

Can anyone in your class tell what the sentences mean?

Does your language use an alphabet different from these? Write some of these letters on the board to share with your classmates.

Ancient Egyptian hieroglyphics and Chinese characters are two different forms of picture writing.

Some languages don't use an alphabet. For example, ancient Egyptian picture writing uses hieroglyphics and Chinese picture writing uses characters, as shown in these photographs.

Does your native language use a form of picture writing? Illustrate and explain some of the signs used in your language.

FREE WRITE
How do you feel about learning English as a second language? Describe some of your difficulties, disappointments, satisfactions, embarrassments, and sense of accomplishment.

Vocabulary in Context. The words in this exercise will appear in the reading passage. Circle the letter of the word that means the same as the italicized word in each of the following sentences.

1. Most civilizations have changed from the ancient *system* of picture writing to an alphabetic system.

   a. machine   b. process   c. discovery

2. If you have not made *sufficient* preparation for your speech, you may bore your audience.

   a. historical   b. simple   c. adequate

3. *Eventually,* as children grow up, they gain a larger vocabulary.

   a. previously   b. finally   c. quickly

4. To perform the jobs required by modern industry, a person must be *literate*.

   a. intelligent   b. able to read   c. skilled in mathematics

5. Spoken language *originated* so long ago that no one knows exactly how the first words were formed.

   a. disappeared   b. was recorded   c. began

6. Beautiful works of art have a *permanent* value that can be enjoyed long after their creators have died.

   a. never-ending   b. emotional   c. fundamental

7. Language students *probably* learn as much from each other as they do from their formal classroom instruction.

   a. absolutely   b. very likely   c. never

8. Shrugging, or lifting the shoulders, is a typical French *gesture* that means one does not know or care about something.

    a. object   b. realization   c. movement of the body

9. The instructions for putting together the radio were clear, but I still needed someone to *demonstrate* the process.

    a. find   b. repeat   c. show

10. The *emotion* of love is probably the most common subject of popular fiction.

    a. intelligence   b. feeling   c. bodily strength

Ⅱ READING

Is One Picture Worth a Thousand Words?

[1]   How did early humans first communicate with each other? In the beginning, they didn't use words at all. They probably used signs or pointed to things that they wanted. For example, perhaps they rubbed their stomachs to show that they were hungry or held their noses to show that something had a bad odor. When they wanted to teach someone how to build a fire or prepare a new food, perhaps they used gestures or demonstrated the action. It was possible to communicate a great deal without words. However, as human culture developed, something more than gestures was needed.

[2]   Nobody knows for certain when people first began to use actual spoken words. Perhaps the first spoken words originated from grunts, moans, sighs, and other sounds of the human voice. These were probably used to signal danger or show basic feelings such as love, hate, fear, pain, or other basic emotions. We do not know exactly how these sounds grew into words, but some scientists believe that this process began about one million years ago. The first actual words in the human vocabulary probably named family members or necessary items such as food. They may have been short, simple sounds for things in nature that human beings saw every day, such as the sun, the moon, a tree, a stone, rain, or water.

[3]   Gestures and basic spoken words were sufficient for the hunter-gatherer societies that existed at the dawn of human history. When human life became more complex, however, and people began to engage in trade, develop systems of government, and create religious organizations, it became necessary to preserve ideas and information in permanent form. Thus, writing was born. The archeological evidence shows us that writing is about eight thousand years

old. The first kind of writing was "picture writing." Egyptian picture writing, one of the oldest in the world, is called hieroglyphics. Hieroglyphics could communicate in a number of ways. They could mean exactly the same thing as the object shown. For example, ⬡ meant *face,* and ⬡ meant *eye.* The hieroglyphic picture could also communicate an act related to the picture. For example, a picture of a pair of legs, ∧ , meant the verb *to go.* Hieroglyphics also suggested ideas and emotions. For instance, the picture of a person leaning over a cane meant *old age.* Furthermore, hieroglyphic signs could also be used for certain sounds. ⌒ , for example, was pronounced as the consonant *t.* Finally, hieroglyphics could be placed before other words as a kind of prefix. For instance, the figure ⬡ in front of a word meant the feminine form of the word.

[4]   The development of picture writing improved communication a great deal. People did not need to see each other to communicate. They could write their picture words on clay tablets, animal skins, or fiber and leave them for others to read when they were absent. They could communicate over long distances by writing down their thoughts and deeds and sending them by messenger to other places. Older members of the culture could write down their ideas and records of past events and pass them on to younger members and to future generations.

[5]   Although picture writing was certainly very useful, it did present some problems. Sometimes the roughness of the writing materials made it difficult to draw the picture signs clearly. In addition, the signs for certain objects, emotions, or ideas were sometimes confusing to the reader because they looked very similar to other picture signs. Moreover, as human thought and society became more complex, a huge picture-sign vocabulary developed. It was a difficult task to create new picture signs for new ideas and to remember all the picture signs in the vocabulary. Also, picture writing required a great deal of time to carve into stone or metal and a great deal of space on precious materials such as animal skins or fiber.

[6]   About 3,500 years ago, language underwent another important change. The alphabet was invented. Picture signs changed to lines and curves called letters, each of which was associated with one sound. Letters were combined together to form words. Alphabetic writing was much easier than picture writing. Writing with an alphabet took less time and space than did writing with picture signs. The alphabetic words were easier to write than were picture signs, and more people could become literate. With the use of alphabetic writing, information could be communicated to greater numbers of people, and ideas were more quickly carried from land to land. With the creation of alphabetic writing, the ancient world had discovered a new tool for knowledge and communication. Most civilizations from India west to Europe and the Americas eventually adopted alphabetic writing. Here is how the letter *A* developed from picture writing to alphabetic writing:

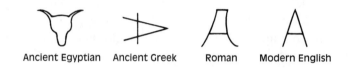

Ancient Egyptian   Ancient Greek   Roman   Modern English

[7]   Today China is one of the few nations that still use a system of picture writing. Chinese picture writing, like Egyptian hieroglyphics, began thousands of years ago with pictures that really looked like the objects they named. For example, the ancient Chinese picture sign for *mountain* was ᴍ. As the Chinese language developed, however, the pictures became simplified and looked less like real objects. Today, the Chinese character for *mountain* is 山. Chinese writing contains nearly fifty thousand separate signs, or characters, each one having a different meaning. To read a newspaper in Chinese, a person has to know about three thousand characters. That means that a great deal of a Chinese child's education is spent just trying to learn the written language. For that reason, some people in modern times have tried to simplify the Chinese written language or replace it altogether with an alphabet. If the Chinese ever do change to an alphabetic writing system, then picture writing, the oldest form of written communication, will almost entirely disappear from human culture.

Guided Summary.   A summary communicates the main ideas of a reading passage. Complete the following sentences to make a summary. Write your new sentences on a separate sheet of paper, in the form of a paragraph.

1. The main purpose of this reading is to tell us about . . .

2. Paragraph [2] describes how . . .

3. Writing developed . . .

4. Hieroglyphics, the ancient Egyptian picture writing, . . .

5. Picture writing made communication easier, but . . .

6. About 3,500 years ago, . . .

7. The conclusion states that the alphabet . . .

8. Only the Chinese . . .

Reacting to the Reading

People have always used gestures to communicate.

a. What are some of the gestures that early humans probably used? Are these same gestures used today?

b. What gestures do you frequently use in conversation? Explain how gestures help get your message across.

c. Describe a situation in which you found gestures helpful in getting or giving information.

Reading Comprehension

1. Understanding the Text. Follow the directions for each item.

a. Mark the following sentences *T* for *true* or *F* for *false,* according to the information in the reading passage. Underline the part of the passage where you find your information.

(1) People at the dawn of human history communicated in picture writing.____

(2) Gestures for communication originated before words. ____

(3) Human language may be about one million years old. ____

(4) Love and fear are emotions that developed about 8,000 years ago. ____

(5) The alphabet was invented about 3,500 years ago. ____

(6) Clay, animal skin, and fiber were used for writing in the ancient world. ____

(7) A person must know about fifty thousand Chinese characters to read a Chinese newspaper today. ____

b. Circle the letter of the correct answer, or answer the question as directed.

(1) The word *however* in the last sentence of Paragraph [1] signals that this sentence

   (a) continues the thought of the previous sentence.

   (b) gives an example of the thought in the previous sentence.

   (c) reverses the thought of the previous sentence.

(2) Paragraph [2] speculates, or makes educated guesses, about the origin of language. Underline at least five words or expressions in this paragraph that the writer uses to show that our information on this subject is not certain or exact.

(3) In the third sentence of Paragraph [2], the expression *such as* signals

   (a) a new thought.

   (b) examples of the previous noun.

   (c) a reason for the previous statement.

(4) Picture writing developed

    (a) long before people talked.

    (b) long after people used signs for words.

    (c) after alphabetic writing.

(5) In Egyptian hieroglyphics, a picture of legs meant

    (a) the feminine form of a noun.

    (b) the verb *to go*.

    (c) the "ing" form of a verb.

(6) In Paragraph [3], two signal expressions that mean the same thing are

    (a) however/thus.

    (b) for example/for instance.

    (c) furthermore/when.

(7) Picture writing

    (a) didn't help people to communicate.

    (b) was the only form of communication in the past.

    (c) was a difficult form of communication.

(8) Alphabetic writing was efficient because

    (a) it was invented after picture writing.

    (b) it saved time and space.

    (c) it developed from picture writing.

(9) Write the sentence or part of the sentence in Paragraph [5] that states the main idea of that paragraph. _____

_____

(10) In Paragraph [7], Sentence 6, what does the expression *each one* refer to?

_____

c. Number the following sentences in their correct time order, according to the reading passage. Your first sentence will be the first event.

    (1) Picture writing is about eight thousand years old. ____

    (2) Alphabetic writing is about 3,500 years old. ____

    (3) The earliest language used signs, not words. ____

    (4) The Chinese may simplify their picture writing. ____

(5) The first words were simple sounds for common things. ____

(6) Spoken language may be about one million years old. ____

2. Answering Information Questions. Write the answers to the following questions in complete sentences.

a. How did early humans communicate?

b. About how old is spoken language?

c. What are hieroglyphics?

d. List three advantages of writing over speech.

e. What happened to language abut 3,500 years ago?

f. Why is alphabetic language more efficient than picture writing?

g. Which modern civilization still uses picture writing?

III THE READING PROCESS

Linking Pronouns. Pronouns are words that link, or tie, the writer's ideas together. The reader needs to know which words the pronouns are replacing.

Read Paragraph [1] of the reading selection again. The subject of Sentence 1 is *early humans*. The next four sentences do not use the subject *early humans*. These sentences use the pronoun *they. They* is a plural subject pronoun that takes the place of *early humans*. Pronouns must agree in number and form with the nouns they are replacing. Review the pronoun chart in Appendix A.

a. Circle or respond with the correct answer.

(1) The word *these* in Sentence 3 of Paragraph [2] takes the place of

(a) human beings.

(b) words.

(c) sounds.

(2) The word *they* in the last sentence of Paragraph [2] replaces

(a) early human beings.

(b) the earliest words.

(c) stones and trees.

(3) The pronoun *they* in Sentence 8 of Paragraph [3] stands for

    (a) Egyptians.

    (b) hieroglyphics.

    (c) numbers.

(4) Write the nouns that replace the following pronouns in Paragraph [4].

    (a) Sentence (3): *them* _____

    (b) Sentence (4): *their* _____

    (c) Sentence (4): *them* _____

    (d) Sentence (5): *their* _____

(5) In Paragraph [5], Sentence 1, what does the pronoun *it* stand for?

_____

b. Read the following paragraph. All the pronouns are circled. Draw an arrow from each pronoun to the noun it is replacing. (The same noun may be used for more than one pronoun.) The first one is done for you.

Most of the first immigrants to America came from England. They spoke the English language. But they discovered many new plants and animals in their new land. These things didn't have English names, but they did have Native American names. The immigrants learned the Native American names. They borrowed them from the Native American languages.

Language is one of the unique characteristics that make human beings different from other animals. All human beings have the ability to learn language. Here, students study in a modern language laboratory to improve their listening comprehension and pronunciation.

VOCABULARY

1. New Words. Pronounce these words, following your instructor.

Verbs	Nouns	Adjectives	Adverbs
originate	gesture	permanent	eventually
demonstrate	emotion	sufficient	probably
	system	literate	

EXPANDING VOCABULARY

a. Use the word in parentheses in answering each of the following questions. Write your answers in complete sentences.

   (1) How did early human beings communicate with each other? (probably)

   (2) According to this chapter's reading selection, where did hieroglyphics begin? (originated)

   (3) Which languages are you able to read and write? (literate)

   (4) If two people do not speak the same language, how can they communicate with each other? (gestures)

   (5) Do you expect to have a temporary job when you graduate? (permanent)

   (6) What kind of job do you hope to get? (eventually)

b. Write a complete sentence for each of the following phrases. Do not change the order or the form of the given phrase.

   (1) the emotion of love

   (2) in our solar system

   (3) demonstrated the computer

   (4) a sufficient food supply

2. Word Families: Negative Adjectives with *in-*, *im-*, and *un-*. Study the following lists of adjectives and their negative forms.

Adjectives	Negative Adjectives
sufficient	insufficient
correct	incorrect
visible	invisible
efficient	inefficient
practical	impractical
possible	impossible

common	uncommon
important	unimportant
original	unoriginal
usual	unusual
emotional	unemotional
related	unrelated

a. The prefixes *in-*, *im-*, or *un-* often go in front of words to make them negative. Choose the correct word in parentheses to fill in the blank space in each sentence.

(1) The English words *morning* and *night* are (related, unrelated) _____ to the German words *morgen* and *nicht*.

(2) It is (practical, impractical) _____ to carry a large desk dictionary with you to class.

(3) No one uses hieroglyphic writing any longer. Therefore, it is difficult to get (correct, incorrect) _____ translations for every hieroglyphic sign.

(4) At night, dark clothing makes a bicyclist almost (visible, invisible) _____.

(5) It is (usual, unusual) _____ for people today to use picture writing as their main form of communication.

(6) Children do not always have a(n) (sufficient, insufficient) _____ vocabulary to express their ideas.

(7) Students learn to type because writing long reports by hand is (efficient, inefficient) _____ .

(8) Instructors like students to write (original, unoriginal) _____ essays that contain students' individual thoughts.

b. Follow the directions for each item.

(1) Put a check (✓) next to the items that might make a teacher *unpopular.*

arrives late to class ____ knows students' names ____ marks home-work carefully ____ never looks at homework ____ doesn't answer students' questions ____ helps students after class ____ gives many tests ____

(2) What kind of weather is *improbable* in New York in January? What kind of clothing is *impractical* for traveling?

(3) In complete sentences, state two things that babies are *unable* to do.

(4) In complete sentences, state whether you are *afraid* or *unafraid* of each of the following things.

the dark   high places   airplanes   strange places
deep water   thunderstorms   loud noises   snakes

(5) Write one sentence telling what makes you *happy* and one sentence telling what makes you *unhappy.* Use one or both of the following patterns.

It makes me happy to see my friends.
Smiling people make me happy.

(6) Put an X next to those items that are *unimportant* for learning a new language.

doing housework ____ using a dictionary ____ practicing new sounds ____ owning a dog ____ exploring space ____ reading a newspaper every day ____ wearing new clothes ____

c. Write a correct, meaningful sentence for each of the following words.

(1) important   (2) insufficient   (3) emotional

(4) uncommon   (5) incorrect

LANGUAGE FOCUS

Simple Past Tense of *To Be*

The simple past tense is used to show that someone or something existed or that something happened or was finished in the past.

> One million years ago language *was* simple.
> The vocabulary *wasn't* large.

Study the simple past tense forms of the verb *to be*.

	Singular	**Plural**
First Person	I was	A writer and I were We were
Second Person	You were	You were
Third Person	Writing was He/She/It was	Things were They were

Notice that only the first person and third person singular forms use *was*. The negative forms are *wasn't* and *weren't*.

1. Sentence Completion.   Fill in the blank spaces in each sentence with the correct form of the simple past tense of *to be*. Use negatives where you are asked to do so. The first one is done for you.

a. (negative) Early people _____*weren't*_____ exactly like us.

b. But they _____ the same as we are in some ways.

c. Water _____ important to them, as it is to us.

d. The sun _____ something they saw every day.

e. Their basic emotions _____ probably similar to ours.

f. (negative) Early humans _____ able to talk.

g. Early language _____ probably sign language.

h. (negative) It _____ easy for early people to communicate.

i. Simple sounds _____ probably the first words.

j. Ideas _____ probably hard to communicate.

k. Clay _____ difficult to write on.

l. (negative) Writing _____ invented until eight thousand years ago.

m. Pictures _____ the first written words.

2. Sentence Building.   Write a correct sentence by putting together a subject from Column A, a verb form from Column B, and one item from Column C. Your sentence should contain information from the text. Write your new complete sentences on a separate sheet of paper.

A	**B**	**C**
a. Early people	was	probably used for basic things.
b. It	wasn't	picture writing.
c. The first spoken words	was were	probably hungry much of the time.
d. The first writing	were	easy to communicate without words.
e. Egyptian picture writing	was	
	weren't	one of the earliest writing systems.
f. ⌒		the first people to use an alphabet.
g. The English		the sign for the sound *t*.

Simple Past Tense of Regular Verbs

The simple past tense of most regular verbs adds *d* or *ed* to the base verb.

Single-syllable base verbs ending in a consonant double the final consonant before adding *ed*: *bat* ⟶ *batted*. The past tense of verbs ending in *y* preceded by a consonant changes the *y* to *i* and adds *ed*: *simplify* ⟶ *simplified*.

> People ***used*** sign language before they ***developed*** picture writing.

1. List Completion.   Study the following list of regular verbs. Fill in the blank spaces with the correct forms.

Basic Verb	Simple Past
talk	talked
use	used
rub	_____
_____	pointed
want	_____
simplify	_____
_____	communicated
_____	showed
name	_____
touch	_____
_____	developed
plan	_____
_____	replied
happen	_____
enjoy	_____
_____	originated
_____	changed
demonstrate	_____

Simplified Chinese characters communicate the message of this cartoon: "Don't waste money on expensive items."

2. Dictation.   Write the following sentences from your instructor's dictation. These things all happened in the past. All the verbs will be in the simple past tense.

  a. Early humans used signs to communicate.

  b. They pointed to such things as rocks, trees, and animals.

  c. Picture writing developed about eight thousand years ago.

  d. People in the Middle East invented the alphabet.

  e. The alphabet changed our way of writing.

  f. The Chinese simplified their written characters in the early 1900s.

3. Recognizing Subjects and Verbs.   Check your dictation, and correct your errors. In the following Subject column, write the subject of each sentence. Mark it *S* for *singular* or *P* for *plural*. In the Verb column, write the verb of each sentence.

	Subject	S or P	Verb
a.			
b.			
c.			
d.			
e.			
f.			

Does the form of a verb in the simple past tense change for a singular or plural subject?

Simple Past Tense of Irregular Verbs

Many English verbs do not form the simple past tense in the regular way. Study the following verb forms.

Basic Verb	Change	Simple Past
begin	change vowel	began
do	change vowel add consonant	did
see	change vowels add consonant	saw
take	change vowel double vowel	took

keep	change vowel	kept
	change consonant	
have	change consonant	had
make	change consonant	made
speak	change vowels	spoke
put	no change	put
understand	change vowel	understood
	double vowel	

You will find a list of commonly used irregular verbs in Appendix A.

1. Sentence Completion. Fill in each blank space with the simple past tense of the verb in parentheses.

Two thousand years ago the Roman people (speak) (1) _____

Latin. Their vocabulary (be) (2) _____ large. The Romans (need)

(3) _____ numbers in addition to words. They (invent)

(4) _____ an interesting number system. They (begin)

(5) _____ with the number I. They (make) (6) _____

numbers 2 to 10 like this: II, III, IV, V, VI, VII, VIII, IX, and X. They (have)

(7) _____ numbers for 100 and 1000. The Roman numbers (be)

(8) _____ common all over the Western world. But later the Western

world (take) (9) _____ over the number system of the Arabs.

The Arabic number system (be) (10) _____ easier to use.

2. Sentence Composing. Answer the following questions in complete sentences. Note the use of time words for the simple past tense. They may occur at the beginning or end of sentences. Use these time words in your writing. The first one is done for you.

   a. Where did you do your homework last night?

   _____ *I did my homework in my room last night.* _____

   b. What did you have for dinner last night?

   c. When did you begin work yesterday?

   d. What program did you watch on TV last night?

   e. Why weren't you in class yesterday?

   f. Why did you miss class this morning?

g. What did you do last Saturday?

h. Which movie did you see last month?

i. What did the picture $\bigwedge$ mean in hieroglyphics?

j. What did human beings do first, speak or write?

k. What time did you come to school today?

3. Controlled Writing.   Rewrite the following paragraph. Change the subject *children* to *I.* Change the pronouns to first person. Change the verbs from simple present to simple past tense.

Your first sentence will be the following: *I didn't talk when I was very young.*

   Children don't talk when they are very young. But they communicate. They make sounds in their throats. They use a lot of sign language. They point to things that they want. Children soon develop ideas. Then they begin to talk. They make simple sounds. They take words from their parents. They name things, and they invent words. That is how they learn to talk.

Simple Past Tense Negative Forms

The negative form of the simple past tense is *didn't* + the basic verb. Study the examples.

The Romans ***didn't use*** Arabic numbers.
Writing ***didn't develop*** quickly.

1. Sentence Composing.   Use the following items to write complete sentences about what you or someone else did yesterday, last night, or this morning. Use time words, adjectives, and prepositional phrases to make your sentences more specific and interesting.

see a movie
I saw a good movie last night.

a. do my homework   b. read a book   c. draw a picture

d. use a pencil   e. need a dictionary   f. buy a coat

g. be at home   h. change my mind   i. take a bus

j. begin a lesson   k. have an exam   l. speak to my instructor

2.Sentence Rewriting.   Now write your sentences using the verb in the negative. Change additional words to make a meaningful negative statement.

> I did my homework in my room. I didn't do my homework in the library.

Article Use

The articles *a*(*an*) and *the* are placed before a noun in some cases. In other cases no article (Ø) is placed before a noun. For singular nouns the possibilities are *a*(*an*), *the*, or Ø. For plural nouns the possibilities are *the* or Ø.

Study the following chart of article use.

	Singular Nouns	**Plural Nouns**
(1) *a* (*an*)	countable indefinite	
(2) *the*	countable/uncountable definite	countable definite
(3) Ø	uncountable indefinite	countable indefinite

Read the corresponding examples and explanations for singular nouns.

(1)
> There is *a **cat*** in my backyard.

This cat is mentioned for the first time. It is indefinite, not a specific cat that we know. The noun *cat* is a countable noun, one individual among many.

(2)
> ***The cat*** looks hungry. It must rely on ***the kindness*** of strangers to feed it.

The noun *cat* in this sentence is countable, but now it is also a definite noun. We know this cat because it was mentioned before. The noun *kindness* is abstract and uncountable, but here it is made definite by the words *of strangers*. Therefore we use *the*.

> *The* best *place* for a cat is in a home.

The noun *place* here is definite, qualified by the word *best*. When there is only one of something, we know it. Therefore, we use *the*.

(3)
> The cat in my backyard seems to be in ∅ poor *health*.
> It needs ∅ *food*.

The nouns *health* and *food* in these sentences are uncountable and indefinite. The noun *health* means a condition; the noun *food* is a general term for nourishment. Therefore, no article (∅) is placed before these nouns.

Now read the corresponding examples and explanations for plural nouns.

(1)   The article *a(an)* is *never* used with plural nouns.

(2)
> I always feed *the cats* that come into my backyard.

These cats are definite. They are the ones who come into the backyard.

(3)
> ∅ *Cats* can be ∅ good *pets*.

Cats and *pets* in this sentence are indefinite. The statement is general, not a comment about particular cats or pets. Therefore no article is used.

Sentence Completion.

a. In the following paragraph, fill in each blank space with *a(an)* or *the*. If no article is needed, put ∅ in the blank.

   Can (1) ____ animals communicate with (2) ____ human beings? We know they do in some ways, but can they really "speak" to us? In (3) ____ 1970s (4) ____ psychologist tried (5) ____ experiment. He decided to raise (6) ____ young ape in his home. He sent (7) ____ ape to (8) ____ school to learn (9) ____ English. His teachers taught him to make (10) ____ signs for (11) ____ English words. After several months (12) ____ psychologist gave different kinds of (13) ____ tests to (14) ____ ape. He was disappointed with (15) ____ results. He decided that this ape couldn't learn to communicate on our level.

b. In the following paragraph there are no blank spaces, but some nouns are underlined. If *a*(*an*) or *the* is needed, insert the article between the words in the appropriate place. If no article is needed, write ∅ above the noun. The first two are done for you.

William McGuffey had ∧*an* important <u>place</u> in American <u>education</u>∅. He was born in Pennsylvania in 1800. As young <u>man</u> he wanted to go to <u>college</u>. So he studied part-time for eight <u>years</u> and received his degree. Then he became interested in <u>subject</u> of education. He began to write <u>books</u> for young <u>children</u>. He wanted to teach good <u>behavior</u> to all <u>children</u> in America's public schools. <u>Books</u> he wrote were very popular. They became most popular <u>schoolbooks</u> in <u>country</u>.

THE COMPOSING PROCESS

1. Sentence Combining to Form a Paragraph.   Combine the following sentences into longer, more interesting statements to form a paragraph about the development of American English. Leave out all the unnecessary words. Use adjective-noun combinations and pronouns to make your sentences flow smoothly. Use signal expressions as directed in the parentheses.

Rewrite your new paragraph on a separate sheet of paper. Use correct punctuation.

    a. Our English vocabulary has many words.

    b. These words are from other languages.

    c. Many English words originated in German.

    d. These are short words.

    e. These are basic words.

    f. Many English words come from Latin. (Use signal for addition.)

    g. These are long words.

    h. These are for communicating invisible things.

    i. These invisible things are ideas.

    j. These invisible things are emotions. (Join Items i and j to Item h by the expression *such as*.)

Latin was the common language of Europe in the Middle Ages. This Latin manuscript, with its decorative capital letter, is from a religious text.

k. Other words in English come from French.

l. These French words relate to fashion.

m. These French words relate to cooking.

n. These French words relate to the arts.

o. American English uses words from many languages. (Use signal for addition.)

p. These languages are immigrant.

q. *Boss* is a Dutch word. (Begin your sentence for Items q and r with the expression *For example,*.)

r. *Cookie* is a Dutch word.

s. *Canyon* is a Spanish word.

t. *Cigar* is a Spanish word.

u. *Cocoa* is a Spanish word.

v. American English owes a lot to languages.

w. These languages are many.

x. These languages are different.

2. Developing a Unified Paragraph with Details.   A good English paragraph should contain only one main idea, or it may follow a few sentences of introduction. To develop the main idea of your paragraph, you should include a number of different details. These details must all relate to the main idea and to each other. They should follow a logical order in your paragraph.

The following exercise will help you develop a paragraph with details in logical order. Use the questions as the basis for your written answers. Write your details in the form of a paragraph, on a separate sheet of paper.

a. Where did you live seven years ago?

b. What language did you speak at home?

c. What language did you usually speak in school?

d. Did you learn to read and write in (name of your language)?

e. In what grade did you begin to study English?

f. Did you use English textbooks and workbooks in school?

g. Did you also listen to English radio programs and tapes?

h. Did you see English films and television programs?

i. Did you frequently use an English dictionary?

j. What kind of information did you look for in the dictionary?

k. Was your English teacher a native speaker of English?

l. Did he or she know English grammar very well?

m. Did he or she assign English paragraphs frequently or rarely?

n. Did you enjoy learning English in your school?

Which sentences form the introduction to your paragraph? Which sentence states the main idea?

3. Sequencing Details in a Paragraph.   In a well-written paragraph, the details follow each other in logical order. All the sentences that deal with a particular item in the paragraph should go together. Time words, repeated topic words, and other kinds of signal words should tie related sentences together. This exercise will help you learn how to link sentences together so that your reader can follow your ideas without difficulty.

Read the following sentences about the development of the English language. Number them in correct order to form a logical paragraph. Put *M.I.* (for *main idea*) next to the main idea sentence. This will be Sentence 1. Look for time expressions, linking pronouns, repeated use of key words, and other signals to help you put the sentences in the correct sequence. Write all the sentences in the form of a paragraph. Then answer the questions.

a. Many of the English words we use in science, education, and government have a Latin origin. ____

b. The English language has also borrowed words from Greek, Hindi, Arabic, and many other languages. ____

c. From about 1200 to 1500, Latin words also entered the English language.

____

d. First of all, English has a Germanic origin. ____

e. The English language owes its development to many different languages. ____

f. Many basic English words are similar to German words. ____

g. Then, in 1066, the French conquered England. ____

h. And, finally, English has created many new words for new inventions. ____

i. French words became very common in English. ____

Questions

(1) What is the topic of the paragraph?

(2) What are some time expressions that were helpful in putting the sentences in order?

(3) How many sentences does the writer use to discuss words of Latin origin? Of French origin? Of German origin?

(4) Which word in Sentence (b) signals that this sentence is adding information to previous sentences?

Paragraph Topics

1. You can learn a new language through many different activities. With your class, think of the different activities you can do to help you learn a new language. After you have a complete list of the various language-learning activities, group together those items that relate to the language skills of listening and speaking, reading and writing. Write a unified paragraph about learning a new language, based on one or more of the groups of items. Make sure your paragraph has a clear main idea statement.

2. Expressing yourself in a foreign language can be a problem at times.

    Write a paragraph describing an embarrassing or humorous incident in language learning. Begin with an introduction identifying the location of the incident and the language involved. Develop your paragraph with appropriate details, and write a conclusion. Review your paragraph for correct grammar.

VII ADDITIONAL READING

The Tower of Babel

[1]   The book of Genesis, in the Old Testament of the Bible, tells the story of how the nations of the world came to speak different languages. The story begins after the great flood that had covered the Earth with water as a punishment for the wickedness of human beings. Only the family of Noah, which had boarded an ark, or large boat, with the male and female animals of every species, was left alive. When the floodwaters finally went down, Noah's ark landed on a mountaintop in the part of the world we now call eastern Turkey.

[2]   After a time, the descendants of Noah multiplied and became numerous. They journeyed south, to a place in the valley of the Euphrates River that was known as Babel, or the kingdom of Babylon. At that time, the Biblical story tells us, these descendants of Noah all spoke the same language and thought of themselves as one people or nation. As the Bible states, "And the whole earth was of one language, and of one speech."

[3]   Now, the descendants of Noah wished to remain as one people speaking one language and to become a powerful nation. So after they settled themselves in the valley of Babylon, they decided that they would build their own city and a great tower whose top would reach up to the highest heavens. They began to build their tower to the sky, using mud bricks that they baked (instead of stone) and a mortar made of mud and water. They called this tower the Tower of Babel because *babel* was a Babylonian word meaning *gate of God*.

[4]   While these descendants of Noah were building their great tower, their Lord looked down from heaven to view its construction. The Lord realized that with one language and one national identity, these people could become very proud and powerful. Perhaps they would think that they could do anything they wanted and create anything they desired. So the Lord decided to prevent them from finishing their great Tower of Babel and their city. He confused their languages so that everyone spoke a different tongue and no one could understand anyone else. Then the people could not communicate with each other about the construction of the city and the tower, and these works were never completed. Eventually, the descendants of Noah left the kingdom of Babylon and spread out

all over the Earth, speaking different languages and becoming different nations of people.

[5]   Was there ever a Tower of Babel such as the biblical story describes? We cannot say for sure, but today, in the land that was ancient Babylon, about thirty such towers, called *ziggurats*, still exist. These ziggurats were artificial mountains built as sacred places for the gods to visit. (In Babylonian, the word *ziggurat* means "to build high.") Usually, ziggurats contained a great exterior staircase that led from the bottom of the mountain to a small temple on the top. Ziggurats were usually built on seven levels, with each ascending level somewhat smaller than the one below. A ziggurat looked like a corkscrew-shaped pyramid.

[6]   We do not know if one of the ziggurats that exists today on the site of ancient Babylon is the biblical Tower of Babel. But the English expression "a babel of languages" remains. It means a confusion of voices and tongues. It reminds us of one ancient explanation of why the different peoples of the world all speak different languages.

Tower of Babel

Reacting to the Reading

According to the story, the Lord confused the language of the Babylonians.

   a. Do all the people of your native country speak the same language? If not, what are the different languages that they speak?

   b. Does your country have an official language? If so, which one? What are some advantages of having an official language?

   c. What are some problems of countries that have more than one language?

Reading Comprehension

Summarizing Through Sentence Completion.   The following paragraph summarizes the biblical story of the Tower of Babel. Fill in the blank spaces with appropriate words and phrases to summarize the story. You may use words from the reading passage or from your own vocabulary.

The biblical story of the Tower of Babel explains why the people of the world

(1) _____ . It tells how the (2) _____

of Noah settled down in the ancient land of Babylon and began to build

(3) _____ and (4) _____ . At this time,

the people all spoke (5) _____ . When their Lord saw them build-

ing (6) _____ , He became (7) _____ .

He did not want them to become too (8) _____.

So He (9) _____ . Then they couldn't (10)_____

with each other, so they never completed their buildings. From this story, we get the

English expression "a babel of languages," which means (11) _____

_____ .

Vocabulary

Expanding Vocabulary. Circle the letters of all the items that mean the same thing as the italicized word in the given sentence.

a. There are over 200 *species* of birds in the United States, each with its own song, coloration, and mating customs.

    (1) kinds   (2) diseases   (3) types

    (4) educational centers   (5) foods

b. Many Chinese immigrants *journeyed* from California to the eastern United States in the late 1800s.

    (1) kept journals   (2) traveled   (3) assisted

    (4) made a trip   (5) celebrated

c. Parents try to *prevent* their children from injuring themselves.

    (1) think   (2) complete   (3) stop

    (4) prepare   (5) keep from

d. Nonnative speakers of English may *confuse* the words "live" and "leave" because their vowel sounds are similar.

    (1) include   (2) mix up   (3) misunderstand

    (4) satisfy   (5) mistake

e. Temples are *sacred* places where gods are believed to live or visit.

    (1) frightening   (2) holy   (3) expensive

    (4) spiritual   (5) religious

f. Do the ruins of ancient temples *exist* in your native country?

    (1) occur   (2) leave   (3) excite

    (4) remain   (5) disappear

g. What *explanation* does the dictionary give for the meaning of the word "babel"?

    (1) result   (2) interpretation   (3) definition

    (4) celebration   (5) communication

h. We should all be *proud* of our national or cultural identities.

    (1) very careful   (2) feel good about   (3) think well of

    (4) become nervous about   (5) put a high value on

CHAPTER FIVE

LANGUAGE FOR LIVING

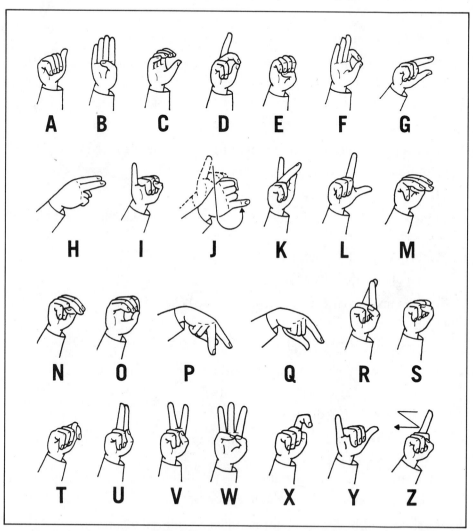

This chart of American Sign Language shows the manual method by which hearing-impaired people can communicate with each other. Some words are spelled out letter by letter, while other common words have short forms.

I   PREREADING

Class Discussion.   Nonverbal means of communication vary from culture to culture. What signs would you use to communicate the following information?

1. To show that you disagree with someone

2. To show that you agree with someone

3. To show anger

4. To show that you don't know something

5. To show that you want a ride from a passing vehicle

6. To show that your team just won its game

Among your classmates, do students from different cultures use the same signs as you? Discuss some of the similarities and differences.

FREE WRITE

Some signs and signals, such as those used for driving, are universal; everyone can understand them. Do you think the world would be a better place if there were a universal language, one that everyone could speak and understand? Why? Would your language be a good universal language? Explain your response.

Vocabulary in Context.   The words in this exercise will appear in the reading passage. Fill in each blank space in the paragraph with a word or expression from the following list that means the same thing as the item in parentheses.

send	necessary	carry
ask for	mainly	is reduced
simple	orders	able to be heard
mix	useful	very surprised
stood for		

   Most people use their voices or words to (1) (transmit) _____

their ideas, feelings, and information to someone else, but it is sometimes

(2) (essential) _____ to use artificial signs or signal languages to

(3) (convey) _____ messages. You would be

(4) (amazed) _____ at the different kinds of voiceless languages people

have created. One hundred years ago, a man named Sodre invented a musical language.

He called it Solresol because the musical notes such as *so*, *la*, and *re* represented words.

But most such artificial languages are not very (5) (effective) _____

for communication because they have only (6) (primitive) _____

vocabularies. They are used (7) (primarily) _____ to give

(8) (commands) _____ or to (9) (request) _____ simple

information, but not to exchange ideas. Naval or military communication often uses

signals, either visible, such as a light, or (10) (audible) _____ , such as the

blast of a foghorn. In some theatrical language, gestures or body movements

(11) (combine) _____ with props such as a fan or scarf to communicate

certain feelings or situations. As an artificial, voiceless, sign or signal language

becomes more complex, the number of people who can understand it

(12) (is diminished) _____ .

II READING

Signs and Signals: Communication Without Voices

[1]   Sign and signal language is a system of communication that does not use the human voice or natural speech. Some sign language is based on a code of hand and arm gestures or movements of other parts of the body. Other sign language, called signaling, refers to the transmission of information by visible and audible signals, electrical communications through wire and radio waves, or the use of messengers and even trained animals. Some gestures and signals in sign language may convey actual ideas or directions. For example, a traffic director blows a whistle and holds up his or her hand, palm facing out, in order to make traffic stop. In contrast, other signals are symbolic; that is, they convey some idea associated with, but not the same as, themselves. In Japanese No theatre, for instance, the fluttering of a fan may stand for violent swordplay.

[2]   Sign language and signaling have many different purposes. Sign and signal language can convey information, give commands, tell stories, or communicate requests and prayers to deities, or gods, in religious ceremonies. Sign and signal language can be used for communication among special groups of people who

cannot use ordinary speech, such as the hearing impaired. Voiceless languages can also be used to communicate in special situations where people cannot see each other, where they are long distances from each other, or where it is important to communicate only a few essential ideas quickly and secretly. Baseball coaches on the sidelines or in the dugout, for example, use signals that the other team does not understand in order to instruct their own players on the field to make certain plays.

[3]   Gestures, or movements of the body, particularly the hands, fingers, and eyes, are frequently used together with dancing, to entertain, or for religious purposes. In the Hindu religion of India and Indonesia, for example, gestures combined with dance movements have been used for over two thousand years to represent emotions, activities of daily life such as eating or drinking, common objects such as the moon or water, and living creatures. The Kathakali school of Hindu dance has a vocabulary of 500 signs, each of which represents a different word, which is sung along with the dance. In Tai Chi Chuan, a Chinese form of physical exercise, the different movements of the hands, legs, and head represent various animals such as the deer or the horse. Among Native Americans of the southwestern United States, certain gestures and body movements are used in the rainmaking dances as requests to the gods to send down rain for the crops.

In this Klana Topeng performance from West Java, Indonesian dancer Deena Burton employs arm and finger movements to represent a boastful attitude in a demon-king.

[4]   Signal communication differs from theatrical or religious sign language in purpose. Signal communication is used primarily to convey useful information. Its origin is in the military, where signals are used to convey the voice of the commanding officer. Audible signals such as the blast of a trumpet or the notes of a bugle have been used for thousands of years to control armies and signal the beginning of battles. Visible signals for military purposes, such as flags, banners, and the waving of swords in different ways, are other means by which commands have been given to armies and navies. In today's navy, for example, semaphore signaling uses two black-and-white flags held in different positions to represent the letters of the alphabet, numbers, and certain special signals. There is also an international flag alphabet in which different shapes and colors of each flag are used to represent the letters of the alphabet and certain special orders.

[5]   Of the various audible signaling languages used in modern times, the most familiar to the average person is the international Morse code. Many films about World War II include a scene in which a soldier or sailor is sitting at his radio transmitter tapping out the dots and dashes of the Morse code. The Morse code was first created by Samuel Morse and his assistant Alfred Vail to communicate messages on their electric telegraph machine. The Morse code consists of long and short pulses, or taps, known as dots and dashes. Each combination of dots and dashes represents a single letter of the alphabet. Because Morse and Vail spoke English, they used the letters of the English alphabet as the basis for their code. They gave the most common letters such as *E* and *T* the easiest patterns of dots and dashes. Thus, an *E* is one dot, or short tap. A *T* is one dash, or long tap. Less frequently used letters, such as *Z*, have more complicated patterns. Thus, the letter *X*, for example, is represented by one long dash, one short dot, and two long dashes. The Morse code can also be used to communicate without electricity by tapping on walls or by using lights.

[6]   The use of Morse code by signal lights is particularly effective in the naval service. Ships can transmit messages to each other across distances as far as five miles at night by using powerful flashlights to make the dots and dashes of the Morse code. These flashlights can transmit Morse code dots and dashes in the sunlight as well, although the distance of communication is lessened to about two miles. One of the biggest advantages of the Morse code is that the person who is sending the message can transmit any message he or she wishes. Messages are not limited to a few basic pieces of information. Furthermore, Morse code is easy to learn and effective in any language that uses an alphabet.

[7]   In Henry Wadsworth Longfellow's well-known poem "Paul Revere's Ride," about the start of the American Revolution, we are told that the Boston silversmith Paul Revere signaled the colonists of the arrival of the British troops with flashing lights: "One if by land, and two if by sea; /And I on the opposite shore

will be/Ready to ride and spread the alarm/to every neighboring village and farm." Today's military and civilian land, sea, and air operations have moved far beyond that primitive signaling system used in the American Revolution. With the perfection of radio, radio telephone, and advanced computer communication systems, even the Morse code has diminished in importance. Now we have signals that can even communicate through outer space. Paul Revere and his fellow revolutionaries would have been amazed.

Oral Cloze.   Number a column in your notebook from 1 to 10. Your instructor will read Paragraph [2] aloud to you twice. Listen very carefully. Then your instructor will read the paragraph aloud again, but he or she will leave out some words. Your instructor will say "blank" where these words are left out. Next to each number on your paper, write the word that correctly fills the blank space. Your instructor will read the paragraph with blanks to you several times. Now close your books.

> Sign language and signaling have "blank" different purposes. Sign and signal language "blank" convey information, give commands, tell stories, or "blank" requests and prayers to deities, or gods, in religious ceremonies. Sign and signal "blank" can be used for communication among special groups of people who "blank" use ordinary speech, "blank" as the hearing impaired. Voiceless languages can "blank" be used to communicate in special situations where people cannot "blank" each other, where they are long distances "blank" each other, or where it is important to communicate only a few essential "blank" quickly and secretly. Baseball coaches on the sidelines "blank" in the dugout, for example, use signals that the other "blank" does not understand to instruct their own players on the field "blank" to make certain plays.

Reacting to the Reading

Learning a new code or language involves reading, writing, and oral practice.

a. What are some ways in which you can develop your language skills in these areas?

b. How important are memorization, concentration, and motivation (desire to learn) when learning a language or code? What are some factors that help or interfere with these aspects of learning a new language or code?

Reading Comprehension

1. Understanding the Text.   Choose or write the correct answer.

a. Which sentence uses the word *directions* as it is used in Sentence 4 of Paragraph [1]?

(1) The four directions are north, south, east, and west.

(2) Please give me clear directions to your house so I won't get lost.

(3) The children ran off in different directions.

b. The expression *in order to* in Sentence 5 of Paragraph [1] means

(1) as a result of.

(2) for the purpose of.

(3) as an example of.

c. The expression *In contrast* that begins the next-to-last sentence in Paragraph [1] suggests

(1) a reason for the previous sentence.

(2) a time relationship with the previous sentence.

(3) a reversal of the idea in the previous sentence.

d. Which two expressions in Paragraph [1] express the same idea?

(1) or/and

(2) in contrast/that is

(3) for instance/for example

e. In Paragraph [2], the expression *such as* introduces an example of the general term *people who cannot use ordinary speech*. What is the example? In the same paragraph, baseball coaches are given as an example. What are they an example of?

f. In Paragraph [2], Sentence 4 adds information to Sentence 3. Which word introduces the idea of addition?

g. In Paragraph [2], Sentence 4, to what does the word *they* refer?

h. Paragraph [3] provides two samples, or examples, of general terms. What are these? What signal expressions of example introduce them?

i. In Paragraph [3], what idea is illustrated by the mentions of the Kathakali school of dance, Tai Chi Chuan, and Native American rain dancing?

j. In Paragraph [4], Sentence 3, to what does the word *Its* refer?

   k. The main idea of Paragraph [4] is that signal languages

      (1) use trumpets or bugles to convey military commands.

      (2) have been used for over two thousand years.

      (3) are used primarily to communicate information.

      (4) are similar to religious and theatrical sign languages.

   l. In Paragraph [5], what is the author's purpose in describing the film scene?

   m. In Paragraph [4], semaphore flag and international flag alphabet signaling are examples of signal languages that

      (1) communicate audibly and visibly.

      (2) require the sender and the receiver to be able to see each other.

      (3) entertain as well as inform.

   n. According to the information in Paragraph [5], which group of letters would have the most complex pattern of dots and dashes?

      (1) *A, E, S*

      (2) *I, M, L*

      (3) *K, X, Q*

   o. In Paragraph [6],

      (1) Sentence 5 contradicts Sentence 4.

      (2) Sentence 5 gives an example of Sentence 4.

      (3) Sentence 5 expands Sentence 4.

   p. In Paragraph [6], Sentence 3, the word *although* suggests

      (1) an opposition of ideas.

      (2) an addition of ideas.

      (3) an illustration of a general term.

   q. In Paragraph [6], two advantages of Morse code are given. Which word signals the addition of a second advantage?

   r. Paragraph [7] suggests that Paul Revere would be amazed because

      (1) Morse code has diminished in importance.

      (2) signaling language has become so technologically advanced.

      (3) the U.S. Navy is still using flashing lights to signal.

2. Answering Information Questions. Write the answers to the following questions in complete sentences on a separate sheet of paper.

   a. List at least three types of communication that can be used in signal or sign languages.

b. What are two purposes of sign or signal languages?

c. Why do baseball coaches use secret hand signals to their players?

d. Give one example of an audible car, plane, or ship traffic signal.

e. Give one example of a visible car, plane, or ship signal.

f. How are signals in Morse code formed?

g. Describe the signal that was used by Paul Revere to announce the arrival of the British troops.

III THE READING PROCESS

Scanning for Specific Information.   To scan means to read a passage quickly to find specific facts. To scan for the answer to a question, you must first pick out the main words in the question.

Answer the following questions by scanning the reading passage for facts. The main question words are italicized for you. Write the number of the paragraph and sentence where you find your answer. The first one is done for you.

a. Is *Morse code* an *ancient or a modern* signaling system?

   Morse code is a modern signaling system.

   Para. 5 Sent. 1.

b. What *signal* is used to *stop auto traffic*?

   _____

c. What is the meaning of a *fluttering fan* in *Japanese No theatre*?

   _____

d. In Chinese *Tai Chi Chuan,* what do one's *body movements* represent?

   _____

e. For what *purpose* did systems of *signal communication originate*?

   _____

f. What *signal system* uses *black-and-white flags* held in different positions to communicate?

   _____

g. *How far* can *Morse code flashlight* signals transmit *at night*?

During the *day*?

_____

h. What are the *three most modern means of military signal communication*?

_____

Ⅳ VOCABULARY

1. New Words. Pronounce these words, following your instructor.

Verbs	Nouns	Adjectives	Adverbs
combine	requests	audible	primarily
convey	transmission	effective	
diminish	commands	essential	
amaze		primitive	

a. *EXPANDING VOCABULARY.* Choose the item that best explains the meaning of each italicized word.

(1) Morse code is *primarily* a military signaling language.

   (a) recently   (b) historically   (c) mainly

(2) Morse code flashlight signals are *effective* up to five miles at night.

   (a) useful   (b) impossible   (c) artificial

(3) The effectiveness of flashlight signals in Morse code *diminishes* during daylight hours.

   (a) is increased   (b) is made easier   (c) is reduced

(4) The *transmission* of a few basic commands is possible by blowing a trumpet.

   (a) celebration   (b) rejection   (c) sending

(5) Dance movements can *combine* with gestures to entertain an audience.

   (a) confuse   (b) mix   (c) come before

(6) Symbolic gestures can be used to *make requests* of deities, or gods.

   (a) bring rain   (b) explore ideas   (c) ask favors

(7) With today's computer communication, earlier signaling languages appear *primitive*.

(a) underdeveloped   (b) most important   (c) splendid

b. *USING VOCABULARY.* Read the following brief passages. Then use each of the vocabulary words in a sentence related to the topic.

(1) In order for armies and navies to move into action quickly and to communicate with each other, they must use signaling languages.

command(s)   audible   essential

(2) People who cannot hear often have problems speaking clearly as well. Yet many hearing-impaired people can communicate with each other through a sign language in which different movements of the fingers represent different letters of the alphabet.

convey   amazed

2. Word Families: Adjectives and Adverb Use.   Adjectives describe nouns or pronouns.

> Speech is the *primary* method of human communication.
> (What kind of method? *Primary* method.)

Adverbs of manner tell how (in what manner) verb action is done.

> Human beings learn language *primarily* through imitation. (How do human beings learn language? *Primarily* through imitation.)

Most adverbs are formed by adding *ly* to adjectives.

Study the following lists of adjectives and adverbs.

Adjectives	Adverbs
natural	naturally
audible	audibly
visible	visibly
actual	actually
violent	violently

certain	certainly
essential	essentially
physical	physically
different	differently
international	internationally
effective	effectively
powerful	powerfully
basic	basically
particular	particularly
secret	secretly

In the blank space, write the correct form of the word in parentheses.

(1) Soldiers used Morse code (particular, particularly) _____

  during World War II.

(2) There are (certain, certainly) _____ notes on the bugle

  that signal the ending of the day's activity.

(3) The finger movements of American Sign Language are all (different,

  differently) _____ from each other.

(4) Semaphore flags can only transmit (essential, essentially) _____

  signals.

(5) Morse code works (basic, basically) _____ with long and short

  electrical impulses.

(6) Newspaper articles can be (powerful, powerfully) _____ means

  of influencing people's ideas.

(7) (Violent, Violently) _____ behavior will not be permitted

  in the classroom.

LANGUAGE FOCUS

Present Continuous Tense

The present continuous tense of verbs is used to express action in progress and action that is limited in duration of time. It tells about activity that is going on now or in the present period of time. It can also communicate future intention. The present continuous tense is formed by *am*, *is*, or *are* + the *ing* ending of the main verb.

> The soldier *is sending* Morse code signals to transmit important information. Now we *are learning* the present continuous tense.

Study the present continuous tense of the verb *to wave*.

	Singular	**Plural**
First Person	I am waving	My friend and I are waving We are waving
Second Person	You are waving	You are waving
Third Person	The sailor is waving He is waving	The sailors are waving They are waving

The negative forms are *am not* (*I'm not, is not, isn't*) and *are not* (*aren't*) + the *-ing* form of the verb. Note that verbs that end in *e* drop the *e* before adding *ing: wave* becomes *waving.*

1. Sentence Completion. Complete each of the following sentences by putting the verb in parentheses in the present continuous tense.

a. You and your classmates (communicate) _____ in English.

b. Perhaps you (use) _____ a tape recorder for pronunciation.

c. The sailor (negative: use) _____ the semaphore flags for entertainment.

d. and e. He (try) _____ to communicate the weather information to another ship, which (sail) _____ two miles away.

f. When armies (move) _____ into battle, they must be in touch with their commanders.

g. Currently, many high school and college students (study) _____ Spanish.

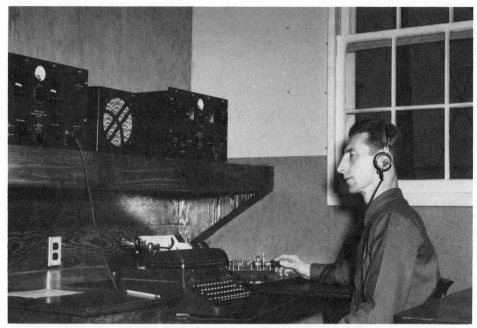

Some soldiers sit in special signaling rooms at army bases all over the country. They tap out military information in Morse code on a radio. They also listen to signals from their receivers on a special headset. Soldiers must pay careful attention when they are sending and receiving Morse code.

h. We hope that you (look) _____ up new words in your

dictionary.

2. Sentence Building.   Write complete sentences by matching the subjects in Column A with the related present continuous verb phrase in Column B. The subjects must agree in number with their verbs. Use the information from the chapter as a basis for your answers.

A

B

a. You

is studying English with me.

b. The soldier

are studying English in England.

c. He

are learning Spanish.

d. Currently, Chinese children

is tapping out Morse code.

e. The Indonesian dancer

are learning English this term.

f. One of my friends

isn't performing Tai Chi Chuan.

g. We

is trying to communicate military information.

h. Many foreign students

are learning a simplified form of Chinese.

i. Many American students

are practicing present continuous tense.

3. Controlled Writing.   Look at the photograph of the soldier tapping out Morse code. The caption is written about soldiers in general, using the simple present tense. Rewrite the caption about this soldier, who is working on an army base in Georgia. Change the main subject to *This soldier*. Change the verbs to present continuous tense to indicate action in progress. Make all necessary noun, verb, and article changes from plural to singular. To practice present continuous tense orally, change your paragraph about *This soldier* to *These soldiers*. Make all necessary plural changes.

Sentence Patterns with *Because*

We answer questions that ask *why* with the connecting word *because*. The word *because* joins together two thoughts. One thought tells what happens, that is, the result. The other thought gives a reason why.

Many people are learning English because it is an international language.
(result)   (reason)

1. Sentence Combining.   In each of the following items, one sentence tells us the result and the other sentence explains the reason. Combine the two sentences into one complete sentence by using the connecting word *because*. Replace nouns with pronouns where necessary. Rewrite each new sentence with correct punctuation and capitalization.

(1) Many people are learning English.
(2) English is an international language.
Many people are learning English because
it is an international language.

a. (1) A traffic controller holds up his or her hand.

   (2) He or she wants traffic to stop.

b. (1) There are so many different languages in the world.

   (2) It is difficult for people from different lands to communicate.

c. (1) Baseball coaches use secret signals.

   (2) They do not want rival teams to understand their instructions.

d. (1) I want to have better English pronunciation.

   (2) I listen to English TV programs.

e. (1) There are many factories near the river.

(2) The river is very polluted.

f. (1) Most scientific writing is produced in English.

(2) Scientists should study English.

g. (1) Archeology takes you to many different lands.

(2) Archeology is an interesting profession.

2. Sentence expansion.   Complete the following result clauses by adding a reason that explains why. Join the two sentence parts with the word *because*. Complete your new sentences in the space provided.

a. Many people are studying Spanish _____

_____

b. Many immigrants come to the United States _____

_____

c. Language changes _____

_____

d. The air in my city is very dirty _____

_____

e. Paris is an important city _____

_____

f. Very little vegetation grows in the desert _____

_____

g. It would be difficult to live on the moon _____

_____

h. I am studying English _____

_____

i. It is interesting to go to college _____

_____

j. It is useful to speak two languages _____

_____

Plural Possessives

You have already learned how to form singular possessives in the apostrophe + *s* form. Study the following model. It shows you how to write plural possessives in the *s* + apostrophe form.

Singular	Singular Possessive	Plural	Plural Possessive
a writer	a writer's decision (decision of a writer)	writers	writers' decisions (decisions of the writers)

With your instructor, talk about how the plural possessive is formed with an *s* + apostrophe. We mainly use this form of the plural possessive with living things.

1. Forming Plural Possessives.   Change the items in the list of singular possessives to plural possessives. The first one is done for you.

Singular Possessives   **Plural Possessives**

a. a friend's tape recorder   *friends' tape recorders*

b. an immigrant's difficulty   _____

c. a man's suit   _____

d. a student's work   _____

e. a scientist's interest   _____

f. a parent's love   _____

g. a child's toy   _____

2. Sentence Rewriting.   Rewrite each sentence, changing the italicized expressions to plural possessives in the *s* + apostrophe form.

> The notebooks of the students were filled with exercises.
> *The students' notebooks were filled with exercises.*

a. *The children of my neighbors* are literate in two languages.

b. *The assignments of my instructors* are usually clear.

c. At first, *the paragraphs of the students* were quite short.

d. The American Constitution protects *the rights of all citizens.*

e. *Opinions of teachers* about that book were mixed.

f. Professor Tannen has written about *the communication problems of women.*

Now identify the subject of each new sentence. Draw an arrow from the subject to its main verb. Do they agree in number?

3. Proofreading.   Some of the following sentences have errors in the formation of the possessive. Some sentences are correct. In the space provided, correct any error in the possessive. If the sentence is *correct*, write C in the space.

   a. Dictionaries are writers' friends. ____

   b. A writers' opinion can help you choose a good TV program. ____

   c. Childrens games often use special vocabularies. ____

   d. It is difficult to understand some professor's pronunciation. ____

   e. English teachers must carefully review their students papers. ____

   f. Babies' first words are learned in their parent's home. ____

   g. The United Nation's official languages are French and English. ____

   h. An Indonesian dancers' movements convey emotion. ____

Ⓥ THE COMPOSING PROCESS

1. Sentence Combining to Form a Paragraph.   Combine the following sentences into longer, more interesting statements to form a paragraph about international languages. Leave out unnecessary words. Use adjective-noun combinations, linking pronouns, plural possessives, and reason-result clauses to make your sentences flow smoothly. Follow the directions in the parentheses.

   a. People have always dreamed of a language.

   b. This is a single language.

   c. This is an international language.

   d. People always want to trade with each other.

   e. The people are from different countries.

   f. People want to have exchanges.

   g. These exchanges are cultural.

   h. This is difficult. (Use signal for changing a thought. Use signal for reason.)

   i. People speak many different languages.

   j. Currently, many people are creating languages.

   k. These languages are artificial.

l.   These languages are international.

m.   Esperanto is one of these languages.

n.   Esperanto uses many words in its vocabulary.

o.   These words are from Romance languages. (Use signal to introduce examples.)

p.   These languages are Spanish.

q.   These languages are Italian.

r.   These languages are French.

s.   Volapuk is another language.

t.   This language is artificial.

u.   Its vocabulary is primarily German.

v.   Its vocabulary is primarily Slavic.

w.   Esperanto and Volapuk do not use words.

x.   These words are from Chinese.

y.   These words are from Korean.

z.   These words are from other languages.

aa.   These languages are Asian.

bb.   Other world languages do not employ words.

cc.   They use signs. (Use signal to introduce examples.)

dd.   They use musical notes.

ee.   They use numbers.

ff.   They use computer codes.

gg.   A sign language might be easy to learn. (Use signal for reason.)

hh.   A sign language would have a small vocabulary.

ii.   A sign language would have a basic vocabulary.

jj.   But could we write poetry in a language?

kk.   This would be a language with only a few basic signs.

2. Developing a Paragraph with Several Points.   One way to develop a subject for an extended paragraph is to think of two or three main points about your subject and support them with details or examples. In this way, you can be sure that your paragraph is really developing, not just repeating itself. The following exercise will help you practice this pattern of composition.

The notes listed below describe the scene in a school cafeteria where a variety of activities is taking place. The introductory notes tell where and when the action is taking place and present the writer's general feeling about the scene.

The notes are grouped by three main points: students alone, pairs of students, and groups of students. Each point is supported by several details that tell what these people are doing.

Read the notes, and then write the given information as a complete paragraph. You will use the present continuous tense for those sentences that tell what people are doing. You will use the simple present tense for those sentences that tell how people look, seem, or are.

Lunchtime — Noon — 2:00 — College Cafeteria
    busy — crowded — lots of different activities
I. students alone
      reading newspaper
      studying textbooks
      look serious — concentrating on work
II. pairs of students
      a couple — holding hands; smiling at each other
      — seem in love — two students arguing
      — loud voices — waving hands around — excited
III. groups of students
      playing cards, video games, reviewing for an
      exam — asking each other questions — discussing answers

Paragraph Topics

  a. Painting, sculpture, music, dance, and architecture are among the many arts that communicate with people. In a composition, choose two or three of these arts and talk about what they communicate to you. Use separate short paragraphs for each different type of art. You may refer to a specific example of each type of art if you wish.

  b. Some people think that English is a difficult language to learn. Some of the more difficult features of English are its spelling, pronunciation, verb tenses and forms, plural noun forms, use of articles, and formation of questions.

Choose two or three items that you find difficult about English, and discuss them in a composition. You should give specific examples of your main points.

Ⓥ ADDITIONAL READING

Learning to Read: Malcolm X

[1]   Malcolm X was an African-American civil rights activist, religious leader, writer, and speaker. He was born in Omaha, Nebraska, in 1925 and was mysteriously assassinated at a religious rally in 1965. By that time, his *Autobiography of Malcolm X* was widely known. Malcolm X was born Malcolm Little, but he took the name Malcolm X after he became a leader of the Black Muslims. This is a religious organization based on the beliefs of Islam, or the Moslem faith. The American Black Muslims have changed some of the practices of Islam to apply more specifically to the lives of African-American people in the United States.

[2]   Malcolm X learned about the Black Muslims while he was in prison. Because he was poorly educated, he felt that he could not adequately teach his new political and religious beliefs to others. On the street, he had been able to express his thoughts and ideas in the slang of the "hustlers." When he tried to inform people about the Black Muslims, however, he found that he did not have an adequate vocabulary and communication skills for his purpose. In his own words, he "wasn't even functional."

[3]   To increase his knowledge and improve his skills, Malcolm X turned to books. But when he tried to read serious books on his own, he found he couldn't comprehend most of the words. "They might as well have been in Chinese," he wrote. And if he skipped all the words he didn't know, he would end up with very little idea of what the book was about. "I became frustrated," Malcolm wrote in his autobiography.

[4]   Malcolm X's frustration at his inability to read and write made him determined to overcome these deficiencies. "I saw that the best thing I could do was get hold of a dictionary," he tells us, "to study, to learn some words. I was lucky enough to reason also that I should try to improve my penmanship. It was sad. I couldn't even write in a straight line. It was both ideas together that moved me to request a dictionary along with some tablets and pencils from the Norfolk Prison Colony school."

[5]   For the first two days, Malcolm X just skimmed through the pages of the dictionary. He tells us of his amazement at the contents of the dictionary: "I'd never realized so many words existed! I didn't know which words I needed to learn. Finally, just to start some kind of action I began copying." In his slow, careful,

uncertain handwriting, Malcolm X copied everything on the first page of the dictionary into a notebook. He even copied the punctuation marks. This copying took him one day. After that, he read aloud everything he had written. "Over and over, aloud, to myself, I read my own handwriting," Malcolm recalled.

[6]   Malcolm X describes how the next morning he woke up thinking about the words he had copied and read aloud the night before. He felt "immensely proud" to realize that he had written more than he had ever written before. He had even written words that he didn't know were in the world. He could even remember the meanings of most of the words he had written. "I reviewed the words whose meanings I didn't remember," he states in this section of his autobiography. "Funny thing, from the dictionary's first page right now, that aardvark springs to my mind. The dictionary had a picture of it, a long-tailed, long-eared, burrowing African mammal, which lives off termites caught by sticking out its tongue as an anteater does for ants."

[7]   Malcolm X was so fascinated that he went on to copy the dictionary's next page and study that by reading it aloud as well. And once again, when he woke the next morning, he had the same experience. With every succeeding page he copied and read aloud, Malcolm X found he was learning and remembering more and more words. In addition, he learned about people, places, and events from history. "The dictionary is like a miniature encyclopedia," he discovered. Finally, when he finished copying the entire *A* section of the dictionary, he had filled an entire writing tablet. Then he went on to the *B*s. "That was the way I started copying what eventually became the entire dictionary."

[8]   As Malcolm X's word base broadened, he began to understand what a book was saying when he picked one up to read. It was the first time in his life that this had ever happened. "Anyone who has read a great deal can imagine the new world that opened. Let me tell you something: from then until I left that prison, in every free moment I had, if I was not reading in the library, I was reading on my bunk. . . . Months passed without my even thinking about being imprisoned. In fact, up to then, I never had been so truly free in my life."

[9]   Malcolm X was imprisoned in an institution that believed strongly in the rehabilitation of its prisoners. The prison philosophy was to prepare its inmates as well as possible for success in life on the outside after their prison terms were over. Therefore, the prison authorities were pleased at any inmate who showed an interest in books. There were many well-read inmates in Malcolm X's prison. Some of them were "practically walking encyclopedias"; they "had devoured more literature than any university would have required." These men were the prison celebrities.

[10]   In this section of his autobiography, Malcolm X reflected on what learning to read meant to him. "I knew right there in prison that reading had changed forever the course of my life," Malcolm wrote. Malcolm X describes in his book how one day an English writer telephoned him from London for an interview.

American sculptor John W. Rhoden's statue of ex-slave Frederick Douglass holding a book beautifully captures Malcolm X's feeling that reading is a means of liberation.

The interviewer asked Malcolm X what college he had graduated from. "Books," Malcolm told him. "I told the Englishman that my *alma mater* [college from which one graduates] was books, a good library."

Reacting to the Reading

1. Malcolm X states that even though he was in prison, his ability to read made him *free*.

    a. What do you think he meant by the word *free* in this context?

    b. Do you agree with him that reading can be a form of freedom?
        Explain your answer.

    c. Has reading made you feel *free*? In what way?

2. Some teachers think that dictionaries are *over*used by English-as-a-second-language (ESL) students. These teachers want students to try to guess the meaning of a word from its use in the sentence. They do not want their students to use the dictionary as a crutch, or something to lean on.

    a. How do you think a dictionary should be used in beginning ESL study? Do you think a student should look up the meaning of every unfamiliar word in a reading passage? Should a student keep lists of vocabulary words learned from the dictionary? Should students write the dictionary meaning of a word in the reading passage where the word occurs?

    b. What do you do if you don't understand the meaning of a word given in a dictionary?

Reading Comprehension

Understanding the Text.   Choose the correct answer, or follow the directions for each item.

    a. In Paragraph [1], Malcolm X's original name is given as well as the name he took as a Black Muslim. Which word signals the contrast between the two names?

    b. In Sentence 2 of Paragraph [2], what thought relationship does the word *Because* signal: contrast? addition of ideas? reason? result? example?

    c. In Paragraph [3], when Malcolm X stated that words in books "might as well have been in Chinese," he meant that
        (1)   he could read Chinese.
        (2)   Chinese was a mysterious language to him.
        (3)   Chinese is as difficult as English.
        (4)   he would have liked to have known Chinese.

    d. In Paragraph [6], Malcolm X describes the aardvark to show
        (1)   that aardvarks are interesting creatures.
        (2)   an important word he learned from the dictionary.
        (3)   how a dictionary is alphabetically arranged.
        (4)   how useful his method of studying the dictionary was.

    e. In Paragraph [8], in the sentence *It was the first time in his life that this had ever happened*, what does the word *this* refer to?

f. In Sentence 6 of Paragraph [8], the use of the word *free* means that
    (1) Malcolm X left prison a free man.
    (2) the library books Malcolm X read were free.
    (3) Malcolm X had freedom to do as he pleased in prison.
    (4) Malcolm X's mind became free through his reading.

g. In Paragraph [9], what is the thought relationship between Sentences 2 and 3?
    (1) Sentence 3 is an example of Sentence 2.
    (2) Sentence 2 is a contrast to Sentence 3.
    (3) Sentence 3 is a result of Sentence 2.
    (4) The two sentences relate to each other in time order.
    Which word(s) signal the relationship?

h. Paragraph [9] uses the expression *prison celebrities* to describe men who
    (1) were very much respected by the other inmates.
    (2) became famous outside of prison after their release.
    (3) were correction officers and administrators of the prison.
    (4) were Malcolm X's friends.

i. In Paragraph [10], it is implied that the Englishman was interviewing Malcolm X because
    (1) he wanted to write an article about Malcolm X.
    (2)   he wanted proof of Malcolm X's college degree.
    (3) he was going into prison himself.
    (4) he wanted the names of some good books.

Vocabulary

Expanding Vocabulary.   Each of the italicized vocabulary items from the passage on Malcolm X is followed by several common synonyms. First, read the given sentence aloud, substituting one of the synonyms for the original vocabulary word. Then write an original sentence using one of the synonyms.

a. *beliefs*:   ideas   notions   tenets   opinions
   The beliefs of the Black Muslims are based on those of Islam.

b. *adequate*:   sufficient   good enough   suitable   acceptable
   Malcolm X did not have an adequate vocabulary to express his ideas.

c. *frustrated*:   baffled   defeated   blocked   stopped
   Malcolm X felt frustrated because he could not read and write well.

d. *amazement*:   surprise   astonishment   wonder
   Malcolm X felt great amazement at the number of words in the dictionary.

e. *fascinated*:   interested   delighted   attracted   charmed
   The dictionary fascinated Malcolm X so much that he went through it to the very end.

CHAPTER SIX

ANIMAL TALES

Ⅰ PREREADING

Class Discussion. All humans are mammals, but not all mammals are human. Humans and other mammals are alike in certain ways. For example, mammals give birth to their babies alive. Mammals take care of their young babies. They protect them by forming family units.

But humans and other mammals are also different in certain ways. Talk about some ways in which humans are different from other mammals. Your answers to the following questions will help you develop your ideas.

1. How do humans move around? How is this different from other mammals?

2. What are some ways that humans protect themselves from cold, heat, and rain? How is this similar to or different from the way other mammals protect themselves?

3. How do humans get some of their basic foods? Do other mammals get their food in the same way?

4. How do humans communicate with each other? Name some things that other mammals do to communicate with each other.

FREE WRITE

What pet animal have you observed in regard to its intelligence and emotions? Did this pet seem to understand and love its owner? Explain, and include a specific incident to illustrate your response.

Vocabulary in Context. The words in this exercise will appear in the reading passage. Circle the word(s) that means the same as the italicized word in each of the following sentences.

1. Some (a) *creatures* communicate through sound waves that cannot be (b) *detected* by the human ear.

   (a) designers   animals of different kinds   plants and animals

   (b) discovered   taken away   argued about

2. Overcoming (a) *obstacles* in getting food and water is (b) *vital* to animal and human survival.

   (a) processes   limits   difficulties

   (b) useful   essential   unnecessary

3. That song was only (a) *slightly* (b) *audible* because the microphone was broken.

   (a) a little bit   quite thin   occasionally

   (b) able to be written   able to be seen   able to be heard

4. A thick (a) *cluster* of birds on a branch may (b) *indicate* the presence of food.

   (a) problem   accident   group

   (b) suggest   arrest   dictate

5. Many (a) *experiments* have been tried to (b) *improve* the (c) *ability* of children to read.

   (a) exciting films   examples   tests

   (b) interest   make worse   make better

   (c) friendliness   capability   appetite

6. The instructor (a) *claimed* that I did not (b) *respond to* the last question on the examination.

   (a) lied   did not know   said

   (b) omit   answer   repeat

Ⅱ READING

Sounds from the Animal Kingdom

[1]   Several years ago, if you were walking past Boston's New England Aquarium late at night, you would hear a noise coming out of the seal pond that sounded like someone yelling, "Come here, come here!" That voice was not a human voice, however. It belonged to a harbor seal named Hoover. Everyone who heard Hoover's "Come here, come here!" thought he sounded just like a human being. Visitors came from all over to hear Hoover "talk." He became so famous that when he died, he had an obituary in the newspaper just like a human being. But scientists say that Hoover was not really communicating as human beings do. He was just copying the sounds he heard his human visitors make every day.

[2]   Many people who own a pet dog or cat, a singing bird such as a canary, or a "talking" bird such as a parrot are certain that their pets can communicate with them. They know that their dog barks differently when it wants to go outside than when it sees a stranger. Cats meow slightly differently when they are hungry than when they have accidentally been locked in a closet. Scientists, too, know that each species of animal has its own "language" for communication with others of its kind. Large mammals such as lions make a variety of noises to indicate hunger, fear, anger, hurt, or a desire to mate. These sounds are audible to human beings, and scientists can easily tell them apart through close observation.

[3]   Birds, of course, communicate with others of their species by vocal calls audible to human beings. We call these sounds "songs," as if birds were singing for pleasure as human beings do. In fact, birds are not really "singing"; they are using these sounds to communicate vital information. With the help of modern technology, scientists can discover a great deal about the meanings of various

Elephants can communicate with each other through ultrasound.

bird songs. Instruments called spectrographs can diagram bird sounds on screens—in color—at the moment they are happening and then print them as maps to be used in bird guidebooks. Diagramming bird communication in this way is a fascinating experience. One scientist has described it as like "listening to water falling past your ear."

[4]   Bernd Heinrich is an ornithologist who studies how birds survive during cold winters. He believes that bird song may play an important role in this survival. Heinrich found, for example, that tiny kinglet birds keep themselves warm at night by clustering close together on a tree branch. He observed that the kinglets make a long, high-pitched sound to signal other birds in the area to join them. Then they make a second call, different from the first, that brings all the birds into a cluster on the branch where they will spend the night. Heinrich claims that the kinglets "sing" almost constantly, making thin, bell-like cheeps that remind him of small pebbles being struck together. One sound that he hears at the beginning of spring is a quick series of twelve happy notes per second, repeated six to nine times per minute. This is a "conversation" that announces the new mating season that will make sure that the kinglets survive as a species.

[5]   Many creatures, however, do not use a system of communication that is audible to human beings. They communicate with each other through high-pitched sound waves, or pulses that human beings cannot detect. This is called ultrasound. One herd of elephants, for example, may detect dangerous weather

conditions in their area. Then they may warn other elephants of this situation by ultrasound. Dolphins, porpoises, and some whales also can communicate by ultrasonic pulses. Some insects, too, use ultrasonic "language" to communicate. For example, the male praying mantis, which is smaller and weaker than the female, uses ultrasound during its mating season to tell the larger, hungry female that he is not food for a meal but a possible mate. Can we say, then, that these animals are "talking" through ultrasonic language?

[6]   Another form of animal "language" is called echolocation. In echolocation, the animal first produces a sound in its voice box, mouth, or some other part of the head. Then the sound repeats itself, or echos, in the animal's highly developed nervous system. Finally, the animal's brain compares the original sound to its echo. Certain species of bats, whales, and birds use echolocation to move around in their environment, especially in the dark. Echolocation can help these creatures detect food sources and avoid obstacles in their paths. Echolocation, unlike ultrasonic sound, may be audible to the human ear.

[7]   We know now that animals have a varied "vocabulary" of signals to communicate with others in their species. However, can we really call these animal communication systems "language"? Most scientists would say "no." When animals signal to each other, they are only using a physical ability. They are not communicating *ideas*, as human language does. It is true that some birds and many mammals can be trained to recognize certain gestures or verbal commands. Many creatures, like Hoover the harbor seal, can even learn to copy human speech. However, recent experiments with apes, the most intelligent of all animals, indicate that even these humanlike creatures cannot create or use language as human beings do.

[8]   In the last twenty years, scientists have conducted many experiments to test the language ability of apes. One New York City psychologist, Dr. Herbert Terrace, tried to teach an ape named Nim Chimpsky to use sign language with English words. He sent Nim to nursery school at Columbia University. Nim worked with his teachers five hours every day, and in four months he had learned the signs for 125 English words. Nim could recognize signs for visible things such as *table* or *apple*. He could recognize the signs for some active verbs such as *bite*, *jump*, or *hurry*. He learned some signs for colors, such as *red* and *blue*. After the first few months, however, Nim did not improve his vocabulary very much. He never created new words, as human language learners do. Nim never began sentences himself; he could only give responses to his teachers' questions. Dr. Terrace's conclusion was that apes cannot learn language as human beings do.

[9]   A few scientists disagree with Dr. Terrace about the ability of apes to communicate with language. Scientists working with a pygmy chimpanzee named Kanzi at the Language Research Center in Atlanta, Georgia, claim that Kanzi has certainly learned language. Kanzi communicates by using geometrical signs for words. He punches out his signs on a computer keyboard. He can ask to go

to his tree house for a banana, to play tag, or to watch a videotape. Kanzi can respond to human commands in a very humanlike way. Unlike Nim Chimpsky, Kanzi sometimes creates his own statements and adds new information to sentences. Kanzi demonstrates high intelligence, but Dr. Terrace still does not believe he is using language in a human way. It seems as if we will be discussing this interesting issue of animal communication for quite a while yet.

Summary Completion.   A summary gives the main ideas of a passage. It also includes the most important supporting details for the ideas in the passage. In the following summary of this reading selection, some items are missing. Choose the correct item from the list following the summary paragraph to complete each numbered blank space.

Some animals, such as seals, can (1) _____ human voices. Other animals such as dogs or cats make (2) _____ for different reasons. The communication systems of many animals are (3) _____ by human beings. The songs of birds, for example, have been carefully (4) _____ by scientists and can be used to identify their various (5) _____ . Some animals, however, communicate by (6) _____ , a system of sound waves that human beings cannot hear. Bats, dolphins, and some insects can communicate by echolocation, in which sounds are (7) _____ in their brains. Many recent experiments have been done to discover whether apes have (8) _____ . Although apes can learn to understand and make (9) _____ , they do not seem to be able to use language in a (10) _____ way.

(1) write/copy/read

(2) different words/different ideas/different sounds/different sizes

(3) able to be seen/able to be heard

(4) avoided/destroyed/recorded

(5) activities/activity's

(6) voice box/ultrasound/ultrasonic

(7) happened/included/repeated

(8) athletic skills/emotions/language ability

(9) sign/signs/sign's

(10) secret/human/beautiful

Reacting to the Reading

According to what you have read, animals possess certain communication abilities.

a. What are some animal communication abilities that human beings lack?

b. What can human beings communicate that animals don't seem to be able to?

c. Do you think that animals have the ability to communicate emotions? Explain.

Reading Comprehension

1. Understanding the Text. Follow the directions for each item.

a. Mark *T* for *true* or *F* for *false* next to each statement. Be prepared to identify the part of the text where you find your answer.

(1) Hoover was an old seal who lived in the ocean. ____

(2) Animals do not have the ability to imitate human voices. ____

(3) Most animals have different sounds for different situations. ____

(4) Birds sing just for pleasure as human beings do. ____

(5) The kinglet bird illustrates the idea of audible communication in animals. ____

(6) Ultrasonic pulses cannot be used to communicate underwater. ____

(7) Dr. Terrace doesn't believe apes have true language ability. ____

b. Choose the correct answer.

(1) In the title of this reading and throughout the passage, quotation marks are used for such words as "talk," "language," and "vocabulary" in connection with animals. These quotation marks indicate that

a. these are words from a foreign language.

b. these words do not really apply to animals.

c. these words should be emphasized.

(2) Hoover the harbor seal sounded like a human being because

a. seal language is similar to human language.

b. he was copying the sound of a human voice.

c. he was more intelligent than most seals.

(3) Hoover had an obituary in the paper because

    a.   he was famous when he died.

    b.   he became famous after he died.

    c.   zoo animals always have obituaries when they die.

(4) The word *however* in Sentence 2 of Paragraph [1] shows that

    a.   Sentences 1 and 2 continue the same opinion.

    b.   Sentence 2 gives a reason for Sentence 1.

    c.   Sentence 2 contrasts with the idea of Sentence 1.

(5) According to Paragraph [2], dogs, cats, and lions

    a.   make the same sounds no matter what the situation is.

    b.   never repeat the same sounds.

    c.   have special sounds for specific situations.

(6) The word *too* in the middle of Paragraph [2] could be replaced by the word

    a.   very.

    b.   also.

    c.   so.

(7) Birds basically sing

    a.   to entertain other birds.

    b.   for the pleasure of human beings.

    c.   to communicate information.

(8) The word *vocal* as it is used in Paragraph [3] probably means

    a.   telling the truth.

    b.   making a sound aloud.

    c.   speaking in anger.

(9) Bernd Heinrich is an ornithologist. An ornithologist is

    a.   a professor who enjoys his students.

    b.   a rude person.

    c.   a scientist who studies birds.

(10) Kinglets call a dozen quick happy notes in sequence when

    a.   they are ready to mate.

    b.   they cluster together to keep warm.

    c.   they are hungry.

(11) *Ultrasound* refers to

    a.   the noise of a thunderstorm.

    b.   sunlight and lightning.

    c.   high-frequency pulses of sound.

(12) According to Paragraph [5], the ultrasonic message communicated by the male praying mantis to the female is

    a.   "I'll hurt you if you come near me."

    b.   "I'm friendly; don't hurt me."

    c.   "We're different species; just leave me alone."

(13) Paragraphs [5] and [6] have similar purposes:

    a.   to explain the difficulties of communicating in water.

    b.   to explain the construction of animal nervous systems.

    c.   to explain different systems of animal communication.

(14) Paragraph [7] implies that

    a.   you could probably train a dog to understand an idea.

    b.   apes are smarter than seals.

    c.   only human beings can communicate ideas.

(15) In Sentence 4 of Paragraph [7], the pronoun *they* refers to

    a.   scientists.

    b.   animals.

    c.   communications systems.

    d.   ideas.

(16) Which expression in Paragraph [9] suggests that Nim Chimpsky and Kanzi are different from each other?

    a.   It seems as if

    b.   Unlike

    c.   Certainly

c. Put an *O* next to the statements that are opinions. Put an *F* next to the statements that are facts.

(1) Seals are very entertaining animals. ____

(2) Dogs and cats make the best pets. ____

(3) Spectrographs can make color diagrams of bird songs on computer screens. ____

(4) The bird song of the kinglet sounds like stones striking each other. ____

(5) Bats use echolocation to find their way in the dark. ____

(6) Echolocation is a hard form of animal communication to understand. ____

(7) Echolocation is audible to the human ear. ____

(8) Many mammals and even birds can be trained to obey human commands. ____

(9) Nim Chimpsky was as cute as a human child. ____

(10) Kanzi could ask his teachers to give him something to eat or play with. ____

2. Answering Information Questions. Write the answers to the following questions in complete sentences.

a. What was Hoover's special ability?

b. Why do birds sing?

c. What is a spectrograph?

d. Why do the kinglet birds cluster together on a branch at night?

e. How can elephants use ultrasound?

f. How does echolocation help the bats and birds who use it?

g. What was the purpose of Dr. Terrace's experiment with Nim Chimsky? Was Dr. Terrace's experiment successful? Explain.

h. How does Kanzi communicate?

Ⅲ THE READING PROCESS

Skimming for Main Ideas. *To skim* means to read a passage quickly to get the main ideas. Every reading selection has an overall main idea. Each paragraph also has its own main idea. A main idea tells you the topic of the passage and the writer's opinion about the topic. Sentences stating main ideas do not tell you specific details about the topic. Often the main idea is the first or second sentence in a paragraph. But sometimes it is the last or next-to-last sentence. Sometimes the main idea is stated in two consecutive sentences.

Skim the first paragraph of the Prereading at the beginning of this chapter. The main idea is in the second sentence. It tells you the topic: humans and other mammals. It also gives you an opinion about the topic: Humans and other mammals are alike.

a. Skim Paragraph [1] of the reading passage. Which of these sentences expresses the main idea?

(1) The first two sentences

(2) The fifth sentence

(3) The last two sentences

b. Skim Paragraph [2]. Which of the following statements restates the main idea?

(1) Dogs have different barks for different situations.

(2) All animals have a way to communicate with others of their kind.

(3) Lions make audible sounds to communicate fear and hunger.

c. Skim Paragraph [3]. In your own words, what is the main idea?

d. What is the main purpose of Paragraph [4]?

(1) To describe the nighttime habits of kinglets

(2) To contrast kinglets to other birds

(3) To give an example of how bird calls communicate information

e. Skim Paragraphs [5] and [6]. In what way are these paragraphs similar in purpose? What is the topic of each paragraph?

f. Skim Paragraph [7]. What is its topic? State the main idea in your own words.

g. Skim Paragraph [8]. Which sentence expresses the main idea?

(1) The first sentence

(2) The next to-last-sentence

(3) The last sentence

h. Skim Paragraph [9]. The main purpose of the paragraph is to

    (1) tell the reader how Kanzi uses signs on a computer.

    (2) indicate that scientists disagree about language learning in apes.

    (3) demonstrate that Dr. Terrace is less intelligent than other scientists.

Ⅳ VOCABULARY

1. New Words.   Pronounce these words, following your instructor.

Verbs	Nouns	Adjectives	Adverbs
indicate	creatures	audible	slightly
cluster	obstacle	vital	
detect	experiments		
improve	ability		
claim			
respond (to)			

EXPANDING VOCABULARY.   Choose the appropriate word from the list to fill in each blank space in the following sentences.

(a) Most people cannot _____ differences in small birds of the same species. Varieties of hummingbirds differ only _____ from each other. Sometimes only their different-colored wings will _____ that they belong to different species.

(b) The teacher told the children not to _____ together when they were taking the test. She wanted to test each child's individual _____ to _____ correctly to the examination questions.

(c) Some scientists _____ that apes and other intelligent non-human _____ can "talk," but scientific _____ have not supported that viewpoint. Apes can _____ their communication with human beings by learning some signs and commands, but they cannot really create language in a human way.

(d) A public speaker's voice will not be _____ if he or she speaks too low. For people in public office, it is _____ to speak well. A poor command of the language is a major _____ to being elected to office.

2. Word Families: Verb Versus Noun Forms.   Study the following list of verbs and their related nouns. Note that these nouns are formed by adding the ending *ion* to the verb form, after dropping the final *e*.

Verb	Noun
a. communicate	communication
b. conclude	conclusion
c. indicate	indication
d. observe	observation
e. create	creation
f. detect	detection
g. inform	information
h. fascinate	fascination
i. describe	description
j. converse	conversation

Choose the correct form of the word from the list to fill in the blank in each sentence.

a. How do birds _____ with each other?

b. Dr. Terrace reached the _____ that apes cannot learn language.

c. The sign _____ that the store is closed.

d. Scientists use careful _____ to study animal life.

e. Can apes _____ sentences?

f. Dogs can _____ the sound of an ultrasonic whistle.

g. Scientists should never publish false _____ .

h. The study of whales _____ many people.

i. The history textbook gave a clear _____ of ancient Rome.

j. I don't like to have a long _____ on the telephone.

LANGUAGE FOCUS

Modals + Base Form of Verbs

A modal is a helping part of a verb. Modals tell about certain conditions related to the main verb. They are used to express ability, possibility, probability, or advisability. The main verb following a modal is always in the base form, with no endings for person or tense.

Study the following explanations and examples of some common modals. The frequently used negatives are in parentheses.

Can (Can't): Present Ability

Many mammals *can* learn simple tricks.

Could (Couldn't): Past Ability; Possibility—usually with complementary clause of condition or reason in the simple past tense

I *could* swim when I was five years old. I *could* meet you at 10:00 A.M. if I've finished my shopping. I *couldn't* understand you because the phone was broken.

Will (Won't): Future Certainty

We *will* study biology next semester.

Would (Wouldn't): Future Probability; Conditional—with *if* clause in the simple past tense

I *would* (*wouldn't*) enjoy working with chimpanzees. You *would* learn many interesting things if you studied zoology.

May: Present or Future Possibility; Permission

Dr. Heinrich *may* do more observations of birds this year. Students *may* leave this class early.

Might: Possibility Less Certain Than May—with complementary clause in simple past tense

> Columbia University *might* continue to support Dr. Terrace's work.

Must: Necessity; Strong Probability/Inference—with complementary clause in present tense

> Animal trainers *must* handle their subjects patiently.
> You *must* find it difficult to work and attend school at the same time.

Must not (Mustn't): Prohibition

> Scientists *mustn't* give false information in their reports.

Should (Shouldn't): Obligation or Advisability; Expectation

> Scientists *should* communicate with others in their profession.
> Since you registered early, you *should* find your classes open.

Diagram of Modal Possibility/Probability.   The following chart may help you understand the different meanings of the modals of possibility or probability.

can/could	25%
may/might	50%
would	100%, based on certain conditions
will	100%

1. Sentence Completion.   Fill in a modal + a main verb in its basic form and whatever other words you need to create complete sentences from the items listed. Write your sentences in the space provided. The first one is done for you.

a. Tomorrow I . . . class . . .

   Tomorrow I can meet you after class.

b. When I was twelve years old, I . . .

   _____

c. (negative) Children . . . touch . . . objects . . . museum . . .

   _____

d. In the future people . . . moon . . .

   _____

e. Immigrants to the United States . . . English . . . job . . .

_____

f. Students . . . for exams . . .

_____

g. (negative) Nim Chimpsky . . . new words . . .

_____

h. I . . . a letter . . .

_____

i. Next summer . . . Jamaica . . . vacation.

_____

2. Paragraph Writing.   Compose a brief paragraph on the topic of pet care. Use appropriate modals to tell what you should/should not or must/must not do if you have a dog, cat, or other creature as a pet. In your conclusion, talk about what can/could or may/might happen if you don't take good care of your pet.

Verbs + Infinitives

An infinitive verb is formed by _to_ + the base form of the verb. Some verbs such as _want_, _like_, _would like_, _hope_, _expect_, _learn_, _plan_, and _begin_ are often followed by infinitives. An infinitive is not the main verb in a sentence.

Dr. Terrace wanted **_to study_** the language ability of apes.
(main verb) + infinitive

Two verb phrases that include infinitives have special meanings. _Has_ or _have to_ + the base verb means _must_. The negative form of _have to_ means the action is optional or not necessary. _Used to_ + the base verb means something that happened in the past but doesn't happen anymore.

Psychologists **_have to do_** their experiments carefully.
Nim **_used to live_** in Dr. Terrace's apartment.
You **_don't have to take_** zoology to graduate.

1. Answering Questions with Infinitives.   Write complete sentences to respond.

    a. What did Hoover the seal learn to do?

    b. What animals do you prefer to see at the zoo?

    c. What science course do you have to complete for graduation?

    d. What does echolocation help bats do?

    e. What did Dr. Terrace want to find out in his experiments with Nim Chimpsky?

    f. Where does Kanzi like to play?

2. Sentence Composing.   For each of the following items, write a complete sentence using an infinitive.

    a. Next term I want _____ .

    b. Next summer I would like (vacation) _____ .

    c. In my English class we_____ .

    d. At age 2/5/12 I used to _____ .

    e. In my future career I expect (salary) _____ .

    f. In the future I plan (place of residence) _____ .

    g. In this class I hope _____ .

Changing the Direction of a Thought: The Use of *But*

But is used to change the direction of a thought or to present a contrasting idea. In academic English the word *but* is used in the middle of a sentence between the two contrasting ideas. A comma goes before the word *but* if both parts of the sentence are independent clauses. Sometimes in newspapers or magazines the word *but* is used to begin a new contrasting sentence.

> Nim Chimpsky learned over one hundred signs, *but* he never really learned language.
> Nim Chimpsky learned over one hundred signs. *But* he never really learned language.

Immigrants of all ages attend college in the United States. They would like to become proficient in the English language. Compose sentences using infinitives to tell what these ESL students hope, want, expect, plan, and would like to do in the future.

1. Sentence Rewriting.   Rewrite each of the following pairs of sentences by using *but* or *But*.

a. (1) Human speech is probably about one million years old.

    (2) Writing is much newer.

b. (1) The earliest writing was picture writing.

    (2) Today most languages use an alphabet.

c. (1) There are thousands of languages in the world.

    (2) The United Nations uses only two official languages.

d. (1) There is no world language today.

    (2) There may be one in the future.

e. (1) Nim learned signs for words.

    (2) He never created new words himself.

f. (1) Children's sentences grow longer all the time.

    (2) Nim's sentences had three words at most.

g. (1) The babies of mammals are born alive.

    (2) Bird babies are born from eggs.

h. (1) Nim was not a human child.

    (2) He attended a nursery school with special teachers.

2. Sentence Expansion.   Change the direction of the thought in each of the following sentences by adding , *but* + a new independent clause. Rewrite each new sentence. You may want to use the words in the parentheses to guide you.

> Millions of people speak Chinese. (few, Welsh)
> _Millions of people speak Chinese, but few speak Welsh._

a. American English is very similar to British English. (pronunciation, different)

b. I would like to live in Paris. (expensive)

c. A pocket dictionary doesn't have every word. (easy, school)

d. Dogs can be trained to do many tricks. (rabbits)

e. I would like to go bowling. (must study)

f. I would like to visit Egypt. (far away)

g. English articles are simple. (verbs, difficult)

h. I am not learning French. (studying, English)

i. There are many planets in our solar system. (one sun)

j. I would like to see a movie tonight. (have to visit)

Series of Parallel Items

A series of parallel items is a group of three or more words that do the same kind of work in a sentence. A sentence may have a series of nouns, adjectives, verbs, or adverbs. Each item in a series is followed by a comma. The word *and* goes before the last item in the series. All the items in a series must have the same form.

> *Bats, dolphins,* and *whales* can communicate by echolocation.
>   (series of nouns)
> Kinglet birds make *frequent, rapid, joyful* sounds.
>   (series of adjectives)
> Nim *slept, ate,* and *played* at Dr. Terrace's home.
>   (series of verbs)

1. Sentence Combining.   On a separate sheet of paper, combine each group of sentences into one complete sentence. Leave out unnecessary words. Add correct punctuation, and make whatever other small changes are needed. Rewrite each new sentence. The first one is done for you.

a. (1) Nim was angry when he was left alone.

   (2) Nim was afraid when he was left alone.

   (3) Nim was unhappy when he was left alone.

   Nim was angry, afraid, and unhappy when he was left alone.

b. (1) Immigrants brought their native cultures to the United States.

   (2) Immigrants brought their native customs to the United States.

   (3) Immigrants brought their native languages to the United States.

c. (1) Some British words differ from American words in spelling.

   (2) Some British words differ from American words in pronunciation.

   (3) Some British words differ from American words in usage.

d. (1) The big *Webster's Dictionary* would be an interesting gift for a friend.

   (2) The big *Webster's Dictionary* would be a valuable gift for a friend.

   (3) The big *Webster's Dictionary* would be a useful gift for a friend.

e. (1) Nim Chimpsky liked to look at magazines.

   (2) Nim Chimpsky liked to play with pencils.

   (3) Nim Chimpsky liked to learn new signs.

f. (1) Archeologists find toys in the earth.

   (2) Archeologists find pots in the earth.

   (3) Archeologists find gold in the earth.

g. (1) The sun is part of our universe.

   (2) The moon is part of our universe.

   (3) The planets are part of our universe.

h. (1) A map shows us the location of rivers.

   (2) A map shows us the location of seas.

   (3) A map shows us the location of oceans.

i. (1) Astronauts need special suits for space travel.

   (2) Astronauts need special shoes for space travel.

   (3) Astronauts need special food for space travel.

j. (1) Most people in England speak English.

  (2) Most people in Australia speak English.

  (3) Most people in Canada speak English.

k. (1) With a world language, people could communicate easily.

  (2) With a world language, people could trade easily.

  (3) With a world language, people could travel easily.

2. Sentence Composing.   Follow the directions for each item.

a. Use a series of parallel adjectives to describe how a main street in your native city looks.

b. Use a series of verbs to state what you usually do after your English class.

c. Use a series of nouns to name three sports or games you like to play.

d. Use a series of proper nouns to tell what special holidays people in your native culture celebrate.

Dogs can be pets and companions or they can work for people.

THE COMPOSING PROCESS

1. Sentence Combining to Form a Paragraph.   Combine the following sentences into longer, more interesting statements to form a paragraph about Kanzi, the pygmy chimpanzee. Leave out unnecessary words. Use adjectives, pronouns, signal expressions, and other types of connectives to make your paragraph flow smoothly. Rewrite your new paragraph on a separate sheet of paper. Use correct punctuation.

a.   Kanzi is a chimpanzee.

b.   Kanzi is a pygmy.

c.   Kanzi is a four-year-old.

d.   Kanzi lives at the Language Research Center.

e.   This is in Atlanta, Georgia.

f.   Kanzi has an area to roam around there.

g.   This area is large.

h.   This area is grassy.

i.   In this area there is a tree house for Kanzi.

j.   In this area there is a trailer for Kanzi.

k.   In this area there is a path for Kanzi.

l.   This path is special.

m.   This path is to the woods.

n.   Kanzi likes to play like a child.

o.   The child is human.

p.   Kanzi has the motor skills of a boy.

q.   Kanzi has the interests of a boy.

r.   Kanzi has the spirit of a boy.

s.   This boy is a seven- or eight-year-old.

t.   Kanzi has eight teachers.

u.   The teachers show Kanzi signs.

v.   The signs are on a keyboard.

w.   The keyboard is on a computer.

x.   Kanzi watches signs on television. (Use signal word for addition.)

   y. There is a television program.

   z. It is special.

 aa. It is for the research animals.

 bb. It shows a bunny.

 cc. The bunny is a giant.

 dd. The bunny talks to the research animals.

 ee. The bunny demonstrates certain signs for the research animals.

 ff. The bunny entertains the research animals.

 gg. The show is not just for fun. (Use signal for reversing a thought.)

 hh. The show is a way.

 ii. The way is pleasant.

 jj. The way is to teach Kanzi English.

2. Sequencing Ideas in a Paragraph.   Put *M.I.* (*main idea*) next to the sentence that states the main idea of this paragraph. Then number the sentences in the appropriate order to form a good paragraph. Look for pronouns, time signals, and other such words to help you find the correct order. On a separate sheet of paper, rewrite the sentences in correct order, *skipping a line between each one.*

   a. He sent him to a special nursery school. ____

   b. Nim enjoyed his days at nursery school because of these activities. ____

   c. Dr. Terrace created a very human environment for Nim Chimpsky. ____

   d. When Nim learned a new sign, his teachers gave him a treat. ____

   e. They taught Nim signs for English words. ____

   f. It had a lot of pictures and magazines in it. ____

   g. The teachers were well trained to work with Nim. ____

   h. The schoolroom was bright and colorful. ____

3. Composing a Paragraph.   The following lists in Columns A and B describe two different types of language classrooms. You may add items to either list by brainstorming.

Review List A. Make up a main idea statement that would apply to the items in that list. Review List B. Make up a main idea statement that would apply to items in that column. Then complete the following informal outline by choosing either List A or B for your topic and adding appropriate details from the chosen list or from your own imagination for each of the given points. One is done for you.

A (Ms. Jones's class)

- classroom looks bright/cheerful
- teacher reads stories to children
- teacher corrects mistakes patiently
- many books/maps/magazines
- children sometimes create own stories/dialogues
- children sometimes get a treat for good work
- children often talk about ideas/feelings/interests
- children sometimes work with each other
- some useful textbooks/dictionaries in class
- children experiment with new words/sounds/symbols

B (Mr. Smith's class)

- classroom looks dull/uninteresting
- teacher never reads stories to children
- teacher corrects mistakes impatiently
- few books/maps/magazines
- children never create own stories/dialogues
- children rarely get a treat for good work
- children rarely talk about ideas/feelings/interests
- children always work alone
- no useful textbooks/dictionaries in class
- children never experiment with new words/sounds/symbols

Informal Outline

(main idea): _____

_____

classroom and equipment: _____ *Many books/maps/magazines* _____

_____

_____

teacher: _____

_____

_____

activities: _____

_____

_____

When you have finished your outline, compose a complete paragraph based on your notes. Use complete sentences and correct paragraph form. Review your writing for grammatical errors.

Paragraph Topics

a.   Training a child for the future is an important responsibility. What are some qualities or characteristics that you think a well-brought-up child should possess? Write about two or three such qualities, using a separate paragraph for each. Include some methods of training a child to develop these qualities.

b.   A higher education is one of the chief ways in which we can prepare ourselves for the future. What are some ways in which your college is preparing you for a better future? What are some things your college might, could, or should do to improve the education of its students?

These Norwegian children are learning their lessons in a bright, cheerful classroom. The children's colorful paintings decorate the classroom walls.

ADDITIONAL READING

"Anansi and the Gum Baby": An African Trickster Tale

Folktales are very often about animals who use their intelligence to get what they want. Such animals are sometimes called tricksters, because they use tricks of speech and behavior instead of physical strength to achieve their purposes. African folklore is full of stories about a spider named Anansi, the trickster hero of this tale. When various African peoples were taken to America as slaves, they carried their traditions with them, and the figure of the spider Anansi became popular in the United States in the form of Brer (Brother) Rabbit.

One year there was a terrible famine in the land, and all the animals were worried about whether they would have enough to eat. The spider Anansi and his family had a farm and sufficient food for a while, but Anansi thought he should plan for the future. So he devised a scheme to get the best part of the new harvest for himself.

One day Anansi said to his wife, "I am not feeling well. I am going to see the sorcerer and find out what is wrong. Maybe he can help me feel better." Anansi went away and did not return until the evening. Then he announced that he had very bad news. The sorcerer had told him that he was going to die. "The sorcerer told me that I should be buried at the far end of the farm, next to the yam patch," Anansi said, "and in my coffin, you should place a pestle and mortar for grinding and dishes, spoons, and cooking pots so that I can take care of myself in the Other World."

After a few days, Anansi lay on his sleeping mat as though he were sick, and in a short time he pretended to be dead. So his wife, Aso, buried him at the far end of the farm, next to the yam patch, as he had requested, and into his coffin she put all the utensils he had asked for.

But Anansi stayed in his grave only while the sun shone during the day. As soon as it became dark, he came out of his coffin and dug up some yams and cooked them in the pot his wife had buried with him. Then he ate and ate until he was full. Afterwards he returned to his coffin and hid in his grave. Anansi continued to do this each day, selecting the best crops from his field and eating them in secret, until his wife began to notice that their yams and corn and cassava were disappearing at an alarming rate. She thought perhaps a thief was stealing their food, so she went with her sons to Anansi's grave and made a special prayer to Anansi's soul to protect their farm.

That night Anansi came out again, and once more he took the best crops and ate them. When his wife and sons saw that Anansi's soul was not protecting their food, they decided to see if they could catch the thief themselves. So they made a figure that looked like a human being out of sticky gum and set it up in the yam patch.

That night Anansi again crawled out of his coffin to eat. He saw the gum figure looking like a man standing there in the moonlight.

"Why are you standing in my fields?" Anansi asked the figure. The gum man didn't answer.

"If you don't get out of my fields, I will thrash you severely," Anansi threatened the figure. But the figure, of course, was silent. When Anansi got no response from the gum man, he was very displeased. "Since you refuse to answer me, I will just have to beat you," Anansi shouted. And he gave the gum figure a hard blow with his right hand. It stuck fast to the figure, and Anansi could not remove it, no matter how hard he tried.

"Let go of my right hand," Anansi cried. "You are making me very angry." But the gum man would not let go. "Perhaps you don't know how strong I am," Anansi boasted fiercely. "I have more power in my left hand than in my right, as you shall see." And he gave a hard knock to the gum figure with his left hand, but that, too, stuck fast.

"You miserable creature!" Anansi said. "I'll give you something to remember me by. See if my right foot doesn't change your mind!" And he kicked the figure sharply with his right foot, but his foot just stuck to the silent figure, and Anansi could not free it. What an awkward position Anansi was in now! Anansi got even angrier. "Try my left foot, then," he shouted, and gave a tremendous kick with that limb, but now he was stuck, both hands and feet.

"Oh, you stubborn man!" Anansi cried furiously, "This is your last chance. I'll let you have it with my head this time!" And he butted the figure with his head, but that too stuck to the gum figure. Anansi couldn't move at all.

In the morning Aso and her two sons went out to their field to see if they had indeed caught the thief with the gum figure, and there they found Anansi stuck helplessly to the gum man. Now they understood everything. They called the other villagers to their yam patch, and everyone mocked and jeered Anansi all stuck up with gum. Anansi was so ashamed that he hid his face in his headcloth, and when everyone had gone, he broke away and fled from the field. He ran to the nearest house, crawled up into the roof rafters, and hid in the darkest corner he could find. And from that day until this, Anansi has not wanted to face people. That is why he is often found hiding in the darkest corners.

Reacting to the Reading

Folktales about animals that talk and act like people often communicate basic ideas about human nature beneath their humorous surface. Anansi, for example, shows that he is intelligent, tricky, and selfish, all at the same time.

    a. Can you give some examples of people you know who are similar to Anansi?

    b. Has anyone ever played a trick on you or tried to outwit you for his or her own selfish purposes? Explain.

Reading Comprehension

Write *T* for *true* or *F* for *false* next to each item, according to the information that is stated or implied in this African folktale. Be prepared to explain your answers with reference to the text.

1. The introduction implies that African folktales became popular in America through being taught in schools. ____

2. Anansi did not feel well because he had not had enough to eat. ____

3. Anansi never really went to visit the sorcerer. ____

4. Anansi needed household utensils in his grave because he was going to the Other World. ____

5. Anansi's wife suspected a thief was stealing their crops. ____

6. The gum figure was set up to protect their crops. ____

7. If the wife had made the figure of wood instead of gum, Anansi would have gotten into the same kind of difficulty. ____

8. Anansi kept hitting the figure because it was stealing his food. ____

9. Anansi's wife called the villagers to the yam patch to help her ridicule the thief. ____

10. The story implies that Anansi is the only spider that likes dark places.____

VOCABULARY

Word Families.

NEGATIVE PREFIX DIS. The story tells us that Anansi was *displeased* with the gum man because he would not answer him. The prefix *dis* attached to a word often means *not* or *the absence of* a quality. Column A gives you some base words whose negatives are formed by adding *dis*. Complete Column B by writing the negative word in full. Then choose five of the negatives and use them in complete original sentences.

A: Base Word Form   **B: Negatives with "dis"**

1. content (noun)   _____

2. like (verb)   _____

3. agree (verb)   _____

4. agreement (noun)   _____

5. appearance (noun)   _____

6. appear (verb)   _____

7. ability (noun)   _____

UNIT III

Our Social World

CHAPTER SEVEN

WOMEN OF THE AMERICAN PAST

I PREREADING

Strip Story. Listen to your instructor read the story "Molly Pitcher, An American Patriot." Then as a class or in groups, copy each of the following sentences onto a separate strip of paper. Put the strips in the proper order to tell the story of Molly Pitcher. Use pronouns, time expressions, and other words as clues for sentence order. When the strips are correctly arranged, number them in sequence. Then read the story aloud from the strips.

Molly Pitcher was a hero of the Battle of Monmouth in the American Revolution.

At camp she was useful in washing clothes, cooking, and keeping the camp clean.

Finally, the battle was over and the Americans had won.

Then, on July 28, 1778, the American army marched out to fight the British army in the Battle of Monmouth.

Much of the credit for this victory belongs to Molly Pitcher, a brave and quick-thinking American woman.

Molly dropped her pitcher and took over her husband's cannon.

During the hard war years of 1777 and 1778, Mary joined her husband in the army camp at Valley Forge.

The heat was so great that day that the soldiers became terribly thirsty.

She fired round after round of shot at the British with it.

Suddenly, during the battle, Molly's husband fainted from heatstroke.

So Mary Ludwig followed the soldiers into battle with a pitcher of water for them to drink.

Mary Ludwig was a hero of the Battle of Monmouth in the American Revolutionary War.

That's why the soldiers gave her the nickname "Molly Pitcher."

She was married to John Hayes, who was a gunner in the American Revolutionary army.

Each time the pitcher was emptied, Mary would run back to a nearby stream to fill it.

FREE WRITE
There is an ancient Chinese proverb that says "Women hold up half the sky."
What do you think this means? Do you think this proverb is true? If so, write
about a woman you know who holds up half the sky. If not, explain why.

Vocabulary in Context.   The words in this exercise will appear in the reading passage. Circle the word(s) in the second sentence of each pair that mean(s) the same as the italicized word in the first sentence. The first one is done for you.

   1. Historians are now writing books that describe the *role* of women in creating the American nation. Most old history books mainly describe the (part) that men took in events of the past.

2. When new *territories* opened up in the American West, the women went along with the men to settle there. In those regions, both men and women suffered hardships.

3. Women *labored* beside their husbands. They worked hard clearing the land and building homes in wild places.

4. It took a great deal of *courage* for families to settle in those lonely areas. Those people were called pioneers, and the story of their bravery is well-known.

5. Pioneer women had to be strong in *spirit*, even if they weren't strong physically. A good mental attitude was necessary to live in the wilderness.

6. Slave women from Africa *survived* hardships and loneliness. Native American women, once called Indians, lived through terrible times when their men were killed in battle with the pioneers.

7. Hundreds of thousands of immigrants came to America from Europe and Asia in the nineteenth century, looking for a more *successful* existence. Many of them were women who wanted a more favorable life for their families.

8. Immigrant women were often *weary* from hard work in big city factories. Even though they were tired most of the time, they tried to care for their husbands and their children, too.

9. The Statue of Liberty in New York Harbor is a monument in *honor* of all the people who came to America and helped build our nation. Each group deserves respect for the traditions it has given to this land.

10. The stories of women and men of the American past *enrich* our lives today. The contributions of the past add value to the present.

Ⅱ READING

Harriet Tubman: The Moses of Her People

[1]   In the development of the United States, many groups of women played an important role. Native American women traveled with the earliest explorers. They guided the men through deep forests and across wide rivers, helping them to find a way to the West. Black women from Africa labored as slaves in the fields and homes of the American South. Although they were not allowed to become educated, slave women used their native skills and intelligence as healers and midwives to help both black and white families. In the 1800s, the West opened up, and pioneer women made difficult journeys with their families to

find new homes. Pioneer women suffered many hardships, and they had to be very strong in body and spirit to survive. In the nineteenth and twentieth centuries, many immigrant women made the long journey across the oceans to settle in America. They, too, had the strength and ability to face difficult times in a strange new homeland.

[2]   Some people may think of women as the "weaker sex," but the history of women in America proves that they are mistaken. We don't have the names of all the individual women who showed their strength of body and spirit. But the stories of some are told in books. The life story of Harriet Tubman, an active leader of escaping slaves, is especially well-known. Her story is an example of all the women who played an important role in creating the American nation.

[3]   Harriet Tubman was born in the southern state of Maryland in 1820. Her parents were slaves and worked on a plantation. When Harriet was only seven years old, she was taking care of a house and a baby on a nearby plantation. Her mistress was harsh and cruel. Every hour that Harriet worked for this mean woman, she dreamed of freedom.

[4]   As a teenager, Harriet was sent out in the fields to labor under the hot sun all day long. While she worked, she continued to dream of freedom. She listened to stories of slaves who had escaped to the North. One day Harriet learned that she was going to be sold. When she heard this, she knew that she had to escape immediately. She could not even say good-bye to her parents because it was too dangerous. That night she walked off the plantation and followed the North Star to freedom. She was hungry, lonely, and frightened. Nevertheless, she forced herself onward and didn't stop until she was out of slave territory.

[5]   When Harriet Tubman reached Pennsylvania, she was free. But she couldn't forget the others who were still living in slavery. She joined a secret organization called the Underground Railroad. This organization helped slaves escape from their masters and find homes in the free states of the North. As an active member and later as the leader of the Underground Railroad, Harriet Tubman made frequent trips back to the South and was successful in bringing out more than three hundred slaves. She even succeeded in leading her aged parents to safety. When there were problems for the runaway slaves in the northern states, she guided them into Canada. For all her extraordinary deeds of courage, Harriet Tubman received high praise from many famous men. John Brown, a well-known leader of the antislavery movement, referred to her as "one of the best and bravest persons on the continent."

[6]   Harriet Tubman was not only a courageous woman but a clever one as well. On one of her trips back South, she was sitting in the waiting room of a railroad station in Maryland. The door was straight ahead of her, and she could see everyone who entered. Suddenly, a man walked in and looked around the room slowly. She immediately knew that the man was a slave catcher looking for a runaway slave. She had to think quickly. There was a book on the bench beside

During the Civil War, Harriet Tubman
served as a nurse, laundress, and spy for
the northern army.

her. She picked it up and held it on her lap as if she were reading it. When the slave catcher looked at Harriet, he saw her with the book. He knew that slaves were never allowed to learn to read, so he thought that she was a northern black person, not a runaway southern slave. Although Harriet Tubman had many such frightening experiences, she remained free through her cleverness and intelligence.

[7]   As the leader of the Underground Railroad, Harriet Tubman was known for her strict discipline. When some of her followers became weary or frightened, she encouraged them with kindness. Sometimes, however, she had to be more forceful, and she would point a loaded gun at them. For the most part, the people under her leadership were proud to obey her rules of conduct. They even called her "General" Tubman. She was strict with herself as well, no matter what kind of work she had to do. During the American Civil War, she served first as a nurse and laundress for the northern army, and later as a spy. She went to South Carolina and helped to get information that the North used successfully in a battle against the army of the South.

[8]   In 1865, when the Civil War was over, all the slaves gained their freedom. Harriet Tubman's journeys were over, but her fame remained. People honored her as "the Moses of her people." Just as the ancient Hebrew Moses led his people out of the desert to freedom, Harriet Tubman guided many of her people to safety in the North. Her life, like those of all the courageous women of the past, instructs us and enriches our own lives today.

Summary Completion.   Fill in each blank space with the appropriate word from the columns following the paragraph.

Women have played an (1) _____ role in the development

(2) _____ the United States. Native American (3) _____ ,

slave women, pioneer women, (4) _____ immigrant women have all

(5) _____ build this country. Harriet Tubman's (6) _____

is an example of (7) _____ brave spirit of many (8) _____

women of the past. As a leader of the Underground Railroad, Harriet Tubman guided

many slaves to (9) _____ in the North. She placed herself in danger, but

because of her cleverness, she (10) _____ never caught. She was strict

with her followers and with (11) _____ also. During the Civil War she

served with the northern army (12) _____ a nurse, laundress, and spy.

(13) _____ the war was over, the slaves were all freed, and Harriet

Tubman was honored for all her courageous deeds.

(1) ordinary/dangerous/important/
   unhappy

(2) from/of/to/with

(3) men/children/owners/women

(4) but/often/and/again

(5) decided/helped/brought/developed

(6) slavery/owner/life/cruelty

(7) a/*leave blank*/the/an

(8) America/the United States/country/
   American

(9) bravery/masters/safety/problems

(10) was/wasn't/is/didn't

(11) them/her/themselves/herself

(12) for/to/as/*leave blank*

(13) At/When/If/Just

Reacting to the Reading

Harriet Tubman is considered a hero.

  a. Are there any heroes such as Harriet Tubman in the history of your culture? Tell about them and the heroic acts they performed.

  b. Some people are called "unsung" heroes because they did not become famous for their acts of heroism. Do you know any such "unsung" heroes? If so, tell why you think they are heroic.

Reading Comprehension

1. Understanding the Text.

  a. Write *T* if the sentence is *true* and *F* if the sentence is *false*. If the reading passage does not give information about the sentence, write *N.I.* (*no information*).

  (1) Native American women helped to open the way to the West. _____

  (2) Slaves in the American South knew something about medicine. _____

  (3) Women who traveled to the West often did not survive childbirth. _____

  (4) Harriet Tubman was a freeborn black woman. _____

  (5) Harriet was the first person to escape from a plantation. _____

  (6) Harriet returned to Maryland to free her parents. _____

  (7) Harriet's husband was a free black man named John Tubman. _____

  (8) John Brown thought highly of Harriet Tubman. _____

  (9) Harriet Tubman became a general in the northern army. _____

  b. Choose the correct answer, or follow the directions.

  (1) Paragraph [1] tells something about the various groups of women who helped in the development of the United States. List the groups mentioned.

   a. _____   c._____

   b. _____   d. _____

(2) The author uses Harriet Tubman's life mainly

    a. as a way of telling some of the history of the American South.

    b. as an example of a courageous and capable American woman.

    c. to describe the work of the Underground Railroad.

(3) The author writes that Harriet was only seven years old when she began to work. The word *only* suggests that the author thinks

    a. seven years old is a good age to start working.

    b. seven years old is too young to start working.

    c. seven years old is the usual age to start working.

(4) In a complete sentence, tell why Harriet couldn't say anything to her parents about her plans to escape from the plantation.

    _____

    _____

(5) The word *Nevertheless* in the last sentence of Paragraph [4] introduces

    a. a reason why Harriet was frightened, lonely, and hungry.

    b. an action that contrasts with Harriet's feelings.

    c. another emotion that Harriet was feeling.

(6) The Underground Railroad was

    a. a real railroad that took people from Maryland to Canada.

    b. started by Harriet Tubman when she reached Pennsylvania.

    c. an organization of people who led slaves out of the South.

(7) In Paragraph [5], the author writes: *She even succeeded in leading her aged parents to safety*. The word *even* is used to show

    a. that it was unusual for old people to make an escape from slavery.

    b. that there was nothing extraordinary about this action.

    c. that Harriet was lonely and wanted her parents with her.

(8) The last sentence in Paragraph [5] tells us that Harriet Tubman was "one of the best and bravest persons on the continent." This part of the sentence is in quotation marks because

    a.   the author thinks it is very important.

    b.   John Brown spoke or wrote those exact words.

    c.   Harriet Tubman didn't believe those words.

(9) John Brown was a well-known leader of the antislavery movement. This means that he

    a.   owned a great number of slaves.

    b.   preferred slave labor to free labor.

    c.   was against the practice of slavery.

(10) Choose the item that states the topic of Paragraph [6].

    a.   Harriet's clever trick to avoid a slave catcher

    b.   Harriet's trip back to Maryland

    c.   Harriet's inability to read

(11) In Paragraph [7], the author's main purpose is to describe

    a.   Harriet's participation in the Civil War.

    b.   Harriet's ability to discipline herself as well as her followers.

    c.   Harriet's knowledge of weapons.

(12) The description of Harriet Tubman in Paragraph [7] proves that

    a.   in action, she was as strong as a man.

    b.   she wasn't well liked or respected by her followers.

    c.   she only did work that a man usually does.

2. Answering Information Questions. On a separate sheet of paper, answer each question in a complete statement.

    a. What did Harriet Tubman dream about while she worked on the plantation?

    b. How did she feel as she walked North to freedom?

    c. What organization did she join when she reached Pennsylvania?

    d. What did John Brown say about Harriet Tubman? (Use your own words.)

    e. What did Harriet Tubman do to escape the slave catcher at the railroad station?

    f. What jobs did Harriet Tubman have during the Civil War?

g. What happened to the slaves when the Civil War was over?

h. How did people honor Harriet Tubman?

Ⅲ THE READING PROCESS

Recognizing Signals of Contrast.   When English writers want to contradict, or state something opposite to what they have just said, they usually use signal words of contrast. These words let the reader know that the writer is going to present two pieces of contradictory, contrasting, or opposite information.

Study this list of signal words of contrast.

, but	in contrast,	although
however,	in contrast to _____ ,	unlike _____ ,
on the other hand,	nevertheless,	

Read the following paragraphs, and underline the signals of contrast in each.

   a.   Harriet Beecher Stowe was another woman named Harriet who fought against slavery. Unlike Harriet Tubman, however, Harriet Beecher Stowe was a free, white, well-educated woman from an old New England family. Harriet Tubman's relatives were poor slaves who could not help her in her work. But Harriet Beecher Stowe's family included a husband who was a professor and a brother who was a famous minister and writer. Harriet Tubman could not read or write; in contrast, Harriet Beecher Stowe was a professional writer. Her book against slavery, *Uncle Tom's Cabin*, awakened many people to the evils of slavery. These two Harriets had very different positions in life. Nevertheless, they both shared a powerful hatred of the system of slavery and had the courage to fight against it.

Now make two lists of the different, contrasting qualities of Harriet Beecher Stowe and Harriet Tubman.

   b.   In contrast to India and England, the United States government has never had a female leader. The wives of some American presidents have been important and well-known in their own right, but none has ever been elected to office herself. The United States has had a few women senators and representatives in Congress. No woman, however, has ever been a vice president. Although the United States presidency has always been occupied by a male, perhaps in the future we will see a woman occupying that position.

Mark *T* if the statement is *true*. Mark *F* if it is *false*.

(1) India and England have never had female leaders. ____

(2) No American president's wife has ever been elected to office. ____

(3) American women have been senators and members of Congress. ____

(4) The United States has had a woman vice president. ____

(5) The president of the United States will always be a male. ____

Ⅳ VOCABULARY

1. New Words. Pronounce these words, following your instructor.

Verbs	Nouns	Adjectives
enrich	courage	successful
honor	spirit	weary
labor	role	
survive	territory	
	discipline	

a. *EXPANDING VOCABULARY.* Fill in the blank space with a word from the list.

(1) Farm women often _____ in the fields with their husbands.

(2) Today, women play an important _____ in the American work force.

(3) The closeness of grandparents can _____ a child's life.

(4) Working people often feel _____ after a long, hard day on the job.

(5) Teachers try to keep strict _____ in the classroom so that children get the most out of their education.

(6) It takes great _____ to leave one's country and emigrate to a strange new land.

(7) Immigrants have to be strong in body and _____ to under-

take life in a new country.

(8) Many pioneer women didn't _____ childbirth because there

was no medical help in the areas where they traveled.

(9) Most children are taught to _____ their parents' wishes.

(10) Wild animals have their own _____ and often fight to keep

it for themselves.

(11) It takes a lot of hard work to be _____ in school, business,

or life in general.

b. *USING VOCABULARY.* Write a complete sentence in answer to each question. Use the italicized words in your sentence.

(1) When people *labor* all day, what do they need to do after work?

(2) Which of the following—reading literature, going to museums, attending concerts, listening to stories of the past—*enriches* your life?

(3) What famous person in the history of your native land showed great *courage* in body and *spirit*?

(4) In which school or grade did your teachers demand strict *discipline*?

(5) Is it necessary to have a lot of money to feel *successful* in life?

(6) If you were an actor, would you prefer to play the *role* of a good person or a mean person?

(7) Can a person *survive* on water alone?

(8) What do you do when you feel *weary*?

(9) How do people usually feel when they enter a strange *territory*?

(10) Why should children *honor* older people?

2. Word Families: Related Word Forms.   The stem, or root, of a word is often found in other related words. The related words may have different forms, prefixes, or suffixes from the stem word. But the meanings of all the words in a word family will have some relationship to each other. Recognizing the root of a word in other words will help you increase your vocabulary. Study the word lists for each of the following paragraphs. Fill in the blank spaces in the paragraphs with the correct word from the list.

a. **verb:** honor   **adjective:** honorable, honest,
                                       dishonorable, dishonest

    noun: honor, honesty,   **adverb:** honorably, honestly,
           dishonesty, dishonor   dishonorably, dishonestly

Slavery was a(an) (1) _____ practice. Men and women who work deserve an(a) (2) _____ day's pay for their labor. Many Americans of the past (3) _____ wished to end slavery. They worked hard to erase the (4) _____ of slavery from the land. We (5) _____ such people as Harriet Tubman for their work against slavery.

b. **verb:** labor   **adjective:** laborious, laboring

    noun: labor, laborer,   **adverb:** laboriously
          laboriousness, laboratory

    related phrases: child labor, labor unions, slave labor

(1) _____ men and women of the past had few rights and little protection. They (2) _____ many hours for very little money. There were no laws against (3) _____ , so children as young as seven often worked in mines and factories. But then (4) _____ in factories began to join together in (5) _____ . They finally got better pay and working conditions.

These female astronomy students of one hundred years ago were very unusual. Most women in the past did not have an education beyond grade school. Discuss the advantages of higher education today.

LANGUAGE FOCUS

Past Continuous Tense

The past continuous tense describes ongoing, continuous action during a limited time in the past. Actions in the past continuous are sometimes interrupted by another action in the simple past tense. The past continuous tense is formed by *was* or *were* + the *ing* form of the main verb.

> Last night I ***was reading*** an interesting book about Harriet Tubman.
> While I ***was reading*** last night, the doorbell rang.

Study the past continuous tense of the verb *move*.

	Singular	Plural
First person	I was moving	My friend and I were moving
		We were moving
Second person	You were moving	You were moving
Third person	Harriet was moving	Harriet and her family were moving
	He/She/It was moving	They were moving

The negative forms are *was not* (*wasn't*) and *were not* (*weren't*) + the *ing* form of the main verb.

1. Recognizing Past Continuous Tense.   Listen carefully as your instructor reads the following paragraph. Underline each verb in the past continuous tense. (The paragraph is part of a letter written by a grandmother to her granddaughter about a winter hike through the mountains of northern California.)

> The snow was falling steadily. We knew we had to walk quickly to reach the road three miles away. Both of us were carrying heavy packs, which were soon wet with snow. Tree branches were hanging down over our path, and our progress was slow. Because the lake was frozen, we decided to walk on it instead of the narrow path. But as we were moving across the lake, we felt cracks and soft spots in the ice. The ice wasn't completely frozen near the edge. Also, the wind was blowing in our faces, and the snow was blinding us. So we returned to the path. After several hard, tiring hours, we finally reached the road.

2. Sentence Completion.   Read each situation. Then complete the given items, using a verb in the past continuous tense. Use as many words as you need to make an interesting sentence.

    a. You were late to your English class yesterday. Tell what was happening when you entered the room.

        (1) The teacher _____ .

        (2) Most of the students _____ .

        (3) A few of them _____ .

        (4) One of the students _____ .

    b. Mr. Baker came home at 6:00 P.M. yesterday. Describe what the various members of his family were doing when he came in.

        (1) His wife _____ .

        (2) His teenage daughter _____ .

        (3) His two-year-old son _____ .

        (4) His dog _____ .

    c. You were on the bus early this morning. Tell what the other passengers were doing while you were riding.

        (1) The man next to me _____ .

        (2) A woman across the aisle _____ .

        (3) Two schoolboys _____ .

        (4) A young mother _____ .

    d. There was a fire in an apartment building in your neighborhood last week. Describe what was going on when you got to the scene.

        (1) Several fire fighters _____ .

        (2) One fire fighter _____ .

        (3) A woman on the third floor _____ .

        (4) The people on the street _____ .

Use of Past Continuous Tense and Simple Past Tense

The past continuous tense is frequently used in conjunction with the simple past tense. In telling a story about the past, we usually use the past continuous tense to set the scene or stop the action to describe what was happening. Often this tense is found at the beginning of the story or as background to a change in action. The simple past tense is used for actions that move the story forward. The actions in the simple past tense are the focus, or main events, of the story.

1. Recognizing Past Continuous and Simple Past Tense.   Read the following paragraph about the assassination of Abraham Lincoln, the president who declared the slaves free after the Civil War. Underline the verbs in the past continuous tense. Circle the verbs in the simple past tense. Then, with your class, discuss the use of the two tenses in the story.

> On the night of April 14, 1865, President Lincoln was sitting in Ford's Theater with his wife and some friends. They were watching a play called *Our American Cousin*. Suddenly, a man appeared in the President's box. He held a knife in one hand and a gun in the other. He pointed the gun at Lincoln's head and fired once. Lincoln fell forward. His head was bleeding slightly. Several people rushed to his side and tried to help. They decided to take him to a house across the street. As they were carrying Lincoln out, the Surgeon General arrived and tried to revive the wounded man, but it was no use. Lincoln died early the following morning.

2. Paragraph Completion.   The following paragraph is about the capture and death of John Wilkes Booth, the man who assassinated President Lincoln. Fill in the blank spaces with the past continuous tense for those actions that describe or set the scene. Fill in the blank spaces with the simple past tense for those actions that move the story forward. Use the verbs in parentheses.

On the night of April 25, 1865, John Wilkes Booth (hide)(1) _____

in a barn near Fredericksburg, Virginia. Suddenly, some soldiers (appear)

(2) _____ outside the barn. They (know)(3) _____ that

Booth (hide)(4) _____ inside. One of the soldiers (go)

(5) _____ just inside the door. Booth (walk)(6) _____ back

and forth in the barn. He (shout)(7) _____ about fighting for his freedom.

The soldier (wait, negative)(8) _____ . He (take)(9) _____

his pistol and (shoot)(10) _____ the assassin. Booth (die)

(11) _____ two hours later.

Complex Sentences with *When* and *While*

A clause is a sentence part that has a subject and a complete main verb. Complex sentences always include an independent clause and a dependent clause. A dependent clause cannot stand by itself as a sentence. Dependent clauses must be joined to independent, or main, clauses.

When and *while* are time words that begin dependent clauses. Dependent clauses with *when* and *while* must join independent clauses to form a complete sentence.

A *when* and *while* clause may appear as the first part of a complex sentence or as the last part. When a *when* or *while* clause begins the sentence, it is followed by a comma.

> When the Civil War was over, all the slaves gained their freedom.
>   (dependent clause)   (independent clause)
> I read the chapter about Harriet Tubman while I was riding on the bus.
>   (independent clause)   (dependent clause)

When tells us about two kinds of time periods: (1) a long period of time during which many different actions take place

> When Harriet Tubman was a slave, she was always dreaming of freedom.

and (2) a point of time when two actions take place together or immediately following each other (at that time).

> When Harriet heard she was to be sold, she planned her escape.

While tells us about actions that take place during the same time period. *While* often introduces clauses using continuous tenses.

> While Harriet was walking to freedom in the North, she thought sadly about her family.

1. Identifying Dependent Clauses. Underline the dependent clause in each of the following sentences.

    a. While I was studying last night, I heard some strange noises.

    b. Immigrants often feel lonely when they first arrive in their new country.

    c. College students may enjoy listening to music while they are studying.

d. I can't concentrate on my work when the television set is on.

e. When my daughter first read about Harriet Tubman, she became very interested in her.

f. Some students were rewriting their papers in class while others were doing grammar exercises.

2. Sentence Completion with *When* and *While*.   The two clauses in complex sentences with *when* or *while* must have the same or related verb tenses. Study the following examples of common pairs of verb tenses in *when* and *while* sentences. Then complete the exercise that follows the charts.

Simple Present   **Simple Present and Future**

When students *enjoy* a certain history book, they often *recommend* it to others.
When we *finish* this chapter, we *will continue* with the next.

Present Continuous   **Simple Present and Present Continuous**

My sister *is working* while her children *attend* school.
Some students *are studying* English as a second language while others *are learning* French.

Simple Past   **Simple Past**

When pioneer women *moved* west, they *suffered* many hardships.

Past Continuous   **Simple Past and Past Continuous**

While Harriet Tubman *was living* in Philadelphia, she *thought* a lot about her family.
Once, some slave catchers *were watching* Harriet while she *was sitting* in a railway station.

Simple Past and Past Continuous   ***Could* and *Would***

When Harriet *planned* her escape, she *couldn't tell* her family.
While she *was laboring* in the fields, she *would dream* of freedom.

Choose the clause that correctly completes the given clause. Write the correct clause in the space provided.

a. Pioneer families suffered many hardships _____

    (1) when they move west.

    (2) when they moved west.

    (3) when they are moving west.

b. _____ when they arrive in their new homeland.

    (1) Immigrants faced difficult problems

    (2) Immigrants were facing difficult problems

    (3) Immigrants face difficult problems

c. I'll apply for a job _____

    (1) while I graduate from this school.

    (2) when I graduate from this school.

    (3) when I will graduate from this school.

d. I like to listen to the radio _____

    (1) while I'm doing my homework.

    (2) when I did my homework.

    (3) when I was doing my homework.

e. _____ when I first came to this country.

    (1) I couldn't speak English well

    (2) I can't speak English well

    (3) I won't speak English well

f. _____ the women were working as nurses

and laundresses.

    (1) While the men are fighting in the war,

    (2) When the men fight in the war,

    (3) While the men were fighting in the war,

g. When I left my house this morning, _____

    (1) the sun was shining.

    (2) the sun is shining.

    (3) the sun shines.`

h. _____ when I got to the station.

    (1) The train was just leaving

    (2) The train is just leaving

    (3) The train will just be leaving

3. Sentence Combining.   Combine each pair of sentences into one complete sentence with a dependent clause and an independent clause. Use *when* or *while* to combine them. Rewrite your complete new sentences.

I was in New York. I decided to visit some historic places.

When I was in New York, I decided to visit some historic places.

We were waiting for the tour bus. We read our guidebook.

While we were waiting for the tour bus, we read our guidebook.

---

a. We were in Washington, D.C. We went to the Lincoln exhibits at Ford's Theater.

b. We got there. The place wasn't open yet.

c. We were waiting for it to open. We read about the exhibits in our guidebook.

d. We were reading. Several other people arrived.

e. The doors finally opened. We bought tickets and walked to the first exhibit.

f. We were looking at photographs of Lincoln. A guide came in and gave us some information about Lincoln's life.

g. It is always interesting to visit historic places. You travel to different areas of the country.

Comparison of Adjectives

Read the following paragraph carefully. Pay special attention to the italicized adjectives.

> Life was much *harder* for American women in 1880 than it is now. In the *earlier* period, there were *fewer* of the household appliances such as vacuum cleaners and refrigerators that make life *easier* today. The *newer*, *richer* houses of the 1880s had indoor plumbing, but the *older*, *poorer* homes did not. Some things were *cheaper* 100 years ago, but men earned much *lower* salaries, and married women usually did not go out to work to earn extra money. In the 1880s, housewives were usually *busier* than they are today because families were *larger*. Today modern women have *fewer* children and *better* medical care than women had 100 years ago. Modern women are *healthier* than their great-grand-mothers were, and modern women live *longer* lives. Modern women have *wider* opportunities for education and careers than their great-grandmothers had. Do you think modern women are *happier* than women were 100 years ago?

The italicized adjectives in the paragraph above are in the comparative form. The comparative form is used when *two* things are being compared. Most adjectives form the comparative as follows:

One-Syllable Adjectives. Adjectives of one syllable add *er* or *r* to the simple form: *old* → *older*; *large* → *larger*.

Two-Syllable Adjectives Ending in y. Two-syllable adjectives that end in *y* drop the *y* and add *ier*: *easy* → *easier*; *busy* → *busier*.

Most Other Two-Syllable and Three-Syllable Adjectives. Two-syllable adjectives that do not end in *y* (or in *ow* or *er*) and three-syllable adjectives keep their simple form but take the comparative word *more* in front of them: *modern* → *more modern*; *interesting* → *more interesting*.

1. List Completion.

Complete the following list of adjectives in their simple and comparative forms.

Simple	Comparative
early	_____
long	_____

Women of the past had harder lives than women do today, but the old proverb may still be true: "Men may work from sun to sun, but women's work is never done."

happy

large

_____

expensive

_____

ambitious

fragile

_____

busy

much

_____

_____

healthier

_____

more popular

_____

_____

stranger

_____

_____

fewer

2. Sentence Composing.

Look at the following pairs of subjects. Write sentences comparing the two subjects and using adjectives in the comparative form. Use the adjectives from Exercise 1 or the additional adjectives that follow the subjects. Remember to use the word *than*.

My uncle is ***more emotional*** than my father.
Housewives in the past were ***busier*** than housewives today.

Subjects

(1) my sister/I	(6) wool/cotton
(2) ancient history/modern history	(7) English/my native language
(3) my native country/the United States	(8) gold/silver
(4) glass/wood	(9) a large city/a small town
(5) women/men	(10) life in the past/life today

Adjectives

difficult	thick	emotional	beautiful	independent
lazy	shiny	expensive	quiet	boring
warm	quiet	fragile	hard	interesting
easy	crowded	cheap	big	careless

Superlative Form of Adjectives

The superlative form of adjectives is used when three or more things are being compared. The patterns for the superlative are the same as for the comparative forms of adjectives, but

er is replaced by *est*: *older* → *oldest*; *poorer* → *poorest*.

ier is replaced by *iest*: *busier* → *busiest*; *healthier* → *healthiest*.

more is replaced by *most*: *more modern* → *most modern*; *more expensive* → *most expensive*.

1. List Completion.

Complete the following list of adjectives in the superlative form. Use *the* before each one.

Simple	Superlative
bright	_____
practical	_____
brave	_____
crowded	_____
dry	_____

comfortable   _____

difficult   _____

serious   _____

cold   _____

creative   _____

quiet   _____

great   _____

talkative   _____

good   _____

2. Sentence Building.

On a separate sheet of paper, write a complete sentence using the words in each set. Add an appropriate adjective in the superlative from the list in Exercise 1, or supply one of your own. Use a different adjective in each sentence. The last part of each sentence will have a prepositional phrase with *in* or *of*.

Mary	person	all my friends

Mary is the quietest person of all my friends.

poverty	one of	problems	world

Poverty is one of the most serious problems in the world.

a. sun   object   sky

b. pollution   one of   problems   our cities

c. Carlos   student   my English class

d. math   subject   all my courses

e. library   place   my neighborhood

f. the Statue of Liberty   one of   monuments   world

g. sofa   piece of furniture   my apartment

h. New York   city   the United States

i. the North and South Poles   areas   world

j. vacuum cleaner   appliance   my house

k. Sahara Desert   one of   places   world

3. Paragraph Completion. Read this paragraph over once. Then fill in the blank spaces by using the directions in the Key following the paragraph. The first one is done for you.

Emily Dickinson (1830–1886) is one of America's (1) ___*most famous*___ poets. As a child she was (2) _____ than most of her friends, but not very different from them. In school she was (3) _____ in writing, but she also studied (4) _____ subjects such as chemistry and physiology. When she was about twenty-five, she had an (5) _____ love affair. After this she became (6) _____ and (7) _____ to people outside her own family than she had been before. It was at this time that Dickinson wrote some of her (8) _____ poetry. Although the language of her poetry appears (9) _____, her thoughts are (10) _____ to understand than they appear at first. Emily Dickinson is still one of America's (11) _____ and (12) _____ poets 100 years after her death.

Key

(1)   superlative form of *famous*

(2)   comparative form of *bright*

(3)   superlative form of *interested*

(4)   comparative form of *unusual*

(5)   simple form of adjective meaning "not happy"

(6)   comparative form of *shy*

(7)   comparative form of *unfriendly*

(8)   superlative form of *beautiful*

(9)   simple form of *simpler*

(10) comparative form of *difficult*

(11) superlative form of *respected*

(12) superlative form of *popular*

THE COMPOSING PROCESS

1. Sentence Combining to Form a Paragraph. The following paragraph about a student's immigrant family has been broken up into short, simple sentences. On a separate sheet of paper, combine the sentences into longer, more interesting statements. Use connectors, signal words, and pronouns where necessary. Leave out unnecessary words, but do not omit any of the important ideas or details. Rewrite your complete new paragraph.

a.   My grandmother was short.

b.   My grandmother was fragile-looking.

c.   My grandmother was proud of her appearance.

d.   My grandmother was a seamstress.

e.   My grandmother sewed dresses.

f.   The dresses were for other people.

g.   My grandmother had a sewing machine.

h.   The sewing machine was in a house.

i.   The house belonged to us.

j.   My grandmother was always at the sewing machine.

k.   That was every day.

l.   My grandmother got a lot of work.

m.   My grandmother sewed very fast.

n.   My grandmother sewed very neatly.

o.   My grandmother's skills were excellent.

p.   My grandmother took care of the housework.

q.   My grandmother took care of me all day.

r.   That was when I was small.

s.   Both my parents worked.

t.   My grandmother played games with me.

u.   The games were interesting.

v.   That was after the housework was finished.

w.   My grandmother made dolls for me.

x.   The dolls were from pieces of material.

y.   I will always have memories.

z.   The memories are beautiful.

aa.   The memories are of my grandmother.

2. Developing a Paragraph of Contrast.

a. From the numbered sets following the paragraph, choose the appropriate signal for the same numbered blank space in the paragraph.

Emily Dickinson and Fay Chiang are different kinds of American poets. Dickinson

lived (1) _____ wrote 100 years ago. (2) _____ Fay Chiang

is a modern poet, alive and writing today. Dickinson was a shy, solitary person.

(3) _____ she was writing, she almost never left her house. Fay Chiang,

(4) _____ is an activist who works in an Asian-American artists'

community in New York's Chinatown. Chiang (5) _____ works with

writers of other minority groups. (6) _____ Dickinson and Chiang are

very different kinds of American women, they both express similarly powerful emotions

through their poems.

(1) but/and/then

(2) Also/In contrast,/While

(3) *leave blank*/But/While

(4) and/however,/in addition,

(5) *leave blank*/on the other hand/also

(6) When/Although/And

b. Study the preceding paragraph carefully. Label all the sentences that tell about the *two* poets *A–B*. Label the sentences only about Emily Dickinson *A*. Label the sentences only about Fay Chiang *B*. Study how the paragraph develops the contrast between the two women by giving us details about one, then about the other, in alternating sentences.

c. Some paragraphs that contrast two subjects are developed in a different way. They do not give details about one thing or person and then another in alternating sentences. Some paragraphs are developed in a series of sentences about one complete subject and then in a series of sentences about the contrasting subject. This kind of paragraph will have two distinct parts. It is often called the block form.

Read this paragraph. Then answer the questions that follow it.

(1) In modern society, women are busy with their responsibilities whether they are full-time homemakers or they work outside the home. (2) Full-time homemakers don't have paying jobs, but they work long hours. (3)

Their primary job is taking care of their children, especially their young ones. (4) These mothers spend a good deal of their time cooking, cleaning, shopping, and doing laundry for their families. (5) Even when their children are old enough to go to school, these mothers remain at home. (6) They feel it is important to be there when their children come home from school because it creates a safe environment. (7) In contrast to these homemakers, some mothers work in offices or factories or have careers in business or the professions. (8) In addition to their jobs, these women must arrange for the care of their children. (9) They may have to hire baby-sitters or place their children in day-care centers. (10) Unlike homemakers, they often have to get someone to clean the house because they don't have the time to do it themselves or they are too tired. (11) Working mothers always have a lot of things to think about while on the job. (12) For example, they may worry about a child getting sick while they are at work. (13) Although it is a difficult situation, many working mothers enjoy the challenge of having a job and a family.

Answer the questions in short note form.

  (1) Which sentence states the main idea of the paragraph? _____

  (2) What two groups of people are being compared? _____

     and _____

  (3) Which sentences describe the first subject? _____

  (4) Which sentence begins the description of the second group? _____

  (5) What expression is used to signal the contrasting group? _____

  (6) Which sentences describe the contrasting group? _____

3. Composing a Paragraph of Contrast.   As a class, brainstorm different types of work or occupations with which you are familiar. Your instructor will list all of these on the board. Combine related items, and eliminate repetitions.

Choose two occupations about which you want to write. (You may want to break one occupation into two different categories, such as dividing *police officer* into *city police officer* and *private security guard*.)

Your purpose will be to compose a paragraph that contrasts the two occupations you have chosen. Some bases for contrast may be the following: physical strength required, salary, education required, potential danger, contact with the public.

Begin your paragraph with a main idea statement that clearly identifies your topic and states an important overall difference between the two occupations. Here are some examples:

Being a secretary is a more interesting job than being a flight attendant (or the reverse).

Doctors and nurses both work in hospitals, but people treat them very differently.

Paragraph Topics

a. Write a paragraph in which you contrast two different people whom you know well. Try to use adjectives in the comparative form about your two subjects. Begin with a main idea sentence that identifies your subjects.

b. Write a paragraph in which you compare or contrast your native city and the city in which you are now living. Choose such points to talk about as the cleanliness; degree of noise, traffic, or crowdedness; number of parks or recreational areas; and safety. Begin with a main idea statement that introduces the topic and identifies the two cities you will be describing.

 # ADDITIONAL READING

Mary Wilkins Freeman: "The Revolt of Mother"

The American writer Mary Wilkins Freeman was born in Massachusetts in 1852 and died in New Jersey in 1930. Her best short stories are concerned with New England village life. Her characters show a strong sense of pride, even though they live a hard life with few material comforts. The following story is an adaptation of Ms. Freeman's tale of a New England farm family in the late 1800s. It tells how a difficult problem was solved thanks to the determination of the mother.

"Father!"

"What is it?"

"What are those men digging in the field for?"

"I wish you'd go into the house, Mother, and attend to your own affairs," the man answered as he saddled his horse.

"I'm not going in till you tell me," said she. She stood waiting in front of the barn door.

The man glanced at his wife. She looked as immovable to him as one of the rocks in his field. "They're digging a cellar, if you've got to know."

"A cellar for what?"

"A barn."

"A barn? You're going to build another barn where we were going to have a house?"

The man said nothing. He hitched the horse to a wagon and rode off. The woman crossed the yard and entered the house, a tiny shelter compared with the great barn and other buildings on the property.

Nanny Penn greeted her mother, "What are they digging for, Mother? Did Father tell you?"

"They're digging a cellar for a new barn."

"Oh, Mother, another barn?"

"That's what he says."

Sammy, the young son of the family, stood in the kitchen, seeming not to pay attention to the conversation.

"Sammy, did you know Father was going to build a new barn?" his sister asked.

Sammy hesitated and then said, "Yes, I suppose I did."

"How long have you known it?" asked his mother.

"About three months, I guess. Didn't think it would do any good to tell you," replied the boy.

Mrs. Penn looked sternly at her son and asked, "Is father going to buy more cows?"

"I suppose he is. Four, I guess." The boy put on his cap, took an old arithmetic book from a shelf and left for school.

While Mrs. Penn washed the dishes, Nanny wiped. "Mother," she said, "Don't you think it's too bad Father's going to build that new barn, much as we need a decent house to live in?"

Her mother scrubbed a dish fiercely. "You haven't found out we're women-folks, Nanny," said she. "One of these days, you'll find out how men think women-folks are supposed to be. Then you'll know that we know only what men-folks think we do. Men-folks think we should consider them in with Providence, and not complain of what they do any more than we should complain about the weather."

"I don't think George is anything like that," Nanny replied. Her face, pretty as a flower, turned red, as if she were going to cry.

"Wait till you marry him. I guess George is no better than other men. You shouldn't judge your father, though. He can't help it, because he doesn't look at things just the way we do. And we've been pretty comfortable here. Father keeps the house in good repair."

"I wish we had a parlor," said Nanny.

"George can come here to see you in this nice clean kitchen. You shouldn't complain. You have a good father and a good home."

"I'm not complaining," said Nanny, taking up her sewing. She was to be married in the fall and was working on her wedding dress. She sewed industriously while her mother did the housework.

Mrs. Penn was an expert housekeeper. The house, small as a box, was never dusty. She cooked and baked and no dirt ever showed when she finished. Today she was going to bake mince pies, which her husband liked better than any other kind. While she worked, she could see the sight that irritated her deeply—the digging of the cellar of the new barn. Forty years ago her husband had promised her their new house would stand in that place. She continued to roll out the pie crust. However deep her resentment she held against her husband, she would never fail in her untiring attention to him.

The pies were done for lunch. Everyone ate quickly, without much conversation. Sammy went back to school, and Nanny went to the store to buy some more thread for her wedding dress. Mr. Penn went into the yard to unload some wood from the wagon.

"Father, I want to see you just a minute," Mrs. Penn called from the door.

"I've got to unload this wood now, Mother."

"Father, come here." Mrs. Penn stood in the doorway like a queen; she held her head as if it bore a crown. Her husband went in.

"I want to know what you're building that new barn for. It can't be you think you need another barn?" Mrs. Penn said.

"I don't have anything to say about it, Mother, and I'm not going to say anything."

"Now Father, look here. I'm going to talk real plain to you. I never have since we were married, but I'm going to now." Mrs. Penn stood before her husband and one by one she spoke about all the things that were wrong with the house they lived in: no carpet on the floor, wallpaper peeling and dirty; the kitchen, the only

Farm families like the one in "The Revolt of Mother" had a strong sense of pride, even though they lived hard lives with little material comfort.

room in which to sit, work, and eat, and where Nanny's wedding would take place. She showed him the tiny room where they slept, only large enough for a bed and a dresser. She pointed upstairs, where the children slept in two unfinished rooms, not as good a place as the horse's stall.

Mrs. Penn continued, "Now Father, forty years ago you promised me a new house over there in the field. You've been making more money, and I've been saving it for you. You've built sheds and cow-houses and one barn and now another. You're keeping your animals better than your own flesh and blood. I want to know if you think it's right."

"I have nothing to say. I've got to unload that wood. I can't stand here talking all day." Mr. Penn went out.

With red eyes, Mrs. Penn took a roll of cloth, spread it out on the kitchen table and started to cut out some shirts for her husband.

Nanny came back with her thread and sat down to do her needlework. Suddenly she looked up, her face and neck all red. "Mother," she said, "I've been thinking—I don't see how we're going to have any wedding in this room."

"Maybe we can have some new paper on the walls; I can put it on."

"We might have the wedding in the new barn," said Nanny with gentle irritation. "Why Mother, what makes you look so?"

Mrs. Penn was staring at Nanny with a curious expression. She turned again to her work. "Nothing," she said.

All through the spring months she heard nothing but the noise of saws and hammers. The new barn grew fast. It was a fine building for this little village. Men came on Sundays to admire it. Mrs. Penn did not speak of it. Mr. Penn did not mention it to her, but he seemed hurt by her silence.

"It's a strange thing how Mother feels about the new barn," he said to Sammy one day. Sammy didn't reply.

The barn was all ready for use by the third week in July. Just then Mr. Penn decided to go off to Vermont to buy a new horse. He would be gone for four days. "When the new cows come, Sammy can drive them into the new barn," he told his wife. "I'll be back by Saturday."

Mrs. Penn prepared clean clothes for her husband, a package of pie and cheese, and saw him off. "Do be careful, Father," she said. She had a strange expression in her eyes.

As soon as he was out of sight, Mrs. Penn began to pack the dishes into a basket. Her children watched. "What are you going to do, Mother?" inquired Nanny in a timid voice.

"You'll see what I'm going to do," replied Mrs. Penn.

During the next few hours a feat was performed by this simple New England mother, equal to the deed of a brave soldier. With the help of her children, she moved all their little household goods into the new barn. By late afternoon, the little house was completely empty. The new barn, designed for the comfort of animals, was more than comfortable for humans. Mrs. Penn saw its possibilities: the stalls for the cows would be better bedrooms than those in the house; the harness room would make a kitchen of her dreams; the great middle space would make a parlor fit for a palace. Upstairs there was as much room as down. With partitions and windows, what a house would there be!

Before the next morning, the news of the move spread in the village. Men and women talked about Mrs. Penn. Some thought she was insane; some thought she had a lawless spirit.

Friday the minister went to see her. "There's no use talking, Mr. Hersey," she said. "I believe I'm doing what's right, just as I think it was right for our forefathers to come over from the old country because they didn't have what belonged to them. I've got my own mind and my own feet, and I'm going to think my own thoughts and go my own way." The minister went away.

The new cows arrived, and Sammy led them into the old barn.

On Saturday Mrs. Penn prepared a special dinner for Mr. Penn's return. The children waited nervously, but with a sense of excitement.

"There he is," Sammy announced, looking out of the barn window.

Mr. Penn was leading his new horse into the yard. When he went to the house door, he found it locked. In a dazed fashion, he crossed the yard to the new barn. The doors rolled back, and he saw his family.

Mr. Penn stared at the group. "What on earth are you all down here for?" he said. "What's the matter over at the house?"

"We've come to live here, Father," Sammy said bravely.

Mr. Penn sniffed the air. "What is it? Smells like cooking. What on earth does this mean, Mother?"

"Come in here, Father," said Mrs. Penn. She led the way into the kitchen area. "Now Father, you needn't be scared. I'm not crazy. There isn't anything to be upset over. But we've come here to live, and we're going to live here. We've got just as good a right here as new horses and cows. The house wasn't fit to live in any longer. I've done my duty by you for forty years, and I'm going to do it now; but I'm going to live here. You've got to put in some windows and partitions; and you'll have to buy some furniture."

"Why Mother!" the man gasped.

"You'd better get washed, and then we'll have supper."

All through the meal, Mr. Penn stopped eating at intervals and stared at his wife, but he ate well. After supper he went out and sat on a step. When the supper dishes were cleared away, Mrs. Penn went out to him. The night was peaceful; the air was cool and calm and sweet.

Mrs. Penn touched her husband on his thin shoulder. "Father!"

His shoulders shook. He was weeping.

"Don't do so, Father," she said.

"I'll put up the partitions, and everything you want, Mother."

Mrs. Penn put her apron up to her face; she was overcome by her own victory.

Mr. Penn was like a fortress whose walls came down the moment the right tools were used. "Why, Mother," he said. "I had no idea you had your heart so set on it, as all this comes to."

Reacting to the Reading

At the time of this story, men were supposed to have the authority in the family.

a. Did Mr. Penn really have the authority in his family? Explain.

b. Is an obedient wife better for a man than one who thinks and acts independently? Illustrate your opinion with the characters from the story.

c. Which aspects of the children's behavior do you agree with? What might you have done differently?

d. What role should children play in family decisionmaking?

Reading Comprehension

Understanding the Text.   Follow the directions for each item.

a. If the statement is *true*, write *T*. If the statement is *false*, write *F*. If the story does not give information about the sentence, write *N.I.* (*no information*). Underline the part of the passage where you find your true or false answers.

(1) This story takes place in the western part of the United States. ____

(2) Mr. Penn's house is small and uncomfortable. ____

(3) Mrs. Penn keeps the house in perfect order. ____

(4) Mr. and Mrs. Penn are forty years old. ____

(5) Sammy Penn is a schoolboy. ____

(6) Nanny sews dresses for a living. ____

(7) Nanny will live with her parents after her marriage. ____

(8) Mr. Penn goes to Vermont to buy some cows. ____

(9) Eventually, the old house will be torn down. ____

b. Circle the letter of the correct answer.

(1) Mr. Penn wants a new barn because

(a) he made a promise to his wife.

(b) he is going to add more animals to his farm.

(c) the old barn is in a bad state of repair.

(2) Mrs. Penn resents her husband because

  (a) he doesn't pay attention to the real needs of his family.

  (b) he doesn't earn enough money to build a new house.

  (c) he doesn't help her with the housework.

(3) Nanny is unhappy about her situation because

  (a) she has to work too hard in the house.

  (b) her wedding will have to take place in the kitchen.

  (c) she can't entertain her girlfriends properly.

(4) Mrs. Penn tries to

  (a) turn Nanny against her father.

  (b) influence Nanny against getting married.

  (c) explain to Nanny the good things about her father.

(5) When Mrs. Penn says ". . . we know only what men-folks think we

know," she means that

  (a) men are naturally superior to women in intelligence.

  (b) men refuse to see women as having independent minds.

  (c) men like women to think and act independently.

(6) When Mrs. Penn talks about the need for a new house, Mr. Penn

  (a) shows no understanding of the problem.

  (b) says he will try to solve the problem.

  (c) walks out before she finishes talking.

(7) For forty years, Mrs. Penn

  (a) has done little to care for the needs of her husband.

  (b) has been dissatisfied as a housekeeper and mother.

  (c) has given in completely to her husband's wishes.

(8) While Mr. Penn is away, Mother "revolts." This means that

    (a) Mrs. Penn is finally able to control her children.

    (b) Mrs. Penn fixes up the house with new wallpaper and new carpets.

    (c) Mrs. Penn changes her life by taking matters in her own hands.

(9) After the move into the barn, Mrs. Penn plans

    (a) to make it into a beautiful, comfortable home.

    (b) to share it with the farm animals.

    (c) to live there until a new house is built.

(10) The village people talk about Mrs. Penn disapprovingly because

    (a) she has gone against her husband's wishes.

    (b) she wants a better house than the one she has.

    (c) she doesn't take good care of the farm while Mr. Penn is away.

(11) At the end of the story, Mr. Penn weeps because

    (a) his family moved without telling him.

    (b) he is unhappy about living in a barn.

    (c) he finally understands his wife's needs and feelings.

(12) The author of this story is trying to show us that in her time and place

    (a) women were usually unreasonable in their demands.

    (b) it was difficult for a woman to revolt against her husband's unreasonable actions.

    (c) men expected women to be equal partners with them in deciding important matters.

Vocabulary

Word Families: Recognizing Word Stems.   Many of our words are formed from a common root or stem. These stems are usually formed from Greek or Latin words. We add prefixes and suffixes to the stem and change the form, but the meanings of all the words in a word family will have some relationship to each other. Recognizing the root or stem of a word will help you to increase your vocabulary. Study the following list.

Stem	Meaning	Example
duc	lead	e*duc*ate, con*duc*tor, intro*duc*e
clud, clus	close, shut	se*clud*e, in*clud*e, con*clus*ion
spect	look, watch	re*spect*, *spect*ator, in*spect*ion
scrib, script	write	de*scrib*e, pre*script*ion
nat	born, birth	pre*nat*al, *nat*ural, *nat*ive
vis	see	*vis*ion, super*vis*or, in*vis*ible
mot	move	*mot*or, pro*mot*ion
dict	say, tell	pre*dict*, contra*dict*, *dict*ation
fin	end, complete	in*fin*ite, *fin*al, *fin*ish
part	separate, divide	de*part*, *part*ition, *part*icular
press	put, push	de*press*, *press*ure, ex*press*ion

CHOOSING DEFINITIONS. Fill in each blank space with a word from the Example column that would make the sentence correct. The italicized words will help you make the correct choice.

a. If you can't *see* without glasses, you have poor _____ .

b. The _____ of an orchestra is the one who *leads* all the musicians together as a group.

c. A _____ over*sees* the work of many people.

d. When a person *moves* up to a better job, we say that he or she receives a _____ .

e. To *say* the opposite of something that was stated before is to _____ the original statement.

f. When a doctor *writes* down symbols for your medicine, he or she is giving you a _____ .

g. Some scientists say that the universe is *without end*; it is _____ in space and time.

h. When just a little water *pushes* through a faucet, we say that the _____ is low.

i. At the *close* of an essay, we find out the author's _____ .

j. _____ care is important if babies are to be *born* healthy.

k. When you *look* into something closely, you make an _____ of it.

l. In a college catalog, there is usually a *separate* list for each course of study; students can then choose the _____ program they prefer.

CHAPTER EIGHT

MEN AND WOMEN:
RELATIONSHIPS OLD AND NEW

❶ PREREADING

Class Discussion.   The following poem was written in China over a thousand years ago by a young groom to his bride.

> A feast being spread in spring-time,
> With a cup of new wine and a joyous song.
> I repeat my salutation and offer my three wishes:
> First, may you have a long life;
> Second, may I have good health;
> Third, may we live as the swallows on the beam,
> Happily together all the year round.

What might the bride's wishes be? What would living happily together mean to you in today's world? Do you think that your own ideas of happiness might be different from those of the Chinese poet? If two people you know are getting married, what kind of message would you compose for them?

FREE WRITE

What type of man or woman do you consider to be the ideal mate? What qualities do you want this person to have? Have you found your ideal mate? Explain.

Vocabulary in Context.   The words in this exercise will appear in the reading passage. Circle or underline the word(s) in the second sentence of each pair that is (are) a synonym for the italicized word in the first sentence. The first one is done for you.

1. In the poetry of the Middle Ages, a popular subject was the *romantic love* between a married woman and a young knight. The (deep feelings) between these two people did not involve a sexual relationship.

2. You may *conquer* most of your difficulties with English compositions by continual practice. You can control your writing problems, for example, by carefully editing your papers.

3. In a court of law, judges are not supposed to let *personal* feelings influence their judgment. The evidence is the most important thing, not the judges' individual emotions.

4. The bank will make an *arrangement* for you to pay your telephone bill by mail. This system can save you time.

5. We all need to *strengthen* our muscles and bones. If you exercise three or four times a week, you will increase the power of those body elements.

6. If you live in a small town, your *reputation* is very important. People know each other well, and if you don't have a good name in the community, you will find it hard to do business or socialize with others.

7. There is no *benefit* to staying up all night to study for an exam. What advantage do you gain by coming to class so tired you can't even remember all you have studied?

8. In some societies, *loyalty* among family members is the most important feeling. A person must show faithfulness to his or her relatives even if he or she does not like them as individuals.

9. It is difficult to teach children *cooperation*. When children are used to doing something in their own way, they may feel unhappy about working with others and giving in on some points.

10. When you practice a second language, you will find that the ability to speak fluently comes *gradually*. You won't be able to pronounce some words correctly at first; it will be a step-by-step process as you master one sound after another.

11. Certain movies are not *suitable* for children because they contain too much violence. Should newspaper ads include information on the appropriate films for various age groups?

Ⅱ READING

Different Ideals of Love and Marriage

[1]   If you listen to American music, watch American television or movies, or read American magazines, you will probably agree that the most popular subject of these forms of entertainment is love. Romantic love always finds an audience in the United States. Falling in love, solving the problems of love, and achieving the happy ending—the big wedding—are subjects of interest to the adult as well as the teenage public. Millions of Americans celebrate Valentine's Day with special cards and gifts that announce their love to their mates, their friends, their coworkers, and their families. Popular songs tell us that "all the world loves a lover." A popular saying is "Love conquers all." Numerous columns in magazines and newspapers offer advice to the lovelorn, those with difficulties of the heart. To most Americans, romantic love is central to a happy life.

[2]   Not only do Americans believe in romantic love, but they also believe that it is the best basis for marriage. Despite the high divorce rate in the United States, young men and women continue to marry on the basis of romantic love. Americans consider marriage a private arrangement between the two people involved. Young Americans feel free to choose their own marriage partners from any social, economic, or religious background. The man or woman may have strong ties with parents, brothers, or sisters, but when he or she falls in love, the strongest feelings are supposed to be for the loved one. When an American couple marries, they generally plan to live apart from both sets of parents and build their own independent family structure. The goal of the young couple is to be each other's best friends and to increase the personal happiness of themselves and their children.

[3]   Marriage, however, isn't always a matter of personal need for love and happiness. In most societies of the world, marriage is an important way to strengthen the main family line by uniting it with another family of the same social, economic, or religious background. In these societies, there are many rules about whom a person can or cannot marry. Parents have a strong interest in seeing that their children continue the family's good reputation and position in society. They also want their children to have a good life. So sons and daughters are not free to choose their mates. By arranging marriages, parents can control the choice of a new member for the benefit of the children, the whole family, and the class to which they belong.

After American couples marry, they generally build a new life apart from relatives, based on love and personal happiness.

[4]   In India, for example, the ideal household includes the parents, the sons, and the sons' wives and children. In this type of arrangement, the strength of the family lies in the respect, loyalty, and cooperation among the children and between the children and their parents. If a son is too interested in his wife, or if the wife is too independent or uncooperative, he or she may cause trouble by breaking the unity of respect and loyalty within the family. A good wife is one who is a good daughter-in-law. She is modest and obedient. She gradually breaks the ties with her own family and becomes completely interested in her husband's. In India many parents arrange a marriage for a son with the right kind of woman.

[5]   Romesh Roy is the son of a successful businessman in Bombay, India. He is a college graduate and thinks of himself as a modern young man. His parents are afraid that he is too independent and might choose his own bride. So while Romesh is busy with his career, Mr. and Mrs. Roy are both looking for a suitable young woman for him to marry. They would like a young woman whose family has a slightly lower position in society than their own so that her family will treat the Roys with more respect. But they want a young woman whose family will offer a good marriage gift. They prefer a woman who is not too tall for their son. She should be well educated but home loving. Her parents must not expect to see much of her once she is married. The ideal wife for Romesh will be the ideal daughter-in-law for the Roy family.

[6]   The Roys know many families with marriageable daughters. However, it isn't easy to arrange a good match. One of the young women is too plain. Another

one is attractive, but she is taller than Romesh. Still another is too "forward" and "thinks too much of herself." Mr. Roy knows a suitable daughter of a business partner. But her parents don't want Romesh for a son-in-law; they are looking for a wealthier family than the Roys for their daughter. Mr. and Mrs. Roy may have to wait a few years before they can make the best arrangement for the benefit of everyone concerned.

[7]   Eventually, Romesh will meet a woman suitable for both him and his parents. He will see her at least once or twice before they marry. The families will exchange gifts of money or jewelry, and then there will be a great wedding ceremony. The couple will live together with Romesh's parents and younger sisters and brothers. The bride will be obedient and cooperative. Because Mr. and Mrs. Roy are kind people, she will be well treated and comfortable in her new environment. Romesh's wife will provide company for Mrs. Roy and help in the management of the household. When Mr. and Mrs. Roy are away on vacation, she will take care of her husband's little sisters and brothers. Someday she will have her own children. When her son is grown, she too will look for a suitable bride for him.

Summary Completion. Fill in each blank space with a word or phrase that is correct in both form and meaning. You may use the exact words from the text or others of your own that communicate the same ideas.

Probably the most common subject of American popular music, films, and magazine columns is (1) _____ . Americans believe that (2) _____ , solving the problems of love and achieving the "happy ending"—(3) _____ —are central to a happy life. Americans also believe that romantic love is the (4) _____ for marriage. Even though the United States has a high (5) _____ , young Americans continue to marry on the basis of their personal feelings of "love." Young American married couples try to (6) _____ from their families and build an independent family structure of their own.

In other parts of the world, however, (7) _____ is not the basis for marriage. Marriage in India, for example, involves the (8) _____ of both the woman and the man. The parents of the young people will try to arrange a (9) _____ based on the economic, educational, and social background of both families. In these kinds of arranged marriages, the young couple will probably live with (10) _____ of either the bride or the groom.

Reacting to the Reading

American marriage has certain characteristics.

    a. List some of these.

    b. Are these characteristics similar to or different from those in your culture? Explain.

Reading Comprehension

1. Understanding the Text.   Follow the directions for each item.

    a. Mark the following sentences *T* for *true* or *F* for *false*, according to the information in the reading passage. Underline the part of the passage where you find your information.

        (1) In some societies sons and daughters are not free to choose their own marriage partners. _____

        (2) In India the ideal household includes married daughters. _____

        (3) An Indian father also takes part in arranging a marriage. _____

        (4) The marriage gift is one of the considerations in arranging a marriage.

        _____

        (5) Romesh Roy will not see his bride before he marries. _____

    b. Circle the letter of the correct answer.

    (1) Paragraphs [1] and [2]

        (a) are both concerned with marriage in the United States.

        (b) offer contrasting views of marriage.

        (c) tell us that love is the most important thing in most marriages.

    (2) The main idea of Paragraph [1] is that

        (a) the music of American teenagers deals mostly with love.

        (b) romantic love is a subject of interest to most Americans.

        (c) Valentine's Day is the most popular American holiday.

This bride and groom from the Indian subcontinent have an arranged marriage. Beautiful wedding jewelry and special clothing are part of the marriage ceremony.

(3) Sentence 1 of Paragraph [2] includes the phrase *not only . . . but also.* This phrase is used to

    (a) show a reason-result thought.

    (b) reverse the direction of a thought.

    (c) give forceful emphasis to a thought.

(4) Sentence 2 of paragraph [2] suggests that

    (a) marriages based on romantic love often end in divorce.

    (b) the writer believes that romantic love is a good basis for marriage.

    (c) the divorce rate in the United States is related to the age at which Americans marry.

(5) In the next-to-last sentence of Paragraph [2], the pronoun *their* in the phrase *build their own independent family* refers to

    (a) parents.

    (b) an American married couple.

    (c) brothers and sisters.

(6) In Paragraph [3], the word *however* in the first sentence signals

    (a) a time sequence.

    (b) a reason for a statement.

    (c) a reversal of a previous thought.

(7) In most societies of the world,

    (a) marriage is a private arrangement between two people.

    (b) married couples break the ties with their families.

    (c) there are many rules about whom a person can or cannot marry.

(8) The information in Paragraph [3]

    (a) gives specific details for Paragraph [2].

    (b) is an example of Paragraph [1].

    (c) introduces a new topic to the reading passage.

(9) The information in Paragraph [4] suggests that the main family line in India

    (a) is broken by marriage.

    (b) is continued through the males in the family.

    (c) is controlled by the daughters-in-law.

(10) In Paragraph [5], the author suggests that the Roys want their son's marriage

    (a) to be in the tradition of Indian culture.

    (b) to be different from their own marriage.

    (c) to be a real love match.

(11) Mr. and Mrs. Roy are looking for a daughter-in-law who is

    (a) short, well-educated, and independent.

    (b) plain, tall, and obedient.

    (c) shorter than their son, home-loving, and well-educated.

(12) In India, a girl's parents

    (a) must accept any offer of a husband for their daughter.

    (b) can reject a man as unsuitable for their daughter.

    (c) may prefer for their daughter to remain unmarried.

(13) In Paragraph [7], indicate the best place for the following sentence:
The groom will wear a business suit, but the bride will wear traditional Indian dress and jewelry.

    (a) after the first sentence

    (b) after the second sentence

    (c) after the third sentence

(14) In Paragraph [7], the author suggests that

    (a)   Romesh's bride will be the ideal Indian daughter-in-law.

    (b)   Romesh will help in the management of the household.

    (c)   Romesh's parents will be away a lot of the time.

2. Answering Information Questions.   Write the answers to the following questions in complete sentences.

    a.   Do married couples in the United States generally live with or apart from relatives?

    b.   In most societies, how does marriage strengthen the main family line?

    c.   Who are the members of an ideal Indian family?

    d.   What are the Roys afraid Romesh might do regarding marriage?

    e.   What will the families do before Romesh's wedding ceremony?

    f.   What will Romesh's wife do when her son is grown?

Ⅲ THE READING PROCESS

Paraphrasing.   Writers may express the same ideas in different ways. A paraphrase is another, usually simpler, way of saying something.

In each group of four sentences, put a check (✓) next to the two sentences that mean the same thing.

  (1) (a) An Indian wife will add to the wealth of her husband's family with gifts given by her parents when she marries. ____

      (b) In India the groom's family offers a small gift to the bride's family before the wedding ceremony. ____

      (c) Money and jewelry are common types of marriage gifts in India. ____

      (d) A bride's parents contribute money or jewelry to their daughter's new family unit as a marriage gift. ____

  (2) (a) The divorce rate is increasing around the world. ____

      (b) Some "love matches" end in divorce. ____

      (c) Even if you marry for love, the marriage may not last. ____

      (d) Love may grow deeply between a couple in an arranged marriage. ____

(3) (a) The Roys think that their son's future bride should be clever and bright. ____

(b) The Roys are looking for an obedient, modest wife for their son. ____

(c) The Roys want their son's bride to have a nice appearance. ____

(d) The Roys are interested in the physical characteristics of a bride-to-be for their son. ____

(4) (a) In the United States, most marriages are "love matches." ____

(b) In most societies, "love matches" are rare. ____

(c) People in the United States generally marry at a later age than they did fifty years ago. ____

(d) "Love matches" are in the minority among the marriage customs of the world. ____

(5) (a) Some Indian sons act independently and marry women of their own choosing. ____

(b) Some Indian sons leave their parents' home to find jobs in other countries. ____

(c) Not all Indian sons marry women chosen by their parents. ____

(d) Indian sons working in other countries often return home to get married. ____

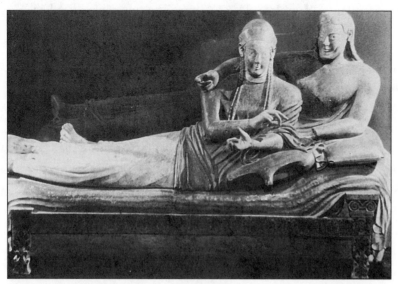

Happy marriages have been an ideal since ancient times, as this tomb sculpture of an Etruscan couple shows.

VOCABULARY

1. New Words. Pronounce these words, following your instructor.

Verbs	Nouns	Adjectives	Adverbs
conquer	reputation	romantic	gradually
strengthen	arrangement	personal	
	benefit		
	loyalty		
	cooperation		

  a. *CHOOSING SYNONYMS*. In the blank space in Column A, write the letter of the
  synonym from Column B.

  A

  conquer _____

  personal _____

  strengthen _____

  suitable _____

  reputation _____

  arrangement _____

  benefit _____

  loyalty _____

  cooperation _____

  gradually _____

  romantic _____

  B

  a. appropriate

  b. little by little

  c. have authority over

  d. an advantageous thing

  e. deeply loving

  f. individual

  g. splendid

  h. position in the community

  i. make stronger

  j. faithfulness

  k. working together

  l. win over

  m. method

  n. success

  b. *USING VOCABULARY*. Follow the directions for each item.

  (1) Circle the items that can only be done *gradually*.

  grow old   become proficient in English

  swallow a pill   run for the bus

  buy a newspaper   learn to walk (as a baby)

(2) Circle the words that are related to the word *strengthen*:

strong   strongly

stretch   strangle

lengthen   strength

(3) Circle the number of the sentence that would correctly follow the given sentence.

Cooperation is very important in planning a family vacation.

    (a) Everyone should do what he or she wants.

    (b) If you go to Europe, you'll have a good time.

    (c) Parents and children should talk about the places they want to see together.

(4) Circle the items that could be considered *benefits* of living in a large city.

bad air   museums   public transportation

lots of cars   small apartments   job opportunities

variety of schools   crowded streets   personal freedom

(5) Complete the following sentence by circling the appropriate phrases.

You can *strengthen* your body by

    playing tennis.   eating sweets.

    smoking cigarettes.   going to the movies.

    eating proper foods.   taking dance lessons.

(6) Check (✓) the sentences that use the word *reputation* correctly.

    (a) An honest businessperson will earn a good reputation. ____

    (b) To learn history you need a good reputation for names and dates. ____

    (c) I filled out two copies of a reputation for a driver's license. ____

    (d) Some politicians have a reputation for dishonesty. ____

2. Word Families: Noun Formation.   Nouns in English sometimes end in *ness*, *ty* (*ity*), *ship*, *ence* (*ance*), and *ment*. Study the following list of sample nouns with these endings.

kindness	loyalty	friendship	experience	arrangement
happiness	majority	partnership	importance	treatment

Follow the directions for each item. Write your answers in the space provided.

a. The verbs *arrange* and *treat* add *ment* to become nouns. Make nouns of the following verbs in the same way.

manage _____   develop _____

govern _____   agree _____

b. What noun ending in *ness* is the opposite of

kindness _____ ?

happiness _____ ?

c. What noun ending in *ness* can be formed from the adjective *lonely*? _____ What noun ending in *ness* can be formed from the opposite of the adjective *messy*? _____

d. What noun ending in *ty* or in *ity* means the opposite of dishonesty? _____ impossibility? _____

e. The noun *majority* means more than 50 percent of something. What is the noun ending in *ity* that means less than 50 percent of something?

_____

f. The suffix *ship* means "the condition of being" or "the skill of." Write the noun forms ending in *ship* for each of the following conditions or skills.

the skill of a leader _____

the condition of being a citizen _____

the condition of being a member _____

g. _____ is the adjective form of the noun *intelligence*.

Independent is the adjective form of the noun _____ .

LANGUAGE FOCUS

Simple Present Tense Conditionals

The word *if* is the sign of a conditional statement. An *if* clause tells us that certain conditions must be true or must happen before something else takes place. The *if* clause states the condition. The other clause in the sentence states the result. The result clause contains a modal + a main verb.

> Children will be helpful to you if you teach them to be cooperative.
>   (result)   (condition)
> If an Indian man marries a woman of his own choice, his parents may be hurt.
>   (condition)   (result)

Note that when the *if* clause begins the sentence, it is followed by a comma. When the *if* clause is the second clause, there is no comma.

When the main verb of an *if* clause is in the present tense, the most common modals in the result clause are these: *can, may, must, should,* and *will*. This type of conditional expresses the idea of possibility.

> If a woman chooses a suitable mate, she may enjoy a happy life.

1. Sentence Completion.   Complete each of the following conditional statements with a second clause containing a modal + a main verb. You may use negatives. Use pronouns carefully. Rewrite your complete new sentences.

     a. If an Indian mother finds a suitable woman for her son . . .

     b. If a bride wants to be a good daughter-in-law . . .

     c. If children watch too much television . . .

     d. If you don't know the meaning of a word . . .

     e. If my friend from India visits me . . .

     f. If parents of small children want to go out in the evening . . .

2. Sentence Building.   There are two items in each set. Make the first item into an *if* clause. Use the verb in the simple present tense. Make the second item into a result clause. Use an appropriate modal with the verb in the second clause. Add appropriate subjects and whatever other words are necessary to make a complete sentence. The first one is done for you.

Even in Western marriages today, family still plays an important role. Left, a Venetian father accompanies his daughter to the church in a gondola. Right, an Australian family shares the happiness of the newly married couple.

a. have enough credits, graduate

If I have enough credits, I will graduate next year.

b. study hard, pass courses

c. have money, visit Greece

d. don't feel well, stay

e. borrow books, return

f. eat too much, do exercises

g. don't cooperate, cause trouble

h. read newspapers, increase vocabulary

i. work long hours, feel tired

j. play active sports, wear suitable clothing

k. watch their mothers, learn to cook

l. do well in school, continue education

m. practice conversation, improve English

3. Sentence Composing.   Write a complete conditional sentence for each of the following items.

  a. Tell what item you will wear or carry if it rains tomorrow.

  b. Tell one thing that may happen if we elect a woman president.

  c. Tell one thing you should do if you are preparing for an exam.

  d. Name one thing you must do if you want to improve your English.

  e. State what you should do if you see an accident.

  f. Tell one thing children can do if they want to help their parents.

  g. Name one thing you may buy if you earn enough money.

  h. Tell what a person must have if he or she wants to drive a car.

  i. Tell how the instructor will feel if everyone passes the course.

Expressing Conditions Contrary to Fact

We use the simple past tense in the *if* clause to express a present condition that is contrary to fact, or unreal. The most common modals in the result clause are these: *could, might, would,* or *had to* (use for the past of *must*). These modals express the idea of improbability.

> If we **had** clean air, we **would live** a healthier life.
> You **would** get better grades if you **studied** harder.

This example expresses the *present* fact that we *don't have* clean air; therefore, the result is improbable.

1. Sentence Completion.   Circle the number of the result clause that best completes the given conditional clause.

  a. If I studied harder,

  (1) I can succeed.

  (2) I could succeed.

  (3) I will succeed.

b. I wouldn't enjoy American movies

    (1) if I can't know any English.

    (2) if I don't know any English.

    (3) if I didn't know any English.

c. I would find out more about different marriage customs

    (1) if I will take a trip to India.

    (2) if I took a trip to India.

    (3) if I am taking a trip to India.

d. If my sister had a higher salary,

    (1) she might move to a larger apartment.

    (2) she shouldn't move to a larger apartment.

    (3) she will move to a larger apartment.

e. If American parents wanted to arrange a marriage for a son,

    (1) the son can't cooperate.

    (2) the son might not cooperate.

    (3) the son shouldn't cooperate.

f. If little girls shared more sports activities with little boys,

    (1) real friendships could develop.

    (2) real friendships will develop.

    (3) real friendships can't develop.

g. You couldn't see your family very often

    (1) if you get a job as a pilot.

    (2) if you got a job as a pilot.

    (3) if you may get a job as a pilot.

h. If you had to travel for your job,

    (1) you would need excellent child care.

    (2) you need excellent child care.

    (3) you must need excellent child care.

   i. If there were more good day-care centers,

     (1) more mothers may work.

     (2) more mothers will work.

     (3) more mothers might work.

   j. If I wanted to be a construction worker,

     (1) I need a lot of strength.

     (2) I would need a lot of strength.

     (3) I will need a lot of strength.

2. Sentence Composing.   Write a complete conditional sentence to answer each of the following questions.

   a. If you became mayor of your city, what would you do to improve public transportation?

   b. If you were the manager of a professional baseball team, would you hire a woman player?

   c. If you had a daughter, what gift might you give her for her seventh birthday?

   d. If your friend gave birth to a boy, what gift would you give the baby?

   e. If your parents needed help around the house, what chores might you do for them?

   f. If a person liked working with children, what job might he or she enjoy doing?

   g. If you called a wrong telephone number by mistake, what expression could you use?

   h. If you won one thousand dollars in the lottery, how would you spend it?

   i. If there were going to be one world language, which language would you prefer?

   j. If scientists found life on another planet, would you go to live there?

   k. If you traveled to Egypt, what language would you need to know?

   l. If you lost your wallet, what would you do?

3. Sentence Completion.   Fill in the blank space with either a conditional clause or a result clause to complete the following statements. Pay special attention to the tense sequence and modal use. The first one is done for you.

a. *If I had children,* I would teach them to cooperate with each other.

b. You can observe many stars _____ .

c. If you want to see a lot of Roman art, _____ .

d. _____ if I traveled a lot.

e. _____ you shouldn't smoke.

f. You could pass this course _____ .

 # THE COMPOSING PROCESS

1. Sentence Combining to Form a Paragraph.

Combine the following sentences into longer, more interesting statements to form a paragraph about wedding gifts in Greece. Leave out all unnecessary words. Use signal words and other connecting expressions to make your paragraph flow smoothly. Rewrite your complete new paragraph on a separate sheet of paper.

a. The *dowry* is a common kind of gift.

b. The gift is for marriage.

c. The marriage is in Greece.

d. Dowries began in ancient times.

e. These times were many centuries ago.

f. The dowry was a gift of money.

g. The dowry was a gift of land.

h. The gift was from the parents.

i. The parents belonged to the bride. (Use possessive.)

j. The gift was to their son-in-law.

k. At that time a wife didn't work.

l. The work was outside the home.

m. She was expected to add to the wealth. (Use signal for reversal of thought.)

n. The wealth belonged to her husband.

o. She was expected to take care of her home. (Use signal of addition.)

   p. She was expected to take care of her children.

   q. The government of Greece wants to do away with dowries. (Use signal of reversal.)

   r. The government is current.

   s. The government says that dowries aren't necessary.

   t. Some women work outside the home. (Use signal for reason.)

   u. Some women earn as much as men do.

   v. Families can't afford to give dowries to all their daughters. (Use signal for addition.)

   w. These families are poor.

   x. To some women, dowries are like buying something. (Use signal for last or final item.)

   y. That something is a husband.

   z. A man may marry a woman.

  aa. The reason might be that she has money. (Use signal for reason.)

  bb. The reason might not be that he loves her.

  cc. Dowries present an interesting question.

  dd. Dowries are a difficult question.

  ee. This is in parts of Europe.

  ff. This is in parts of Asia.

2. Developing a Paragraph

RECOGNIZING GENERAL IDEAS AND SPECIFIC DETAILS. After each sentence in the following paragraph there is a blank space. As your instructor reads each sentence aloud, mark G in the blank space if the sentence is a *general* idea or opinion. Mark S in the blank space if the sentence is a *specific* detail or example.

    In India traditional society is divided into groups called castes. ____ The different castes are related to certain occupations. ____ The Brahmins are priests and scholars. ____ The Kshatriyas are soldiers. ____ The Vaisya are businessmen or merchants. ____ The Sudras are factory workers and craftspeople. ____ Traditionally, a person belongs to one of these castes by birth. ____ For example, a child born of a father who makes jewelry is a Sudra. _____ In the past, a person from one caste didn't marry someone from another. _____ A Brahmin never married a Vaisya, and a Sudra couldn't marry a Kshatriya. _____ However, under modern Indian law, all the groups are equal. _____ So the caste system has become weaker, and people sometimes marry outside their traditional group. _____

3. Developing a General Idea with Specific Details.   Read the following paragraph on the topic of wedding gifts. Then answer the questions.

> (1) In the United States, couples usually receive gifts from their relatives and friends when they get married. (2) Wedding guests usually give gifts to express their good wishes to the couple, but gifts are not necessary for the marriage itself. (3) In other societies, however, gifts are very important, and the marriage may not take place without them. (4) One type of necessary gift is called bride service. (5) A young husband must work for a period of time for his wife's family. (6) He may work as long as fifteen years or until their third child is born. (7) Bride service may seem strange to us, but it is important in societies where people don't have money or material goods to exchange at marriage.

QUESTIONS.   Place a check (✓) before the correct answer to the following questions.

(1) Sentence (1) states the topic of the paragraph: marriage gifts. What is the relationship of Sentence (2) to Sentence (1)?

_____ It contradicts the idea of Sentence (1).

_____ It gives a reason for the idea in Sentence (1).

_____ It gives an example of the idea in Sentence (1).

(2) What is the relationship of Sentence (3) to Sentence (2)?

_____ It contradicts the idea of Sentence (2).

_____ It gives a reason for the idea in Sentence (2).

_____ It gives an example of the idea in Sentence (2).

(3) Which word in Sentence (3) signals its relationship to Sentence (2)?

_____ gifts

_____ however

_____ marriage

(4) What is the purpose of Sentence (4)?

_____ It gives an example of an important marriage gift.

_____ It gives a reason for an important marriage gift.

_____ It shows the time sequence of giving important marriage gifts.

(5) What do Sentences (5) and (6) do in relation to Sentence (4)?

_____ They give the author's general opinion about the topic of Sentence (4).

_____ They give reasons for the topic in Sentence (4).

_____ They give specific details for the topic in Sentence (4).

(6) What does Sentence (7) do?

_____ It gives more specific details for the main idea.

_____ It gives a general reason for the main idea.

_____ It gives another example of the main idea.

With your class and instructor, review on the board the pattern of this paragraph's development.

4. Composing a Paragraph with General and Specific Statements.   The following list includes some items that are considered important for a wedding ceremony.

location of the celebration	flowers
bridesmaids' dresses	groom's suit
time of day and the season	food
music and dancing	guests
wedding dress	

Write a paragraph describing a wedding you observed. Choose three of the listed items on which to focus. Introduce each item with a general idea statement or opinion. Develop each item with specific and concrete details. Completing the following outline will help you write your extended paragraph.

Overall Main Idea _____

_____

I. General Statement, First Item _____

_____

Details 1: _____

2: _____

3: _____

II. General Statement, Second Item _____

_____

Details 1: _____

2: _____

3: _____

III. General Statement, Third Item _____

_____

Details 1: _____

2: _____

3: _____

Concluding Statement _____

_____

Paragraph Topics

a. Large weddings cost a lot of money. Some couples prefer to have a smaller wedding with just close relatives and a few friends, and use the money that they save to begin their new life together. In your opinion, which is the better way? Be sure to support your general idea statements with specific details, examples, and reasons.

b. In the United States and many other cultures, it is traditional to give gifts to the bridal couple—the bride and groom. These gifts may be useful, beautiful, or interesting. Describe the kind of wedding gifts most common in your culture. Include a main idea sentence at the beginning of the paragraph that identifies your culture and states the topic of your paragraph.

Ⓥ ADDITIONAL READING

Men's Roles, Women's Roles: A Changing View

[1]   In the traditional American society of the past, male and female roles were easily defined by the division of labor. Men worked outside the home and earned income to support their families. Women cooked the meals and took care of the home and the children. Those roles were firmly fixed for most people, and there was not much opportunity for men or women to exchange their roles. By the middle of this century, however, men's and women's roles were becoming less firmly fixed.

[2]   In the 1950s, economic and social success was the goal of the typical American, but in the 1960s a new force developed called the counterculture. The people involved in this movement did not value the middle-class American goals. The counterculture presented men and women with new role choices. Men became more interested in child care. They began to share child-rearing tasks with their wives. In fact, some young men and women moved to communal homes or farms where the economic and child-care responsibilities were shared equally by both sexes. In addition, many Americans did not value the traditional male role of soldier. Some young men refused to be drafted as soldiers to fight in the war in Vietnam.

[3]   In terms of numbers, the counterculture was a small group of people. But its influence spread to many parts of American society. Working men of all classes began to change their economic and social patterns. Industrial workers and business executives alike cut down on overtime work so that they could spend more leisure time with their families. Some doctors, lawyers, and teachers turned away from high-paying situations to practice their professions in poorer neighborhoods. Some young people joined the Peace Corps to share their skills with people in nonindustrialized countries around the world.

[4]   In the 1970s, the feminist movement, or women's liberation, produced additional economic and social changes. Women of all ages and at all levels of society were entering the work force in greater numbers. Most of them still took traditional women's jobs such as teaching, nursing, and secretarial work. Some women, however, began to enter traditionally male occupations: police work, banking, dentistry, and construction work. Women were asking for equal pay for equal work and equal opportunities for promotion. Women's groups were organizing more day-care centers for the children of working mothers.

[5]   Women and men began to join groups and attend meetings where these new roles were discussed. Women in particular needed to hear about the problems of other women who were working in nontraditional areas. At Rutgers University, for example, a conference of some of America's most creative women writers attracted a large crowd. Most of the speakers were older women who had

Some women have entered traditional male occupations such as police work. Here a policewoman handles a traffic accident.

achieved success in their field many years ago. They spoke about some of their greatest difficulties as women in a "man's world." Novelist and playwright Lillian Hellman and magazine writer Emily Hahn, two popular speakers at this conference, encouraged the women in their audience to try new roles and activities in their lives.

[6]   Even among older Americans, the grandmother and grandfather generation, there was a broadening of the roles that men and women could play. Advances in medicine and health care were allowing older people to live longer and experiment with new kinds of social activities. Men who retired from work began to take up hobbies such as cooking, painting, or crafts. Previously, these activities had been thought of as "women's work." At the same time, anthropologist Margaret Mead was making Americans more aware of the important part older women played in other cultures. And American grandmothers themselves were changing the definition of their roles. Many, of course, remained traditional grandmothers. Baking cakes, knitting sweaters, and baby-sitting for their grandchildren were their chief activities. But other grandmothers took up jogging, dancing, and writing. They joined senior citizen centers for social activities, either with or without their husbands.

[7]   Today the experts generally agree that important changes are taking place in the roles of all classes and age groups of men and women. Naturally, there are difficulties in adjusting to these changes. It is not easy for men and women

to learn to share the labor of the workplace. It is not easy for women to meet the demands and pressures of work outside the home and still take care of a family. Not all men are willing to share home and child-care responsibilities with their working wives. But perhaps more men are beginning to feel like Rafael Suarez, Jr., a New York City college student who looks forward to the new type of society. "Who needs the pressure of being a typical male?" asks Rafael. "It's more fun being a human being first."

Reacting to the Reading

1. a. Think about a traditionally male occupation such as fire fighting, construction work, or dentistry. Discuss why people might think a woman could or could not do one of those jobs as well as a man.

    b. Think about a traditionally female occupation such as school teaching or nursing. Discuss why people might think a man could or could not do one of those jobs as well as a woman.

2. a. In your native culture, what are some of the activities that are traditional for males? What activities are traditional for females?

    b. Do men and women usually socialize together in your culture? Explain. Are female-male roles changing in your culture? What are some specific changes you can point out?

Reading Comprehension

1. Understanding the Text.   Circle the number of the correct answer.

a. Which sentence best expresses the main idea of Paragraph [1]?

   (1) Men's and women's roles were usually quite separate in the past.

   (2) Women usually worked outside the home for wages.

   (3) Men's and women's roles were easily exchanged in the past.

b. The sentence that best expresses the main idea of Paragraph [2] is

   (1) the first sentence.

   (2) the third sentence.

   (3) the last sentence.

c. In Paragraphs [2] and [3], the author suggests that the counterculture

  (1) destroyed the United States.

  (2) changed some American values.

  (3) was not important in the United States.

d. The main idea of Paragraph [4] is stated in

  (1) the second sentence.

  (2) the fifth sentence.

  (3) the last sentence.

e. In Paragraph [4], indicate the best place for the following sentence:
  They also became taxi drivers, pilots, and college presidents.

  (1) After the first sentence

  (2) After the fourth sentence

  (3) After the last sentence

f. The main idea statement of Paragraph [5] is

  (1) the first sentence.

  (2) the second sentence.

  (3) the last sentence.

g. Women *in particular* needed to hear about other women in nontraditional fields probably because

  (1) the whole idea of women working in a "man's world" was new.

  (2) women needed to earn more income than men.

  (3) men gave a lot of support and encouragement to working women.

h. In Paragraph [6] the main idea is in

  (1) the first sentence.

  (2) the second sentence.

  (3) the sixth sentence.

i. In Paragraphs [5] and [6], two expressions that introduce specific supporting illustrations of general statements are

Some modern fathers are becoming more involved in caring for their children.

    (1) previously/at the same time.

    (2) for example/such as.

    (3) of course/in particular.

j. In Paragraph [7], the author suggests that

    (1) men and women will never share the same goals.

    (2) most men will be happy to take care of their children.

    (3) some men may be willing to change their traditional male roles.

k. The quotation by Rafael Suarez, Jr., in Paragraph [7] suggests that

    (1) he would not permit his wife to hold a job.

    (2) he would share some of the household responsibilities with his wife.

    (3) he wants a job with a lot of pressure.

2. Paraphrasing. Writers may express the same ideas in different ways. A paraphrase is another, usually simpler, way of saying something. Follow the directions for each item.

In each group of four sentences, put a check (✓) next to the two sentences that mean the same thing.

    (1) (a) More American households are headed by a woman than ever before.

        ———

(b) There has been an increase in the number of women who return to work after having children. ____

(c) Many American women leave their jobs when they have children. ____

(d) The number of American homes with no adult male member is increasing. ____

(2) (a) In many colleges in the United States, men and women live in the same dormitories. ____

(b) Most formerly all-male colleges now admit female students. ____

(c) Women are starting to enter some colleges that used to be only for men. ____

(d) Women in some colleges are taking part-time jobs that used to be held by men. ____

(3) (a) Divorced mothers are returning to college in increasing numbers. ____

(b) More divorced men are asking to have their children live with them. ____

(c) Most children of divorced parents live with their mothers. ____

(d) The number of divorced men raising their children is growing. ____

(4) (a) In the United States, secretaries are usually women. ____

(b) In European and South American offices, secretaries are frequently male. ____

(c) Male secretaries are common in the offices of Europe and South America. ____

(d) European offices are usually better run than American offices. ____

(5) (a) Research shows that the more education a woman gets, the fewer
children she usually has. ____

(b) Research reveals that many women now combine going to college
with having children. ____

(c) Research shows that educated women have high educational goals for
their children. ____

(d) Research indicates an increase in the number of mothers going back
for higher education. ____

Vocabulary

Using Vocabulary. The following list contains new vocabulary words or forms of
words from the reading. Use each word correctly in one of the blank spaces in the
paragraph.

involve	responsibilities	leisure	typical
influenced	industry	economic	goals
occupations	promotion	pressure	

In a (1) _____ American business office, men's jobs and women's
jobs are different from each other. Typing, filing, and other secretarial work usually
(2) _____women. A female typist may get a (3) _____
to a secretary's position, but she will find it harder to move into management.
In most firms, men still have the major (4) _____ and enjoy a higher
(5) _____ level. But in these higher-level (6) _____, there
is more (7) _____ and less (8) _____ time. The
women's movement has (9) _____ women to set higher occupational
(10) _____ for themselves. But women who move up in
(11) _____ or business often find they have two full-time jobs: the
one they are paid for and their housework and child care at home.

CHAPTER NINE

REACHING OUT

I PREREADING

Pair Discussion. Short sayings, which include proverbs, maxims, and quotations from literature, have been used throughout the centuries to express some popular truth or useful thought. Sometimes these sayings express contrasting points of view.

Read the following items to discover the contrasting points of view about the two subjects: *neighbors* and *charity*. With a partner, discuss your preference for either *a* or *b* in each item, based on your own experience or your common sense.

1. a. Thou shalt love thy neighbor as thyself.
    The Bible

    b. Good fences make good neighbors.
    Robert Frost

2. a. Charity begins at home.
    Sir Thomas Browne

    b. The essence of charity is troubling oneself for the community.
    Laws of Passover

FREE WRITE

Read the following letter to "Dear Abby," and free-write your response to Jill H.

Dear Abby,

*   I am a sixteen-year-old girl, busy with school and my friends. My mother thinks I should spend some time at a community center volunteering my services to the elderly. In my spare time I would rather hang out with my friends and have fun. This makes me feel guilty—not contributing to my community. But I can't bring myself to work with old people. I think it would be too depressing. Is something wrong with my attitude?*

Sincerely yours,

Jill H.

Vocabulary in Context.   The words in this exercise will appear in the reading passage. Choose the word(s) that mean(s) the same as the italicized word in each sentence.

1.   To be a good parent, I *realize* that I must have a lot of patience with my children.

a. pretend   b. understand   c. hope

2.   I listen *sympathetically* to my children's problems because they rely on me to help them.

a. with compassion   b. impatiently   c. with little interest

3.   Our teenage daughter wants to play the saxophone. I think it's a great idea, but my husband says it's *ridiculous*.

a. silly   b. clever   c. important

4.   For a costume party, my teenager dressed as a clown. Her friends looked at her, but without *recognition*.

a. remembrance   b. responsibility   c. emotion

5.   Our young son was angry and, acting on *impulse*, ran away from home, but only for an hour.

a. fear   b. sudden desire   c. command

6.   If you feel *self-conscious* at a party, you might sit by yourself in a corner of the room.

a. at ease   b. in a good mood   c. uncomfortable

7. Adults can get very *distressed* over the wild behavior of some teens in their neighborhood.

   a. proud   b. anxious   c. dependent

8. The ice cream was gone from the freezer. When asked about it, Grandma *confessed to* eating it all, saying it was delicious.

   a. blamed others for   b. told a lie about   c. admitted to

9. Grandma *denied* eating the pie, however.

   a. complained about   b. didn't admit to   c. liked

10. Getting together on a picnic gives my family a chance to relax and eat *leisurely* in the fresh air.

    a. unhurriedly   b. in haste   c. without company

11. Students in college know it takes hard work to become *qualified* in their field.

    a. settled   b. creative   c. competent

12. Don't get *discouraged* if you can't find a job right after graduation; it takes a good deal of time these days.

    a. in low spirits   b. emotional   c. careless

Ⅱ READING

Russell Davis: "Love"

Russell Davis is a contemporary American writer. This short story is an adaptation of Mr. Davis's tale recalling a time in the 1920s when he was growing up in a small town. It gives us a picture of neighborhood life at that time and place and the interaction of some members of that community.

Next door to us lived the Holloways. There was Sam Holloway, a pale, moon-faced bachelor, and his two gray sisters, Faith and Love, both also unmarried. That was all there was to the Holloway family. There had once been a Mrs. Holloway, the mother. My mother remembered her, but just remembered her and that was all. There had been a Mr. Holloway too, but that was back before we moved there.

Sam didn't do anything. He had worked in a steel mill but he retired from that job with a small pension. Now he didn't do anything but mow his lawn or shovel the snow, depending on the time of the year. He was a mild, untroubled sort of person. One morning he dropped dead walking leisurely past Sheehan's Meat Market. We kids heard about it in school. "Hey," someone said. "Do you suppose they put him in the meat wagon?" We all laughed. "Sure," said another kid. "They probably did, so he could *meet* his maker." I thought this remark was pretty funny and told it to my parents at the supper table that night.

My mother frowned. "Now that's not nice at all," she said. My father looked thoughtful. "I wonder how they're fixed for money," he said as he nodded toward the Holloway house.

"I'm sure I don't know," said my mother, still displeased at me for my remark.

And that was the end of the conversation.

We didn't play in the Holloway yard much. We just cut across it once in a while when it seemed convenient. It wasn't that the Holloways forbade us over there, but we knew the two sisters were a little nervous about us. They were, after all, just two old women who lived by themselves and hardly ever went out. Their place seemed strange to us, a house without a mother or father, without any kids, a place so quiet, so old-looking. The newest thing about the house was a window cooler made out of a wooden box. They never had an ice box.

They also had the reputation of being very stingy. Occasionally they would call for me or one of the neighborhood kids to come and do a chore like mowing the lawn or shoveling snow. But we soon learned not to respond. I shoveled them out of a two-foot snowfall one January morning at my mother's order. When I finished, I rang the bell and waited a long time for an answer. At last Miss Faith, the plump one, opened the door just enough to extend her gray hand and drop a rather wrinkled apple into my hand. Then she closed the door and disappeared. I went home and held the apple up to my mother with a disapproving expression on my face. My mother smiled a little but then she said, "You shouldn't be so hard on them, dear. I don't think they have much money."

"Why don't they get some?" I asked.

My mother looked distressed. "I don't know that they have a way to get money," she replied.

"Why don't they *get* a way, then?" I demanded.

My mother bit her lip. "It's not that easy, you know."

"Huh!" I said.

But then the sisters did find a way, though not a way in which they were qualified. They began to take in foster children. First there were two young girls who fought each other all day, threw mud against the windows and finally set fire to the cellar. The girls were taken away. Then there were two other children, a young boy Richard and his baby sister Ola. We played with them while they were living there. We even helped Richard to construct a pushcart in which he would push Ola around. He liked to watch us over at our house as we worked on various projects in our yard.

Suddenly one day Richard and Ola were gone. They too were taken away by the Foster Care Agency because forty dollars disappeared from the kitchen closet and the Holloway sisters thought it had to be Richard who took the money. Richard denied it and only a month later a neighborhood kid confessed to the robbery. After this incident the Agency wouldn't give the sisters any more foster children.

They took in boarders now, but the boarders didn't stay. One boarder told us what the problems were. "It's just a lot of little things. Not enough to eat, small worn-out towels, lack of any real hot water, even the soap is always tiny. And of course, they don't have electricity, only gaslight, so I couldn't see well to read my books at night. And well, all their chairs were uncomfortable." The boarder smiled and added sympathetically, "I suppose they can't afford better."

Certainly I didn't give the Holloway sisters much thought. I was interested in basketball and baseball, and I had a newspaper delivery route I traveled on my bicycle every afternoon. I also had a girlfriend who didn't believe in having only one boyfriend as I believed she should.

One day I came home from school and my mother was wiping tears out of her eyes because one of the Holloway sisters had died that morning. It was Faith, the plump one, although she hadn't been so plump in recent years. She had become almost as thin as her sister Love, who was thin as a hat rack. My mother said Love had come over for help but there hadn't been anything she could do to save Faith.

I stood still and my mouth dropped open. "You mean Miss Love came out of her house?"

My mother nodded.

"Came over here?"

"Yes," said my mother.

What a surprise! We had never known Miss Love to go out except once in a while for a funeral, and never alone.

"After all," said my mother, "her sister was dying."

I thought it over. "What'll she do now?" I said.

My mother shrugged sadly. "Live on there alone, I guess."

But Love didn't. Her house was put up for sale by the state authorities. Then a woman in a business suit came in a taxi and took Love out of the house while the taxi driver brought out a high narrow trunk. Love was taken away. We heard soon enough where she went. The poorhouse.

Unlike Love in the poorhouse, older people in today's nursing homes reach out to each other for companionship.

I used to see Love Holloway in the window of the second floor of the poorhouse as I passed it on my paper route. She was always there looking out, not apparently looking at anything, just looking, staring. Once I waved to her, but stopped suddenly because I worried about what someone might think of a full-grown high school boy waving to an old woman in the poorhouse.

I was at a self-conscious age. My love affair was not going well. My girlfriend had found another. He was mature, he could dance, he could play the ukulele and sing, and I couldn't. One day I was riding by the poorhouse on my paper route, feeling particularly discouraged about my life. I decided to stop at the poorhouse door and knock. The door was opened by a small woman who stared at me uncertainly. I handed her a newspaper and said, "It's for Miss Love. It's free. Take it. It's for Miss Love."

I did this every day afterward. Now and then I wondered if she really got the paper, if she really wanted it, what she thought.

Then everything in my life went to pieces. The girl I loved moved away. I wrote; she didn't answer. I gave up my newspaper route for the summer to take an out-of-town job. In my last delivery I told the woman at the poorhouse that I was leaving and the newspaper would come no more.

The next day was the last day of school. I was dressing for a school dance. I was taking a "spare-tire" girl—just someone to take to the dance—when my mother announced that there was a letter for me. I raced down the stairs and tore open the envelope.

Dear Sir:

Love wishes you to call at your earliest opportunity.

What the devil! From the poorhouse, not from the girl.

"Bad news?" inquired my mother.

"No, nothing," I said disgustedly and went slowly back upstairs.

But the next day, with nothing better to do with my last hours in town before leaving for my summer job, I went out the road to the poorhouse and went up and knocked once more. I thought: Probably she wants me to keep bringing the paper. Well, I can't, that's all.

The same small woman opened the door. Now her eyes were lit with recognition. "Come in," she said. She led me up steep wooden stairs, down a corridor to a door, and I entered Miss Love's very small room.

Its bareness shocked me. No rug on the floor, no curtain, just a faded window shade, an iron bed, small table and a cardboard box on it. "Hello," I said. I think this was perhaps the only time in my life I had ever spoken to her.

She stood still, her small eyes glittering, flashing a little. I wondered what emotion was passing through her, fear, anger. I saw that there were tears in her eyes. She said nothing.

"I'm glad to see you," I said awkwardly. "I'm sorry I can't keep dropping you the newspaper, but I'm going away for the summer." I stopped and waited for her to speak.

She didn't. Her thin mouth trembled a little. She moved now a few steps. I realized suddenly that she was lame or feeble, old. Her hands trembled violently as she fumbled with the cardboard box, getting the lid off. She took out a pair of scissors and turning her head sidewise she grasped a wisp of her coarse gray old hair, snipped off a lock of it, and held it out to me.

"Do—do you want me to take it?" I stammered.

She held it, her hands trembling.

I took it. "Thank you," I said a little loudly, with a brief false smile. "Thank you."

She stood staring at me, her eyes still glittering with their tears. After a moment I turned and, saying goodbye, left the room.

On my way home I had an impatient impulse to throw the lock of hair away, but could not somehow. When I got home I could not even tell my mother. It was too ridiculous. I didn't want to explain anything to her. I took the lock of hair up to my room and started to put it in my tin box of souvenirs, mostly of the girl I lost, but that didn't seem right. I put it in a seldom used box in a drawer with some old stamps, a broken comb and some crayons.

Plot Summary.   A plot is a plan of events in a narrative. In the following plot summary, fill in the blanks with appropriate phrases to make a logical and smooth reading of the story.

Faith and Love Holloway are (1) _____ who live next door to (2) _____ . Their brother has died, and they don't have (3) _____ . Their teenage neighbor doesn't like to (4) _____ for them because he thinks (5) _____ . The sisters try to earn money by (6) _____ and later by taking in boarders, but they don't suc- ceed. When Faith dies, Love loses (7) _____ and is taken (8) _____ . The teenager begins to feel sorry (9) _____ , so he decides to (10) _____ every day. After a while he has to stop because (11) _____ . Just before he leaves, Love sends him (12) _____ requesting him (13) _____ . The teenager visits Love and receives a gift of (14) _____ from her. As he leaves the poorhouse, he thinks of throwing it away, but decides instead (15) _____ .

Reacting to the Reading

1. This story takes place in a small town in the 1920s.

    a. In your experience, is life in a small town today similar to the one in this story? Give examples of similarities or differences.

    b. In what ways are town neighborhoods different from city neighborhoods?

2. In the Holloway family there are no children.

    a. Do you know a family where children and their grandparents live in the same household? Describe how they get along.

    b. What are the mutual advantages for youngsters and the elderly in having strong ties?

Reading Comprehension

1. Understanding the Text.   Choose the correct answer, or follow the directions.

a. This story is written from the point of view of

(1) two elderly unmarried women.

(2) a boy in his teens.

(3) the mother of a teenager.

b. The focus of the story is

(1) the strong ties between a teenager and his parents.

(2) the troubles of a teenager with his girlfriend.

(3) the relationship between a teenager and his elderly neighbors.

c. The teenager's description of the Holloways' house suggests that his house

(1) is as old as theirs.

(2) has more modern conveniences than theirs.

(3) doesn't have a yard as big as theirs.

d. We can infer from the story that

(1) while he was alive, Sam Holloway supported his sisters with his pension.

(2) the sisters' financial situation did not change after Sam's death.

(3) the sisters had their own pensions.

e. According to the narrator, Faith and Love were not *qualified* to take care of foster children. This is true because

(1) they didn't have proper documents from the Foster Care Agency.

(2) they couldn't provide enough space for children to play.

(3) they had no previous experience with handling children's problems.

f. The sisters' job as foster parents ended because

(1) they accused a child of stealing money.

(2) the neighbors objected to the children's poor behavior.

(3) the children had no other kids to play with.

g. A boarder describes all the problems of living in the Holloway house. Write the sentence from the story that shows the boarder's sympathetic understanding of the situation. _____

_____

h. At this time in his life, the teenager seems very concerned about

(1) his relationship with his girlfriend.

(2) making money on his paper route.

(3) helping the foster children next door.

i. When the boy learns about Faith's death, he

(1) expresses sadness at the event.

(2) offers to go to her funeral.

(3) shows some concern for Love's future.

j. It is clear from the story that the Holloway house is sold because Love

(1) doesn't want to live there alone.

(2) can't afford to keep it up.

(3) wants the money from the sale.

k. The teenager loses his girlfriend to another boy. The problem seems to be that

(1) he hasn't paid enough attention to her.

(2) he doesn't have talent in social situations.

(3) he wants to take another girl to the school dance.

l. At one point the boy tells us that everything in his life *went to pieces*. He is saying that

(1) his home life was going badly.

(2) he was having physical problems.

(3) great changes were taking place in his life.

m. Even as he feels discouraged about his life, the teenager reaches out to Love in a spirit of giving. List the events that show the boy's sympathy for Love. The first one is done for you.

(1) *starts to wave to Love as he passes the poorhouse*

(2) _____

(3) _____

(4) _____

(5) _____

n. He doesn't tell his mother about Love's gift to him because

(1) it is supposed to be a secret.

(2) he is uncomfortable about it.

(3) his mother would disapprove of it.

o. Which two statements apply to this story?

(1) Giving helps make the other person a giver also.

(2) The ability to sympathize depends on the character development of the person.

(3) The gap between the young and the old is too wide to bridge.

2. Answering Information Questions. Write the answers to the following questions in complete sentences.

a. According to the boarder, what were some of the problems with living in the Holloways' house?

b. Why was the boy surprised that Love came over to his house?

c. Why did he stop waving to Love in the poorhouse window?

d. Why was he disappointed when he read the note from Love?

e. Describe Love's room in the poorhouse.

f. What did the boy suddenly realize about Love when he saw her in the room?

Ⅲ THE READING PROCESS

Descriptive Language. Narrative writers may use a verb like *frown* or *shrug* to describe a character's reaction to a situation. They also use adjectives like *pale* and *glittering* to reveal something about the character beyond the word itself. Noting this descriptive language will help you form vivid pictures of characters and objects, and will add to your understanding and enjoyment of a story.

Read the following descriptions from the story, and answer the questions. The first one is done for you.

a. Sam Holloway was a *pale,* moon-faced bachelor. What does the adjective *pale* imply? *Sam might not be very strong or healthy; perhaps he doesn't eat well.*

b. He had two *gray* sisters, Faith and Love. What might the color *gray* signify?

_____

c. When the boy told his mother the joke about Sam dying, his mother *frowned.* What was the mother expressing by this *frown?* _____

_____

d. Faith gave the boy a *wrinkled* apple. Describe this apple in your own words.

_____

e. When the boy asked his mother why the sisters didn't find a way to get money, his mother *bit her lip* before she answered. What does *biting the lip* express? _____

f. When the boy learned that Love came out of her house and visited his house, his *mouth dropped open.* Why did his *mouth drop open?* _____

_____

g. The boy wondered what Love would do after Faith died, and his mother *shrugged* sadly. What is she expressing by *shrugging* her shoulders? ____

_____

h. Love stood still, her small eyes *glittering, flashing* a little when the boy entered her room in the poorhouse. Were her eyes *glittering, flashing* from fear, anger, or for another reason? Explain. _____

_____

i. Her thin mouth *trembled* a little. . . . Her hands *trembled* violently. Was Love *trembling* because she was nervous, or was it another reason? Explain.

_____

Ⅳ VOCABULARY

1. New Words. Pronounce these words, following your instructor.

Verbs	Nouns	Adjectives	Adverbs
deny	recognition	distressed	leisurely
confess	impulse	qualified	sympathetically
realize		self-conscious	
		discouraged	
		ridiculous	

a. *EXPANDING VOCABULARY.* Check (✓) the terms in each item that mean the same as the italicized word in the sentence.

(1) The adviser listened *sympathetically* to the student's problem.

with humor ____   doubtfully ____   in a compassionate way ____

hurriedly ____   with feeling ____   with understanding ____

(2) It is *ridiculous* to think you can graduate without working hard in

your courses.

laughable ____   easy ____   silly ____

absurd ____   a good idea ____   popular ____

(3) Teenagers often feel *self-conscious* on their first date.

comfortable ____   awkward ____   ill at ease ____

selfish ____   proud ____   bored ____

(4) We all *realize* the difficulties that elderly sick people face when they

are alone.

are unhappy about ____   understand fully ____   comprehend ____

oppose ____   reject ____   know well ____

(5) On summer evenings I like to walk *leisurely* around my neighborhood.

fearfully ____   in haste ____   at an unhurried pace ____

slowly ____   in company ____   taking my time ____

(6) A neighborhood thief was caught recently and *confessed to* several robberies.

admitted ____   acknowledged ____   denied ____

committed ____   prevented ____   owned up to ____

(7) I confess that when a car blocks my path at an intersection, I have *an impulse* to kick it, but don't.

an opportunity ____   the right ____   the strength ____

a sudden desire ____   an abrupt urge ____   a wish ____

(8) My sister is the president of our neighborhood block association, a position for which she is greatly *qualified*.

suited ____   appreciated ____   capable ____

thankful ____   competent ____   concerned ____

(9) She has received *recognition* for her work in the community.

complaints ____   advice ____   attention ____

acceptance ____   approval ____   gifts ____

b. *USING VOCABULARY.* Answer the following questions in complete sentences, using the italicized words.

(1) When did you first *realize* you wanted to go to college?

(2) Whose problems would you listen to *sympathetically*? (name a person)

(3) What article of clothing did you buy on *impulse* that you didn't really need?

(4) When do you eat in a hurry, and when do you eat *leisurely*?

(5) What classroom situation makes you feel *discouraged* about your progress?

(6) In what kind of social situation do you feel *self-conscious*?

(7) What kind of job are you *qualified* for at this time?

(8) Your friend has told a lie. If you questioned her, do you think she would eventually *confess* to it or *deny* it?

(9) In which situation would you feel more *distressed*: taking an unannounced math test or driving alone on a dark road?

2. Word Families: Number Prefixes.   The prefixes *di(a)*, *du*, and *bi* mean "two."

> This reading passage contains several *dialogues* between the boy
> and his mother.
> My brother is *bilingual*; he speaks French and English.

Other prefixes that show numbers are the following:

mono- 1	quint- 5	oct- 8	cent- 100
tri- 3	sext- 6	nov- 9	mille- 1000
quad(r)- 4	sept- 7	dec- 10	

Answer the following questions, or complete the sentences in the space provided.

a. *Logue* is a part of a word that means "speech." If a dialogue is the speech of two people, how many speakers are there in a monologue?

_____

b. The word-part *tonous* means "having a tone or sound." If a person speaks in one tone without variations, we say that person's speech is

_____.

c. *Cycle* means "wheel." Older children ride a _____; little ones usually begin on a _____.

d. *Ped* is a part of a word that means "foot." Is a horse a *biped* or a *quadruped*? _____ Is a human being a *biped* or a *quadruped*? _____ What kind of insect is a *centipede*? _____

e. Why would a mother with *quintuplets* find it difficult to have a career?

_____

f. If you played the drums in a *sextet*, how many other people would be in your band? _____ A _____ is a song for two people.

g. A quarter is _____ of a dollar. One _____ is 1/100 of a dollar.

h.   September, October, November, and December are the number names of months taken from the early Roman calendar. These months are correct in that calendar because the Roman year did not start in January, but in

_____.

i.   A *decade* is _____ years. A *century* is _____ years. A *millennium* is _____ years. On July 4, 1976, the United States celebrated its *bicentennial* birthday. How old was the United States on that date? _____ The woman was one hundred years old. Her family celebrated her _____ anniversary with a big party.

j.   How many sides does an *octagon* have? _____ How many angles does a *quadrangle* have? _____ How many angles does a *triangle* have? _____

V   LANGUAGE FOCUS

Complex Sentences with *Before* and *After*

Complex sentences sometimes include activities that happen at different times. One part of the sentence happens *before* or *after* the other. The part of the sentence that begins with the time word *before* or *after* is called the *dependent clause*. The dependent clause must be joined to a main, or independent, clause to complete the sentence.

> Before my brother goes to school, he delivers newspapers.
>   (dependent clause)   (independent clause)
> He likes to play basketball after he finishes his homework.
>   (independent clause)   (dependent clause)

Note that when the dependent clause begins the sentence, it is followed by a comma.

The main verb in both parts of a complex sentence must be in the same or related tenses.

Simple Present   **Simple Present and Future**

> My sister *expects* to work with the elderly after she *graduates.*
> Before she *graduates*, she *will do* volunteer work in a hospital.

Simple Past   **Simple Past and Past Continuous**

> Before I *graduated* from college, I *was working* as a volunteer.
> After I *passed* my license exam, I *got* a well-paying job as a nurse.

1. Sentence Combining.   Join the two sentences in each set by adding *before* or *after*. Make whatever small changes are necessary for sentence correctness. Rewrite each new complete sentence. The first one is done for you.

a. (1) Some families move many times.

(2) They find a suitable place to live.

Some families move many times before they find a suitable place to live.

b. (1) We were living near my aunt's house.
   (2) We moved next door to my grandparents' house.

c. (1) My grandmother used to read me a story every night.
   (2) I went to sleep.

d. (1) My grandfather retired from his job.
   (2) He took up gardening.

e. (1) Many older people don't like living alone.
   (2) Their spouses die.

f. (1) Some couples sell their house.
   (2) Their children are out on their own.

g. (1) We were living in our house a while.
   (2) We made new friends among our neighbors.

h. (1) The house next door was empty a long time.
   (2) Our neighbor moved away.

i. (1) My children used to play in the empty yard.
   (2) A new family bought the house.

j. (1) My older daughter finishes her homework.
   (2) She will baby-sit for the neighbors' children.

2. Sentence Building.   Use each pair of items in a complex sentence with the word *before* or *after*. Use the items logically, and add as many words as you like to make a complete, interesting sentence. You may use the words in any tense or in the negative. The first one is done for you.

a. have a test, review my notes

   Before I have an English test, I always review my grammar notes.

b. eat dinner, go to a movie

c. take a course, see an adviser

d. take a shower, go to bed

e. finish this exercise, do another

f. graduate, apply for work

g. read, give my opinion

3. Sentence Composing.   Follow the directions for each item.

a. Tell where you lived before you came to this city.

b. Tell where you plan to live after you finish school.

c. Tell what you will do after this class is over.

d. In two separate sentences, tell two things you should do before you write a paragraph. Then combine the two sentences, making all the necessary changes.

e. In three separate sentences, tell three things you do before you leave the house each morning. Then combine the three sentences into one complete sentence, using a series of items.

f. In two separate sentences, tell two things you must not do after a test has started. Now combine the two sentences into one, making all the necessary changes.

Adverbs of Manner

Some adverbs tell how, *in what manner*, verb action is done.

> Students who work part-time plan their schedules *carefully*.
> (Students *plan*. How do they plan? *carefully*)

Most adverbs of manner are formed by adding *ly* or *ally* to the adjective: *careful* ⟶ *carefully*; *sympathetic* ⟶ *sympathetically*. Note some exceptions: *fast* ⟶ *fast*; *hard* ⟶ *hard*; *leisurely* ⟶ *leisurely*; *good* ⟶ *well*.

1. Sentence Rewriting .   Rewrite each sentence, changing the italicized phrase into an adverb that describes the verb action. The first one is done for you.

    a. The number of older Americans is increasing *in a steady manner*.
        The number of older Americans is increasing steadily.

    b. Many older people are living *in a modest way* on small incomes.

    c. Some live with relatives and others live *in an independent way*.

    d. The elderly may behave *in a fearful way* if they live alone.

    e. Some of them live *in a comfortable way* in retirement communities.

    f. My children always speak *in a respectful manner* to their elders.

    g. Sometimes teenagers and older people don't communicate *in an easy manner*.

    h. Most people on my block work *in a cooperative way* with their neighbors.

2. Sentence Expansion.   First locate the main action verb in each sentence, and underline it. Then add an adverb of manner that will explain the way in which the verb action was done. Use the adjective in parentheses as the base for the adverb. Think about the best position in the sentence for the adverb. The first one is done for you.

    a. The doctor <u>listened</u> to the patient's complaint. (sympathetic)
        The doctor listened sympathetically to the patient's complaint.

    b. We worked all afternoon to solve the math problem. (hard)

    c. My children speak English and Spanish. (fluent)

    d. The couple danced on their first date. (awkward)

    e. My son does his household chores. (cheerful)

    f.   Our daughter plays with other children in the neighborhood. (good)

    g.   The bus stopped to avoid an accident. (sudden)

    h.   We enjoy walking in the park on weekends. (leisurely)

Punctuation: Quotations

Quotations are the exact words spoken by someone. These quoted words and their punctuation are written within quotation marks (" "). The part of the sentence that tells us who is speaking is called the narration. The quoted part of a sentence and the narration are separated from each other by a comma.

> One mother said, "I encourage my children to help our neighbors."
> "Sometimes they get a small tip for their work," she added.

Some common verbs used in the narration are *said*, *stated*, *asked*, *replied*, and *answered*.

1. Proofreading.   Proofread the following lines from the reading selection, and insert any quotation marks or commas that are missing. Then check your work on page 247.

I stood still and my mouth dropped open. "You mean Miss Love came out of her house?

My mother nodded.

Came over here?

"Yes," said my mother.

What a surprise! We had never known Miss Love to go out except once in a while for a funeral, and never alone.

"After all" said my mother, "her sister was dying."

I thought it over. What'll she do now? I said.

My mother shrugged sadly. Live on there alone, I guess."

2. Composing.   Write a brief dialogue relating a conversation you recently had with a relative, neighbor, or friend. Use quotation marks for the exact words of the speaker. Use the previous exercise as a model for punctuation.

> Today I met my neighbor in the hallway. "Someone left a bag of garbage on the staircase," I said.
> "I didn't do it," replied my neighbor.

You may extend your dialogue with a partner.

 # THE COMPOSING PROCESS

1. Sentence Combining to Form a Paragraph.   Combine the following sentences into longer, more interesting statements to form a paragraph about students who are helping the elderly. Leave out unnecessary words. Use adjective-noun combinations, the word *and*, time clauses, reason-result clauses, and correct punctuation for items in a series to make your sentences flow smoothly. Some suggestions are given in parentheses.

a. Some high school students are enrolled in courses.

b. The courses are special.

c. They are in the Health Services program.

d. These courses are preparing the students.

e. This is for work with the elderly.

f. The students study biology in regard to aging.

g. They study sociology.

h. They study psychology.

i. These subjects are important. (Combine using a reason-result clause.)

j. They help the students understand the physical problems of the elderly.

k. They help them understand the social problems.

l. They help them understand the mental problems.

m. Their studies include fieldwork.

n. This is in hospitals.

o. This is in nursing homes.

p. They visit the elderly to talk to them.

q. They listen to them.

r. They read to them.

    s. They do whatever they can to make their lives more pleasant.

    t. The patients greatly appreciate having ties with the young students.

    u. The patients are often alone in the world. (Combine using *because*.)

    v. Their families may live far away. (Use *or*.)

    w. For the students, too, it is a relationship.

    x. The relationship is satisfying.

    y. Someone asked a student in the program about her feelings. (Use a time clause.)

    z. The student replied sympathetically. (Combine using punctuation for quotations.)

    aa. When I see an elderly woman, I see my grandmother.

    bb. The student continued. (Combine bb, cc, and dd using quotations and a connecting word.)

    cc. These people need me.

    dd. I need them too.

2. Developing a Paragraph. In composing a paragraph, you must pay attention to both the content of the paragraph and the correct formation of the sentences that develop it. In the following exercise, notes for the paragraph are given to you. The topic relates to a teenager's life. Follow the directions for developing this paragraph.

Read the following list of items about the life of the teenager in the story "Love."

- relationship with parents—good

- attends school

- has job—earns money

- friendly to children

- concerned with neighbors

- interested in sports

- is in love

- feels self-conscious

- has trouble with girlfriend

- life is changing—makes new plans

Young people who work with the elderly have a feeling of satisfaction.

These notes will be used to develop a paragraph about this boy. Refresh your memory about the notes by rereading the story.

Now read the beginning of the paragraph. It includes a main idea statement stating the topic and the point of view. This sentence is followed by supporting details developed from the first few items in the list. Notice how some items are combined into one sentence. Complete the paragraph by using the remaining items as the bases for your sentences.

> The teenager in the story "Love" is a typical boy living in a small town in the 1920s. He lives with his mother and father, and he seems to have a good relationship with them. He attends school and also earns money from his newspaper delivery route. He is friendly and helpful to the children in his neighborhood.

For the conclusion, choose the appropriate item and write it as the last statement(s) in your paragraph.

   a. This teenager has too many problems growing up. He will probably have a lot more problems as an adult.

b. This teenager is already mature in all aspects of his life. His adult life will be free of difficulties.

c. Although this teenager has some problems in growing up, he doesn't have a bad life. His character is developing steadily.

3. Composing a Paragraph.   The topic for composing is the following: *a teenager I know*. Read the list of items.

- relationship to parents, brothers, sisters

- household chores

- school attendance

- job

- relationship to friends and neighbors

- community service

- interests: sports, hobbies, music, etc.

- troubles

- handling changes in life

These notes will guide you in composing a paragraph about a teenager you know. Perhaps your paragraph will be similar to the previous one; perhaps it will be in contrast to that one. Follow the directions.

a. Begin with a main idea statement that includes the topic and your point of view. *Example:* My cousin Pam is a (difficult, typical, very nice) teenage girl.

b. Use the notes to describe this teenager's life. You may include information not on the list.

c. Write a conclusion that reflects your thoughts about the teenager's future.

d. When you have finished, proofread your paragraph. Be sure that your details support your main idea and that you have used correct sentence structure.

Paragraph Topics

1. Write a paragraph that describes a special relationship you have with a member of the older generation in your family, such as an aunt, an uncle, or a grandparent. Describe the person, tell where he or she lives and how the relationship developed. Tell what the advantages are and how both of you benefit. If the

relationship is in the past, use the appropriate tense and time expressions. Begin your paragraph with a main idea sentence that includes a feeling or opinion about this relationship.

2. Some parents think an older person is better able to care for small children than a younger person. If you were a parent who needed help with your children, whom would you choose? Give specific reasons for your choice.

ADDITIONAL READING

Men and Women: Do They Speak the Same Language?

[1]   Earlier chapters of this book included several readings about language and communication. One discussion was about the different communication systems among animals. Another passage discussed the methods some scientists are using to teach human language to animals. We know, of course, that human language itself takes many forms. Written language is not the same as spoken language. Some communication systems such as the Morse Code or American Sign Language use audible signals or hand gestures to communicate. There are hundreds of different languages used in different areas of the world. And now, according to American sociologist Deborah Tannen, there seem to be important differences between the languages of men and women.

[2]   Deborah Tannen's recent book, *You Just Don't Understand*, has become a best-seller in the United States. This book discusses the many difficulties men and women have in communicating with each other. Ms. Tannen believes that men and women have problems in conversing with each other because they are raised to see the world in different ways. Because men and women have such different life experiences, they don't speak the same language. Just like people from different cultures, men and women have problems with "cross-cultural communication."

[3]   According to Tannen, men generally see the world as a competitive place. People "win" or "lose" in life just as teams win or lose baseball games. People rank "first, second, or third" just like competing athletes in the Olympics. Many men see life as a contest in which they are struggling to become independent and avoid failure. American men in particular believe that it is important to "make it on their own." They feel that they must struggle against being "put down" or "pushed around" by other people. Because men see the world as a contest, they use words as a way of helping them "come out on top" or "be number one." One common image men use about themselves is that they are "climbing the ladder of success." This image suggests that an individual must act *separately* from other people in order to achieve his goals.

[4]   Women, on the other hand, often view themselves primarily in connection with other people. Their image is more a network or web of relationships than a ladder with separate steps. Women try to get close to other people and reach agreement with them. Perhaps this is because throughout history women have been responsible for raising children, who are dependent and require emotional support. According to Tannen, while men use language to show independence, status, and power, women use language to establish connection and intimacy.

[5]   Because men and women speak "different languages," they often misunderstand each other. These misunderstandings frequently lead to anger and hurt feelings. For example, men often give advice in a situation where a woman really wants emotional support. Tannen tells about one woman, for instance, who was in pain from an operation but wanted to come home from the hospital as soon as possible to be with her family. Her husband said, "Why don't you stay in the hospital where you would be more comfortable?" He thought he was giving his wife helpful advice, but his wife's feelings were hurt because she thought he did not value her being at home.

[6]   Professor Tannen notes in her book that Americans often make jokes about women talking too much. Her research shows, however, that men, in fact, talk much more than women in *public* situations. Men talk to show their skills and knowledge. They hold their listeners' attention by giving out information. Men often tell stories in which they are the main character, or they tell jokes that make fun of other people. From earliest childhood American men learn to use talk as a way to focus attention on themselves.

[7]   Women, in contrast, use both public and private speech to build relationships with other people rather than separate themselves from others. That is why, according to Tannen, women rarely tell jokes in public. Telling jokes is a way to get attention, to make other people look inferior, and to control the emotions of the listener. Women have not been raised to do these things, so they are not as comfortable in telling jokes as men. Furthermore, when women do tell stories, they are usually about other people. When a woman does tell a story about herself, it is often about some foolish or silly thing she has done. Even women with professional or technical knowledge tend to talk less about what they know than do men in the same field.

[8]   Conflict is a feature of every person's life, but men and women are brought up to handle conflict differently. Therefore, when conflict arises, men and women use different language to handle it. Generally, women try to avoid open argument in conversations. They will not disagree strongly with other people in public. They look for common ground, or points on which they can agree and express support for the other speaker. Men, in contrast, view conflict as a way to compete with others and "win" their points. They will voice disagreement openly, and even when they ask a question they may imply a challenge to the speaker.

Even when women communicate on a professional level, they tend to use language in a cooperative and supportive way.

[9]   When men and women converse with each other, women are more likely to use language in a cooperative way. Women will frequently use phrases such as "*Let's* go to the movies" or "*Why don't we* go out for dinner?" Men, however, do not want to feel that others are telling them what to do. They often misinterpret women's words as efforts to "boss them around." Yet research shows that even in the speech of children, it is boys rather than girls who tell others what to do. Thus, it is not surprising that as adults, men and women have different conversational styles and problems in communicating with each other. By presenting her research on men's and women's language, Professor Tannen hopes to clear up some of the misunderstandings between the sexes. Perhaps her work will help both men and women to improve their communication with each other. When women and men "speak the same language," they can work toward better personal and professional relationships.

Reacting to the Reading

Briefly list some of the different personality traits of men and women, according to the article.

   a. Do you agree with Tannen's views on this subject? Be specific about your points of disagreement.

   b. Are any of Tannen's points about the different personalities of men and women true in your native culture? Explain. Do men and women in your native culture use language the way Tannen claims American men and women do? Give specific examples.

Italian American men play the traditional game of boccie ball in New York's Lower East Side. When men get together for sports and games, they often develop a style of communication that women don't share.

c. In your cultural group, do men and women follow different "rules" and use different kinds of language in expressing conflict? Provide some specific examples.

Reading Comprehension

1. Understanding the Text.   Choose the correct answer, or follow the directions.

a. The main idea of the entire reading passage as stated in Paragraph [1] is found in

(1) the first sentence.

(2) the fifth sentence.

(3) the last sentence.

b. The main idea of Paragraph [2] is that

(1) Deborah Tannen wrote a best-selling book.

(2) men and women from different cultures have problems in communicating.

(3) men and women have difficulties in communication because they are raised differently.

c. The main point of Paragraph [3] is that

  (1) men are lonelier than women.

  (2) men experience life as a competition with others.

  (3) men are better athletes than women.

d. In Paragraph [4], the words *network* and *web* suggest that

  (1) women keep secrets better than men do.

  (2) women have more difficult lives than men do.

  (3) women look for relationships with others more than men do.

e. In Paragraph [5], what is the purpose of the story of the woman in the hospital?

  (1) to show the communication problems between men and women

  (2) to show that women value their families more than men do

  (3) to show that men have more common sense than women do

f. Mark *T* for each statement that is *true*, according to Paragraphs [6] and [7].

  (1) In the United States, men make fun of women for talking too much. _____

  (2) Research shows that American women talk more in public than men do.

    _____

  (3) The fact is that women talk more on the telephone than men do. _____

  (4) Giving out information is a way of getting people to listen to you. _____

  (5) Women are usually good at telling jokes. _____

  (6) Women often tell stories that make themselves look dumb. _____

  (7) Men have more professional knowledge than women do. _____

g. In the second sentence of Paragraph [8], the pronoun *it* refers to

  (1) men.

  (2) women.

  (3) conflict.

  (4) language.

Men and women in the workplace must speak the same language.

h. State the main idea of Paragraph [8] in your own words.

_____

_____

i. The last sentence of Paragraph [8] states that "even when [men] ask a question they may imply a challenge to the speaker." This means that

(1) men ask questions because they don't understand the speaker.

(2) men may question a speaker as a form of disagreement.

(3) men question speakers more frequently than women do.

j. In the first sentence of Paragraph [9], the phrase *in a cooperative way*

(1) suggests that women are comfortable doing things with others.

(2) is illustrated by the expression "go out to dinner."

(3) both of the above

(4) neither of the above

k. Paragraph [9] implies that men and women learn social and language behavior

(1) when they mature.

(2) early in life.

(3) in school.

l. In your own words, why did Deborah Tannen write her book on the language of men and women? _____

_____

_____

_____

_____

_____

_____

_____

_____

_____

_____

_____

_____

_____

_____

_____

_____

_____

_____

2. Signal Expressions.   In discussing complex ideas, authors use signal expressions to help the reader follow the relationship between thoughts. Match the relationships in Column B with the signal expressions in Column A by writing the correct letter in the blank space. Some thought relationships are used more than once. Use the context of the signal expression in the reading to help you make your choice.

A: Signal Expressions

(1) (Para. 1, Sent. 6) such as _____

(2) (Para. 1, Sent. 8) And _____

(3) (Para. 2, Sent. 3/4) because _____

(4) (Para. 3, Sent. 2/3) or _____

(5) (Para. 4, Sent. 1) on the other hand _____

(6) (Para. 4, Sent. 5) while _____

(7) (Para. 5, Sent. 4) for instance _____

(8) (Para. 5, Sent. 4/6) but _____

(9) (Para. 6, Sent. 2) however _____

(10) (Para. 6, Sent. 2) in fact _____

(11) (Para. 7, Sent. 1) in contrast _____

(12) (Para. 7, Sent. 4) so _____

(13) (Para. 7, Sent. 5) Furthermore _____

(14) (Para. 8, Sent. 2) Therefore _____

(15) (Para. 9, Sent. 1) When _____

(16) (Para. 9, Sent. 5) Yet _____

(17) (Para. 9, Sent. 6) Thus _____

B: Thought Relationships

a. contrast/reversal of thought

b. time

c. addition of similar items

d. choice

e. example or illustration

f. reason

g. result

h. emphasis

Answers

CHAPTER ONE: Uncovering the Past

I. PREREADING

Vocabulary in Context

2. not too long ago
3. distant past
4. forebears
5. remarkable
6. tell
7. packed
8. look closely at
9. interferes
10. save

II. READING

Summary Completion

1. remains
2. tests
3. society
4. against
5. museums
6. disrespect
7. problem
8. cemetery
9. mixed
10. agreed
11. lives
12. reburied

Reading Comprehension

1. Understanding the Text

a. (3)
b. (1)
c. get information from
d. (1)
e. (3)
f. (2)
g. (2)
h. (3)
i. (1)
j. disturb
k. (2)
l. (2)
m. make clear

2. Answering Information Questions (sample responses)

a. Archeologists use measurements, X-rays, and chemical tests to get the answers.

b. Native Americans are against the study of their ancestors' bones.

c. The Smithsonian has about 18,500 human bones in its collection.

d. The discovery was made in lower Manhattan in New York City.

e. Archeologists discovered pottery, glassware, tools, and toys.

f. The African-American community agreed to the study of its ancestors' bones.

g. Professor Blakey says, "To learn from archeology is another form of respect for our ancestors."

III. THE READING PROCESS

General and Specific Words: Topics

a. (2) city G, New York, S
   (3) notebook S, book G
   (4) ball S, doll S, toy G
   (5) chair S, furniture G
   (6) scientific tool G, X-ray S
   (7) tooth decay S, arthritis S, disease G
   (8) occupation G, farming S, teaching S
   (9) silver S, metal G, gold S

b. (2) countries   (7) clothing
   (3) people   (8) art
   (4) furniture   (9) musical instruments
   (5) jewelry   (10) weapons
   (6) kitchen items

c. (1) b   (2) c   (3) a   (4) c   (5) a

IV. VOCABULARY

1. New Words

USING VOCABULARY. Answers will vary.

2. Word Families

SENTENCE COMPLETION

a. archeologist/archeology   f. writer/writing
b. artist/art   g. science/scientist
c. farming/farmers   h. teacher/teaching
d. history/historian   i. psychologist/psychology
e. photographer/photography   j. astronomy/astronomer

V.   LANGUAGE FOCUS

Sentence Kernels

1. Verbs

RECOGNIZING VERBS

a. holds   c. examine   e. learn
b. looks   d. keep

2. Subjects

RECOGNIZING SUBJECTS

a. earth   c. Archeologists   e. We
b. archeologist   d. They

3. Identifying Verbs and Subjects

a. Subject	Verb
2. He	has
3. (His) students	help
4. They	follow
5. They	receive
6. (The) professor	writes

Simple Present Tense

1. Sentence Completion

a. (1) works   (5) lives   (9) lie
   (2) dig   (6) digs   (10) says
   (3) bring   (7) looks   (11) walk
   (4) discovers   (8) give

2. Scrambled Sentences

a. Archeologists tell us a lot about the past.

b. Archeologists sometimes find bones and tools.

c. They also discover written records of the past.

d. Archeologists bring all the objects to museums to study.

e. The museums carefully preserve these ancient objects.

Plurals

1. Regular Plurals—List Completion

Singular	Plural
—	actions
—	bones
a community	—
—	bodies
—	pieces
an object	—
—	boys
—	countries
a box	—
a game	—
—	dishes
—	stories
—	brushes
a life	—

2. Irregular Plurals—Sentence Completion

a. places

b. plans

c. Children

d. object

e. bones

f. teeth

g. woman

h. men

i. stories

Prepositions

1. Prepositional Phrases of Direction

ANSWERING QUESTIONS WITH PREPOSITIONAL PHRASES. Answers will vary.

2. Prepositional Phrases of Place

a. *RECOGNIZING PREPOSITIONAL PHRASES OF PLACE*

Inside the doorway ... in the center ... under the opening ... on the ground. ... Around the courtyard. ...At the back of the courtyard ... behind that room ... by the fishpond ... among the fruit trees ... in a dining room ... on the side of the garden...

c. Answers will vary.

3. Prepositional Phrases of Time—Sentence Completion

a. at

b. On/at

c. At

d. at/in

e. at

f. in

g. on

h. on

i. at/in

j. at/at

Punctuation and Capitalization

My friend Robert is a field worker for the Museum of Natural History in New York. Every summer he goes out west to Montana. He looks for the remains of ancient life in the rocks. He usually discovers animal bones. Sometimes he finds the remains of plant life. He never finds human bones in that part of the United States. Next summer I am going to Montana. I want to see Robert at work in the field.

V. THE COMPOSING PROCESS

1. Sentence Combining to Form a Paragraph

The potter works every day in his shop next to his house. He keeps the clay in a tub in a corner of the shop. There is a potter's wheel near the window on the other side of the shop. To make a pitcher, the potter throws a lump of clay on the wheel. The clay spins around by means of a pedal under the wheel. The potter moves his hands over the clay to form a beautiful shape. He uses his fingers around the neck of the pitcher to create an interesting design. Sometimes he paints a design around the body of the pitcher, or just on the neck. He dries his pitchers outside the workshop in the sun.

2. Developing A Central Topic (sample response)

a. Tuesday is my busiest day. I get up at 7 o'clock, get dressed, and have breakfast. Then at 8 I go to school. I stay in school until noon. After my classes, I have a lunch break for half an hour. Then I usually go to the library and review my class notes. I leave for home at about 2 o'clock. I go shopping for my family on my way home. At about 5 o'clock I relax and watch the news on TV. After dinner I do my homework. I rarely go out in the evening on Tuesday. I usually go to bed early.

3. Composing A Paragraph Answers will vary.

VII. ADDITIONAL READING

Reading Comprehension

Understanding the Text

1. (a)
2. (b)
3. He hears everything, he breathes fire, and he never sleeps.
4. (b)
5. (b)
6. (c)
7. but sadness soon follows

8. (c)
9. (c)
10. (c)
11. (b)
12. the proud features of Uruk—G; all others—S
13. (c), (d), (f), (h), (i), (j)
14. (c)

Vocabulary

1. Expanding Vocabulary

a. (3)	c. (3)	e. (3)	g. (1)	i. (3)
b. (1)	d. (2)	f. (1)	h. (2)	

Chapter Two: North America: A Continent of Many Cultures

I. PREREADING

Vocabulary in Context

1. b	4. c	7. b
2. a, c	5. a	8. b
3. b, a	6. a	9. b

II. READING

Summary Completion

1. North American
2. English
3. original
4. immigrants
5. traditions
6. Je me souviens (I remember)
7. failed, did not succeed
8. China, India, and Japan
9. problems, difficulties
10. different

Reading Comprehension

1. Understanding the Text

a. The main point is that Canada and the United States use English as their basic language.

b. (1) but, however

c. because Canada was not a slaveholding society

d. the French

e. [3] the French   [4] the Finns   [5] Asians   [7] the Inuit

f. (1)

g. (2)

h. The main purpose of the film is to show some problems of Indian immigrants in Canada.

i. (1) recently   (2) however   (3) For example

j. (3)

k. (2)

l. (3)

2. Answering Information Questions (sample responses)

a. Both countries speak English as the primary language.

b. People follow French traditions in the northeastern part of Canada and in Louisiana.

c. The Finns came to Canada to escape a hard life in Finland.

d. Asians from China, Japan, and India settled in Canada and the United States.

e. The film *Marsala* is about Indian immigrants in Canada.

f. The Inuits live by hunting and fishing.

III. THE READING PROCESS

Identifying Main Ideas.

a. (1) Topic: Montreal's Winter Festival
    Main Idea: Montreal's Winter Festival celebrates the winter season.
  (2) Topic: Immigrants to Canada
    Main idea: Immigrants to Canada come from many different cultures.

Vocabulary

1. New Words

EXPANDING VOCABULARY

(1) celebrate, occasion   (5) represent
(2) immigrant, native   (6) perform, delicious
(3) inhabitants   (7) settle
(4) weapons

USING VOCABULARY. Answers will vary.

2. Word Families

a. western   d. tradition   g. richness
b. culture   e. ancestral   h. Mexico
c. American   f. kind

V. LANGUAGE FOCUS

Answering Questions with Simple Present of *To Be*

a. The Alaskan islands are in the Pacific Ocean.
b. The smallest island on the map is Kuiu Island.
c. Canada is on the border of Alaska.
d. No, Mt. Gallatin and Mt. Lewis Cass are on the mainland/in Canada.
e. Juneau is the capital of Alaska.
f. The capital is on the Alaskan mainland.
g. Ketchikan is on Revillagigedo Island.
h. The Clarence Strait is between the mainland and Prince of Wales Island.
i. No, Chicagof Island and Admiralty Island are in the northern part of Alaska.

1. Choosing the Correct Form

(1) are   (5) there is   (9) is
(2) is not   (6) there is not   (10) is not
(3) is   (7) are
(4) there are   (8) there is

2. Sentence Composing Answers will vary.

To Be + Adjective + Noun

1. Sentence Building

(a) (1) Japanese is an Asian language.
    (2) A lion is a wild animal.
    (3) Gold is an expensive metal.

(4) *Igloo* is an Inuit word.

(5) A trout is a delicious fish.

(6) Montreal is a Canadian city.

(7) Chemistry is a difficult subject.

(b) (1) Japanese and Chinese are Asian languages.

(2) Lions and tigers are wild animals.

(3) Gold and silver are expensive metals.

(4) *Igloo* and *umiak* are Inuit words.

(5) Trout and bass are delicious fish.

(6) Montreal and Ottawa are Canadian cities.

(7) Chemistry and astronomy are difficult subjects.

2. Sentence Completion Answers will vary.

3. Sentence Combining

a. Anticosti is a beautiful island in the St. Lawrence River.

b. There are wild animals in some of the Canadian forests.

c. There are splendid beaches along the coast.

d. There are interesting seashells on the beach.

e. There are lots of cultural activities during the summer.

f. There are skillful workers in my native country.

VI. THE COMPOSING PROCESS

1. Sentence Combining to Form a Paragraph

New Orleans is a city in Louisiana. There is an exciting festival there in the winter called Mardi Gras. During Mardi Gras there are parades throughout the city. There are marching bands and floats with people in extraordinary costumes. The people on the floats toss out trinkets and candy for the children watching the parades. People dance in the streets all day and night. They wear interesting masks to cover their faces. Everyone enjoys eating the delicious French-Creole food outdoors or in restaurants. There are other carnivals such as this in different parts of the country. But New Orleans has the largest and most colorful celebration in the United States. It is a wonderful place to visit at Mardi Gras time.

2. Developing a Unified Paragraph

a. Many Inuit are skilled workers in arts and crafts. (main idea) Detail sentences may follow in any order.

b. 3 (main idea), 1, 6, 5, 9, 4, 2, 8, 7

3. Composing a Paragraph Answers will vary.

VII. ADDITIONAL READING

Reading Comprehension

1. Understanding the Text

a. (3)   b. (2)   c. (3)   d. (1)   e. (2)

f. He was a tall man with white hair and a weather-worn face.

g. He was dressed in a neat blue shirt, faded overalls, and high-top shoes.

h. (1) F   (3) T   (5) T   (7) T

(2) F   (4) N.I.   (6) F   (8) N.I.

   i. (1)

   j. (1) anything   (3) It's about ... spring

     (2) Just   (4) It ... ever

   k. (2)

2. Sequencing events in Time Order

a. (1) 3   (2) 5   (3) 2   (4) 4   (5) 1

b. First he cut a switch from a hickory tree. He held the stick with both hands so that it formed a loop. Then he began to walk back and forth over the property. In some places the stick would shake slightly. But he paid no attention to those spots. He walked around some more. Then he found a strong spot. He told Mrs. Maron to dig there.

Vocabulary

1. Expanding Vocabulary

a. (3)	d. (2)	g. (3)
b. (3)	e. (1)	h. (3)
c. (1)	f. (3)	i. (1)

Chapter Three: Steps To The Future

I. PREREADING

Class Discussion

A dictionary entry such as the example gives the syllables, phonetic pronunciation, accent, part of speech, definitions, and related forms of the entry word.

Abbreviations: v. = verb, n. = noun.

Vocabulary in Context

1. a	3. c	5. a	7. a	9. a
2. c	4. b	6. b	8. c	10. c

II. READING

Summary Completion

1. planet	5. climate	9. rules
2. species	6. recreation	10. activities
3. problems	7. upsetting	11. home
4. air	8. healthful	

Reading Comprehension

1. Understanding the Text

a. (3)	e. (2)	i. (1) (3) (4) (5) (8) (9)
b. (2)	f. (3)	j. (l)
c. (2)	g. (3)	
d. (1)	h. (2)	

2. Answering Information Questions (sample responses)

a. The ozone layer protects us from the sun's dangerous rays.

b. The earth was a dead object made of rock, without air or water.

c. The U.S. National Park and Forest Service manages federal wilderness areas.

d. Venus is a world of carbon dioxide, acid rain, and 900° temperatures.

e. Edward Abbey wrote those words.

III. THE READING PROCESS

Identifying Specific Information

a. (1) examples of something

(2) in the parklands; on the lakes and rivers; in the forests

(3) because overcrowding causes damage to the environment

(4) because it makes the soil poor; *because* signals a reason why

(5) by keeping watch for danger signals

(6) the animals in the forest and the visitors too

(7) yes

b. (1) (a) nine   (c) over 13 million

(b) over 4 billion years   (d) 125 cabins

(2) (a) at home; at beaches; in oceans, rivers, streams; on farmlands and woodlands

(b) Wildlife species become homeless, and the climate changes.

(c) higher temperatures, droughts, and severe storms

(d) coal and oil

(3) electricity, flush toilets, chopping down trees, digging up rocks, burning or burying garbage, powerboats

(4) sailboats, rowboats, canoes

(5) (a) because the Forest Service wants to prevent overcrowding.

(b) because they would pollute the lake.

(c) because chemicals in soaps and detergents can pollute the lake.

IV. VOCABULARY

1. New Words

a. *EXPANDING VOCABULARY*

(1) environment   (6) variety

(2) observe   (7) balance

(3) destroy   (8) irresponsible

(4) necessary   (9) protect

(5) explore   (10) revolve

b. *USING VOCABULARY.* Answers will vary.

2. Word Families

a. homeless   f. star

b. sunless   g. sleepless

c. pain   h. waterless

d. meatless   i. treeless

e. hope   j. care

V. LANGUAGE FOCUS

Simple Present Tense Negative Forms

1. Sentence Building (sample responses)

c. My school library charges a late fee for overdue books.

d. Art museums don't allow people to touch the paintings.

e. Most of my friends go to bed before midnight.

f. The moon doesn't have air or water necessary for life.

g. A salesperson doesn't earn as much as the company's boss.

h. Banks don't offer interest-free loans.

i. Traffic noise bothers me very much.

j. I don't consult a doctor when I have a mild headache.

k. Smoking harms a person's health.

l. The National Forest Service doesn't permit the use of electricity at Echo Lake.

2. Sentence Composing Answers will vary.

Verbs + Adjectives

1. Recognizing Verbs + Adjectives

… looks bright…are strong and would be dangerous… would appear gray… isn't smooth… is fine and dusty… is calm and peaceful

2. Sentence Composing Answers will vary.

Singular Possessives

1. Sentence Completion

b. doctor's office

c. city's laws

d. country's past

e. friend's house

f. father's boss

g. instructor's explanations

h. secretary's desk

i. sun's rays

j. person's health

k. child's progress

2. Proofreading

(2) his child's room

(3) her neighbor's garbage pile

(4) his wife's collection

(7) Mr. LaPlante's instruments

(8) everyone's idea… one person's garbage… another person's treasure

VI. THE COMPOSING PROCESS

1. Sentence Combining to Form a Paragraph

Lake Minnewaska is a beautiful, unspoiled nature preserve in New York state. People go there to picnic by the waterfalls in the lakeside forests. Nature lovers follow the trails through the forests to observe the variety of plants and birds. Now this area is in danger because some hotel owners want to build cabins by the lakeside. The hotel owners would like to clear some of the forest for tennis courts and a golf course. They would pave over a part of the lakeside for parking lots, and they would need to build a pumping station near the waterfall. Nature lovers are trying to keep Lake Minnewaska unspoiled by raising money for lawyers to make a case against the hotel owners. It is important to preserve Lake Minnewaska for all nature lovers now and in the future.

2. Developing A Paragraph

a. *OUTLINING.*

Main Idea: Some people are predicting that in the near future there will be many good solutions to the world's problems.

Details: —sun and wind to heat homes and run factories

—ability to grow food in dry and cold places

—faster and cheaper public transportation

—electric cars

—cleaner air in cities

—stronger laws against chemicals on crops

—cures for serious illness

VII. ADDITIONAL READING

Reading Comprehension

1. Understanding the Text

a. (3)

b. how it will improve their lives; if it can be harmful to them

c. (2)

d. (1)

e. Sentence 1

f. For example

g. (2)

h. (3)

i. take temperature readings, measure the composition of the gases, and collect samples of minerals

j. (1)

k. gas-station attendants, dressmakers, personal robots for the home

l. Machines will take over jobs and leave people unemployed; machines will become smarter than humans and become evil monsters.

m. (2)

Vocabulary

1. Expanding Vocabulary

a. (2)	d. (1)	g. (3)
b. (1)	e. (2)	h. (1)
c. (3)	f. (1)	i. (3)

UNIT II: OUR WORLD OF LANGUAGE

CHAPTER FOUR: Echoes of the Past

I.   PREREADING

Vocabulary in Context

1. b	3. b	5. c	7. b	9. c
2. c	4. b	6. a	8. c	10. b

II.   READING

Guided Summary (sample answers)

1. The main purpose of this reading is to tell us about the development of language.
2. Paragraph 2 describes how human beings first learned to speak.
3. Writing developed long after people learned to speak. Or: Writing developed about eight thousand years ago.
4. Hieroglyphics, the ancient Egyptian picture writing, was one of the oldest systems of writing.
5. Picture writing made communication easier, but in some ways it was still difficult to communicate.
6. About 3,500 years ago, the alphabet was invented.
7. The conclusion states that the alphabet was very efficient. Or: The conclusion states that the alphabet is used all over the world.
8. Only the Chinese still have a picture writing system.

Reading Comprehension

1. Understanding the Text

a. (1) F   (3) T   (5) T   (7) F
   (2) T   (4) F   (6) T

b. (1) c   (5) b
   (2) ...nobody...for certain; perhaps; probably;   (6) b
       do not...exactly; scientists believe;   (7) c
       may have been   (8) b
   (3) b   (9) ...it did present some problems
   (4) b   (10) every single Chinese character

c. (3) (6) (5) (1) (2) (4)

2. Answering Information Questions (sample responses)

a. Early humans used signs to communicate.
b. Spoken language is about one million years old.
c. Hieroglyphics are the ancient Egyptian picture writing.
d. It is permanent; it can be interrupted and referred to again by the reader; it can be continually revised.
e. The alphabet was invented.
f. Alphabetic language is more efficient because it takes up less space and it is easier to understand.
g. The Chinese still have a picture language.

III. THE READING PROCESS

Linking Pronouns

a. (1) c   (4) (a) picture words   (5) picture writing
   (2) b   (b) people's
   (3) b   (c) thoughts and deeds
                             (d) older members

b. Sent. 3, they = immigrants; their = belonging to the immigrants
   Sent. 4, they = things
   Sent. 6, They = immigrants; them = names

IV. VOCABULARY

1. New Words

EXPANDING VOCABULARY Answers will vary.

2. Word Families

a. (1) related   (5) unusual
   (2) impractical   (6) sufficient
   (3) correct   (7) inefficient
   (4) invisible   (8) original

b. (1) arrives late to class, never looks at homework, doesn't answer students' questions.
   (possible answer: gives many tests)
   (2) Answers will vary.
   (3) Answers will vary.
   (4) Answers will vary.
   (5) Answers will vary.
   (6) doing housework, owning a dog, exploring space, wearing new clothes

c. Answers will vary.

V. LANGUAGE FOCUS

Simple Past Tense of *To Be*

1. Sentence Completion

b. were	e. were	h. wasn't	k. was
c. was	f. weren't	i. were	l. wasn't
d. was	g. was	j. were	m. were

2. Sentence Building

a. Early people were probably hungry much of the time.
b. It wasn't easy to communicate without words.
c. The first spoken words were probably used for basic things.
d. The first writing was picture writing.
e. Egyptian picture writing was one of the earliest writing systems.
f. ⌓ was the sign for the sound *t*.
g. The English weren't the first people to use an alphabet.

Simple Past Tense of Regular Verbs

1. List Completion

Basic Verb: add to list: point, communicate, show, develop, reply, originate, change

Simple Past: add to list: rubbed, wanted, simplified, named, touched, planned, happened, enjoyed, demonstrated

2. Recognizing Subjects and Verbs

a. Early humans/plural/used

b. They/plural/pointed

c. writing/singular/developed

d. People/plural/invented

e. alphabet/singular/changed

f. Chinese/plural/simplified

The form of the simple past tense verb does not change for singular or plural.

Simple Past Tense of Irregular Verbs

1. Sentence Completion

(1) spoke

(2) was

(3) needed

(4) invented

(5) began

(6) made

(7) had

(8) were

(9) took

(10) was

2. Sentence Composing Answers will vary.

3. Controlled Writing

I didn't talk when I was very young. But I communicated. I made sounds in my throat. I used a lot of sign language. I pointed to things that I wanted. I soon developed ideas. Then I began to talk. I made simple sounds. I took words from my parents. I named things, and I invented words. This is how I learned to talk.

Simple Past Tense Negative Forms

1. Sentence Composing Answers will vary.

2. Sentence Rewriting Answers will vary.

Article Use

Sentence Completion

a. (1) $\varnothing$

(2) $\varnothing$

(3) the

(4) a

(5) an

(6) a

(7) the

(8) $\varnothing$

(9) $\varnothing$

(10) $\varnothing$

(11) $\varnothing$

(12) the

(13) $\varnothing$

(14) the

(15) the

b. As a young <u>man</u>

go to <u>college</u> ($\varnothing$)

for eight <u>years</u> ($\varnothing$)

<u>the subject</u>

<u>books</u> ($\varnothing$)

<u>children</u> ($\varnothing$)

<u>behavior</u> ($\varnothing$)

The books all <u>the children</u>

<u>the</u> most popular <u>schoolbooks</u>

<u>the country</u>

VI. THE COMPOSING PROCESS

1. Sentence Combining to Form a Paragraph

Our English vocabulary has many words from other languages. Many English words originated in German. These are short, basic words. Many English words also come from Latin. These are long words for communicating invisible things such as ideas and emotions. Other words in English come from French. These French words relate to fashion, cooking, and the arts. American English also uses words from many immigrant languages. For example, *boss* and *cookie* are Dutch words. *Canyon*, *cigar*, and *cocoa* are Spanish words. American English owes a lot to many different languages.

2. Developing A Unified Paragraph with Details Answers will vary.

3. Sequencing Details in a Paragraph

Main Idea = e = Sentence 1

  2. d. "First of all," signal for beginning detail

  3. f. repetition of word *German*

  4. g. signal of time *then...in 1066*

  5. i. repetition of word *French*

  6. c. 1200 to 1500 time signal—*Latin*

  7. a. repetition of word *Latin*

  8. b. signal *also* for addition

  9. h. signal *finally* for a last item

Questions

(1) The topic is the development of English through many different languages.

(2) First of all, also, then, finally

(3) Two sentences for each language

(4) also

VII. ADDITIONAL READING

Reading Comprehension

1. Summarizing Through Sentence Completion (sample responses)

  (1) all speak different languages

  (2) the descendants

  (3) a city

  (4) a tower

  (5) the same language

  (6) a tower to the sky

  (7) angry at them

  (8) proud

  (9) confused all their languages

  (10) speak and communicate

  (11) a confusion of voices and tongues

Vocabulary

Expanding Vocabulary

a. (1) (3)

b. (2) (4)

c. (3) (5)

d. (2) (3) (5)

e. (2) (4) (5)

f. (1) (4)

g. (2) (3)

h. (2) (3) (5)

Chapter Five: Language for Living

I. PREREADING

Vocabulary in Context

(1) send

(2) necessary

(3) carry

(4) very surprised

(5) useful

(6) simple

(7) mainly

(8) orders

(9) ask for

(10) able to be heard

(11) mix

(12) is reduced

II. READING COMPREHENSION

1. Understanding the Text

a. (2)

b. (2)

c. (3)

d. (3)

e. the hearing impaired; people who communicate essential ideas quickly and secretively

f. also

g. people

h. common objects; various animals. Signal expression: such as

i. gestures combine with dance movements to communicate

j. signal communication

k. (3)

l. to show that people are familiar with Morse Code

m. (2)

n. (3)

o. (3)

p. (1)

q. Furthermore

r. (2)

2. Answering Information Questions

a. e.g., flags, lights, hand signals

b. e.g., to communicate information, to transmit secret ideas

c. so the other team won't know their plays

d. e.g., car horn, foghorn

e. e.g., car signal lights, ship flags

f. by dots and dashes

g. flashing lights

III. THE READING PROCESS

Scanning for Specific Information

b. whistle blowing; hand held up: Para. 1, sentence 5

c. violent swordplay: Para. 1, last sentence

d. animal movements: Para. 3, sentence 4

e. to communicate military orders: Para. 4, sentence 3

f. naval semaphoring: Para. 4, sentence 6

g. 5 miles; 2 miles: Para. 6, sentences 2 and 3

h. radio, radio telephone, computer: Para. 7, sentence 3

IV. VOCABULARY

1. New Words

a. *EXPANDING VOCABULARY*

(1) c   (3) c   (5) b   (7) a

(2) a   (4) c   (6) c

2. Word Families: Adjectives and Adverb Use

a. *CORRECT WORD FORM*

(1) particularly   (5) basically

(2) certain   (6) powerful

(3) different   (7) Violent

(4) essential

V. LANGUAGE FOCUS

Present Continuous Tense

1. Sentence Completion

a. are communicating   f. are moving

b. are using   g. are studying

c. isn't using   h. are looking

d–e. is trying/is sailing

2. Sentence Building (sample responses)

a. You are learning English this term.

b. The soldier is tapping out Morse Code.

c. He is trying to communicate military information.

d. Currently, Chinese children are learning a simplified form of Chinese.

e. The Indonesian dancer isn't performing Tai Chi Chuan.

f. One of my friends is studying English with me.

g. We are practicing present continuous tense.

h. Many foreign students are studying English in England.

i. Many American students are learning Spanish.

3. Controlled Writing

This soldier is sitting in a special signaling room at an army base (omit *all over the country*). He is tapping out military information in Morse code on a radio. He is also listening to a signal from his receiver on a special headset. This soldier is paying careful attention while he is sending and receiving Morse Code.

Sentence Patterns with "Because"

1. Sentence Combining

a. A traffic controller holds up his or her hand because he or she wants traffic to stop.

b. Because there are so many languages in the world, it is difficult for people from different lands to communicate.

c. Baseball coaches use secret signals because they do not want rival teams to understand their instructions

d. I listen to English TV programs because I want to have better English pronunciation.

e. The river is very polluted because there are many factories near it.

f. Scientists should study English because most scientific writing is produced in English.

g. Archeology is an interesting profession because it takes you to many different lands.

2. Sentence Expansion Answers will vary.

Plural Possessives

1. Forming Plural Possessives

b. immigrants' difficulties	e. scientists' interests
c. men's suits	f. parents' love
d. students' work	g. children's toys

2. Sentence Rewriting

(a) a. My neighbors' children	d. all citizens' rights
b. My instructors' assignments	e. Teachers' opinions
c. the students' paragraphs	f. women's communication problems
(b) a. children are	d. not applicable—possessive is object
b. assignments are	e. opinions were
c. paragraphs were	f. not applicable—possessive is object

3. Proofreading

a. C	e. students'
b. writer's	f. parents'
c. Children's	g. Nations'
d. professors'	h. dancer's

VI. THE COMPOSING PROCESS

1. Sentence Combining to Form a Paragraph (sample response)

People have always dreamed of a single international language. People from different countries always want to trade with each other and have cultural exchanges. But this is difficult because people speak many different languages. Currently, many people are creating artificial international languages. Esperanto is one of these languages. Esperanto uses many words from Romance languages such as Spanish, Italian, and French in its vocabulary. Volapuk is another artificial language. Its vocabulary is primarily German and Slavic. Esperanto and Volapuk do not use words from Chinese, Korean, or other Asian languages. Other world languages do not employ words. They use signs. For example, they use musical notes, numbers, or computer codes. A sign language might be easy to learn because it would have a small basic vocabulary. But could we write poetry in a language with only a few basic signs?

VII. ADDITIONAL READING

Reading Comprehension

Understanding the Text

a. but

b. reason

c. (2)

d. (4)

e. that he understood what a book was saying

f. (4) (Note different use of *free* in Sentence 4 to mean leisure time.)

g. (3) Therefore

h. (1)

i. (1)

Vocabulary

2. Expanding Vocabulary. Answers will vary.

Chapter Six: **Animal Tales**

I.   PREREADING

Vocabulary in Context

1. (a) animals of different kinds
   (b) discovered
2. (a) difficulties
   (b) essential
3. (a) a little bit
   (b) able to be heard

4. (a) group
   (b) suggest
5. (a) tests
   (b) make better
   (c) capability
6. (a) said
   (b) answer

II. READING

Summary Completion.

(1) copy
(2) different sounds
(3) able to be heard
(4) recorded
(5) activities

(6) ultrasound
(7) repeated
(8) language ability
(9) signs
(10) human

Reading Comprehension

1. Understanding the Text

a. (1) F   (2) F   (3) T   (4) F   (5) T   (6) F   (7) T

b. (1) b   (2) b   (3) a   (4) c   (5) c   (6) b   (7) c

    (8) b   (9) c   (10) a   (11) c   (12) b   (13) c   (14) c

    (15) b   (16) c

c. (1) 0   (2) 0   (3) F   (4) 0   (5) F   (6) 0   (7) F

    (8) F   (9) 0   (10) F

2. Answering Information Questions (sample responses)

a. Hoover's special ability was copying the human voice.

b. Birds sing to communicate to other birds of their species.

c. A spectrograph is an instrument used to record bird song.

d. Kinglet birds cluster on a branch at night to keep warm.

e. Elephants use ultrasound to tell other elephants about the weather.

f. Echolocation helps bats and birds find food.

g. Dr. Terrace was trying to see if apes could use human language. His experiment was not successful.

h. Kanzi communicates on a computer.

III. THE READING PROCESS

Skimming for Main Ideas

a. (3)

b. (2)

c. The main idea is that birds sing to communicate messages to each other.

d. (3)

e. They discuss different kinds of inaudible communication systems in animals. Paragraph (5) topic: ultrasound; Paragraph (6) topic: echolocation.

f. Topic: animal communication in contrast to human communication. Main idea: Animals cannot communicate ideas the way human beings can.

g. (3)

h. (2)

IV. VOCABULARY

1. New Words EXPANDING VOCABULARY

a. detect; slightly; indicate

b. cluster; ability; respond

c. claim; creatures; experiments; improve

d. audible; vital; obstacle

2. Word Families

a. communicate   e. create   i. description
b. conclusion   f. detect   j. conversation
c. indicates   g. information
d. observation   h. fascinates

V. LANGUAGE FOCUS

Modals + Base Form of Verbs

1. Sentence Completion Answers will vary.

Verbs + Infinitives

1. Answering Questions with Infinitives. (sample responses)

a. Hoover learned to copy the human voice.

b. I prefer to see lions, tigers, and bears.

c. I have to complete biology for graduation.

d. Echolocation helps bats find food.

e. Dr. Terrace wanted to discover if Nim could learn human language.

f. Kanzi likes to play in his tree house.

2. Sentence Composing Answers will vary.

Changing the Direction of a Thought: The Use of "But"

1. Sentence Rewriting

a. Human speech is probably about one million years old, but writing is much newer.

b. The earliest writing was picture writing. But today most languages use an alphabet.

c. There are thousands of languages in the world, but the United Nations uses only two official languages.

d. There is no world language today, but there may be one in the future.

e. Nim learned signs for words, but he never created new words himself.

f. Children's sentences grow longer all the time, but Nim's sentences had three words at most.

g. The babies of mammals are born alive, but bird babies are born from eggs.

h. Nim was not a human child, but he attended nursery school with special teachers.

2. Sentence Expansion (sample responses)

a. American English writing is very similar to British English writing, but the pronunciation is very different.

b. I would like to live in Paris, but the rents are too expensive.

c. A pocket dictionary doesn't have every word, but it's easy to carry to school.

d. Dogs can be trained to do many tricks, but rabbits can't.

e. I would like to go bowling, but I must study this evening.

f. I would like to visit Egypt, but it is too far away.

g. English articles are simple, but English verbs are difficult.

h. I am not learning French now, but I am studying English intensively.

i. There are many planets in our solar system, but there is only one sun.

j. I would like to see a movie tonight, but I have to visit my sister.

Series of Parallel Items

1. Sentence Combining

b. Immigrants brought their native cultures, customs, and languages to the United States.

c. Some British words differ from American words in spelling, pronunciation, and usage.

d. The big *Webster's Dictionary* would be an interesting, valuable, and useful gift for a friend.

e. Nim Chimpsky liked to look at magazines, play with pencils, and learn new signs.

f. Archeologists find toys, pots, and gold in the earth.

g. The sun, moon, and planets are part of our universe.

h. A map shows us the location of rivers, seas, and oceans.

i. Astronauts need special suits, shoes, and food for space travel.

j. Most people in England, Australia, and Canada speak English.

k. With a world language, people could communicate, trade, and travel easily.

2. Sentence Composing Answers will vary.

VI. THE COMPOSING PROCESS

1. Sentence Combining to Form a Paragraph (sample response)

Kanzi is a four-year-old pygmy chimpanzee. He lives at the Language Research Center in Atlanta, Georgia. Kanzi has a large, grassy area to roam around there. There is a tree house, a trailer, and a special path to the woods for Kanzi. Kanzi likes to play like a human child. He has the motor skills, the interests, and the spirit of a seven- or eight-year-old boy. Kanzi has eight teachers. They show him signs on a computer keyboard. Kanzi also watches signs on television. There is a special television program for the research animals. It shows a giant bunny. The bunny talks to the animals, demonstrates certain signs for them, and entertains them. But the show is not just for fun. It is a pleasant way to teach Kanzi English.

2. Sequencing Ideas in a Paragraph

c. main idea	g.
a.	e. (detail of g)
h. (schoolroom follows school)	d. (further detail of learning signs)
f. (gives details of "bright and colorful")	b. conclusion

3. Composing a Paragraph (sample response)

A: main idea: It would be fun to be a student in Ms. Jones's class.

   classroom and equipment: comfortable chairs and tables

   Large windows for light and air

   teacher: interested in children's feelings

        gives treat for good work

        has a good sense of honor

   activities: reading aloud

        working in groups

B: main idea: Mr. Smith's class needs a lot of improvement

　　　　　　classroom and equipment: few books/maps/magazines
　　　　　　　　　　　　　　room looks dull
　　　　　teacher: impatient and uninterested in children
　　　　　　　　　　never reads aloud
　　　　　　　　　　comes late to class
　　　　activities: boring drills work alone
　　　　　　　　　children always work alone
　　　　　　　　　children never write their own stories

VII. ADDITIONAL READING

Reading Comprehension

a. (1) F　　　　(3) T　　　　(5) T　　　　(7) F　　　　(9) T
　(2) F　　　　(4) F　　　　(6) F　　　　(8) F　　　　(10) F

Vocabulary

2. Word Families

Negative Prefix dis.

　　1. discontent　　　　　5. disappearance
　　2. dislike　　　　　　 6. disappear
　　3. disagree　　　　　　7. disability
　　4. disagreement

UNIT III: OUR SOCIAL WORLD

CHAPTER SEVEN: Women of the American Past

I. PREREADING

Strip Story

　　Mary Ludwig was a hero of the Battle of Monmouth in the American Revolutionary War. She was married to John Hayes, who was a gunner in the American Revolutionary army. During the hard war years of 1777 and 1778, Mary joined her husband in the army camp at Valley Forge. At camp she was useful in washing clothes, cooking, and keeping the camp clean. Then, on June 28, 1778, the American army marched out to fight the British army in the Battle of Monmouth. The heat was so great that day that the soldiers became terribly thirsty. So Mary Ludwig followed the soldiers into battle with a pitcher of water for them to drink. Each time the pitcher was emptied, Mary would run back to a nearby stream to fill it. That's why the soldiers gave her the nickname "Molly Pitcher." Suddenly, during the battle Molly's husband fainted from heatstroke. Molly dropped her pitcher and took over her husband's cannon. She fired round after round of shot at the British with it. Finally, the battle was over and the Americans had won. Much of the credit for this victory belongs to Molly Pitcher, a brave and quick-thinking American woman.

Vocabulary in Context

2. regions   5. mental attitude   8. tired
3. worked hard   6. lived through   9. respect
4. bravery   7. favorable   10. add value

II. READING

Summary Completion

(1) important   (6) life   (11) herself
(2) of   (7) the   (12) as
(3) women   (8) American   (13) When
(4) and   (9) safety
(5) helped   (10) was

Reading Comprehension

1. Understanding the Text

a. (1) T   (4) F   (7) N.I.
   (2) T   (5) F   (8) T
   (3) N.I.   (6) T   (9) F

b. (1) a. Native American women
     b. Black women
     c. Pioneer women
     d. Immigrant women

  (2) b
  (3) b
  (4) sample response: She couldn't reveal her plans because the slave owners might find out and try to keep her.

  (5) b   (7) a   (9) c   (11) b
  (6) c   (8) b   (10) a   (12) a

2. Answering Information Questions (sample responses)

a. While Harriet Tubman worked on the plantation, she dreamed about being free.

b. As Harriet Tubman walked North to freedom, she felt hungry, lonely, and frightened.

c. In Pennsylvania, Harriet Tubman joined a secret organization called the Underground Railroad.

d. John Brown said that Harriet Tubman was one of the best and bravest persons he knew.

e. Harriet Tubman pretended to read a book.

f. Harriet Tubman was a laundress, a nurse, and a spy during the Civil War.

g. After the Civil War the slaves became free.

h. People honored Harriet Tubman by calling her "the Moses of her people."

III. THE READING PROCESS

Recognizing Signals of Contrast

a. Signals of contrast: unlike, but, in contrast, nevertheless /

<u>Harriet Beecher Stowe</u>	<u>Harriet Tubman</u>
white	black
free	slave
well-educated	no formal education
professional family background	parents slaves
New England writer	Southern field worker

b. Signals in contrast: in contrast to / but / however / Although

(1) F   (2) T   (3) T   (4) F   (5) F

IV. VOCABULARY

1. New Words

a. *EXPANDING VOCABULARY*

(1) labor   (5) discipline   (9) honor
(2) role   (6) courage   (10) territory
(3) enrich   (7) spirit   (11) successful
(4) weary   (8) survive

b. *USING VOCABULARY* Answers will vary.

2. Word Families

a. (1) dishonorable   (4) dishonor
   (2) honest   (5) honor
   (3) honestly

b. (1) Laboring   (4) laborers
   (2) labored   (5) labor unions
   (3) child labor

V. LANGUAGE FOCUS

Past Continuous Tense

1. Recognizing Past Continuous Tense

was falling / were carrying / were hanging / were moving / was blowing / was blinding

2. Sentence Completion Answers will vary.

Use of Past Continuous Tense and Simple Past Tense

1. Recognizing Past Continuous and Simple Past Tense

<u>was sitting</u> / <u>were watching</u> / appeared / held / pointed / fired / fell / <u>was bleeding</u> / rushed / tried / decided / <u>were carrying</u> / arrived / tried / was / died

2. Paragraph Completion

(1) was hiding   (5) went   (9) took

(2) appeared   (6) was walking   (10) shot
(3) knew   (7) was shouting   (11) died
(4) was hiding   (8) didn't wait

Complex Sentences with *When* and *While*

1. Identifying Dependent Clauses
a. While I was studying last night
b. when they first arrive in their new country
c. while they are studying
d. when the television set is on
e. When my daughter first read about Harriet Tubman
f. while others were doing grammar exercises

2. Sentence Completion with *When* and *While*
a. (2)   c. (2)   e. (1)   g. (1)
b. (3)   d. (1)   f. (3)   h. (1)

3. Sentence Combining
a. When we were in Washington, D.C., we went to the Lincoln exhibits at Ford's Theater.
b. When we got there, the place wasn't open yet.
c. While we were waiting for it to open, we read about the exhibits in our guidebook.
d. While we were reading, several other people arrived.
e. When the doors finally opened, we bought tickets and walked to the first exhibit.
f. While we were looking at photographs of Lincoln, a guide came in and gave us some information about Lincoln's life.
g. It is always interesting to visit historic places when you travel to different areas of the country.

Comparison Of Adjectives

1. List Completion

Simple	Comparative
—	earlier
—	longer
—	happier
—	larger
healthy	—
—	more expensive
popular	—
—	more ambitious
—	more fragile
strange	—

—	busier
—	more
few	—

2. Sentence Composing Answers will vary.

Superlative Form of Adjectives

1. List Completion

Superlative

the brightest	the most comfortable	the quietest
the most practical	the most difficult	the greatest
the bravest	the most serious	the most talkative
the most crowded	the coldest	the best
the driest	the most creative	

2. Sentence Building (sample responses)

a. The sun is the brightest object in the sky.

b. Air pollution is one of the most serious problems in our cities.

c. Carlos is the best student in my English class.

d. Math is the most difficult subject of all my courses.

e. The public library is the quietest place in my neighborhood.

f. The Statue of Liberty is one of the most famous monuments in the world.

g. The sofa is the most expensive piece of furniture in my apartment.

h. New York is the most crowded city in the United States.

i. The North and South Poles are the coldest areas in the world.

j. The vacuum cleaner is the most practical appliance in my house.

k. The Sahara Desert is one of the driest places in the world.

3. Paragraph Completion

(1) *most famous*	(5) unhappy	(9) simple
(2) brighter	(6) shyer	(10) more difficult
(3) most interested	(7) more unfriendly	(11) most respected
(4) more unusual	(8) most beautiful	(12) most popular

VI. THE COMPOSING PROCESS

1. Sentence Combining to Form a Paragraph (sample response)

   My grandmother was short and fragile-looking, but she was proud of her appearance. She was a seamstress; she sewed dresses for other people. There was a sewing machine in our house. My grandmother was at the sewing machine every day. She got a lot of work because she sewed very fast and neatly and had excellent skills. She took care of the housework and took care of me all day when I was small because both my parents worked. She played interesting games with me after the housework was finished. She made dolls for me from pieces of material. I will always have beautiful memories of my grandmother.

2. Developing a Paragraph of Contrast

a. (1) and   (4) however,

(2) In contrast,   (5) also
(3) While   (6) Although

b. Number each sentence. There are eight sentences.
   A-B sentences are sentences 1 and 8.
   A sentences are 2, 4, 5.
   B sentences are 3, 6, 7.
c. (1) Sentence 1
   (2) full-time housewives and women who work outside the home
   (3) Sentences 2, 3, 4, 5, 6
   (4) Sentence 7
   (5) In contrast
   (6) Sentences 8, 9, 10, 11, 12, 13

VII. ADDITIONAL READING

Reading Comprehension

Understanding the Text

a. (1) F   (4) F   (7) N.I.
   (2) T   (5) T   (8) F
   (3) T   (6) F   (9) N.I.

b. (1) b   (4) c   (7) c   (10) a
   (2) a   (5) b   (8) c   (11) c
   (3) b   (6) a   (9) a   (12) b

Vocabulary

Word Families

a. vision   e. contradict   i. conclusion
b. conductor   f. prescription   j. Prenatal
c. supervisor   g. infinite   k. inspection
d. promotion   h. pressure   l. particular

Chapter Eight: Men and Woman: Relationships Old and New

I.   PREREADING

Vocabulary in Context

2. control   7. advantage
3. individual   8. faithfulness
4. system   9. working with others
5. increase the power   10. step-by-step
6. good name   11. appropriate

II.   READING

Summary Completion

(1) romantic love
(2) falling in love
(3) a big wedding
(4) best basis
(5) divorce rate

(6) become independent
(7) romantic love
(8) families
(9) good marriage
(10) with the parents

Reading Comprehension

1. Understanding the Text

a. (1) T   (2) F   (3) T   (4) T   (5) F

b. (1) a   (4) a   (7) c   (10) a   (13) c
   (2) b   (5) b   (8) c   (11) c   (14) a
   (3) c   (6) c   (9) b   (12) b

2. Answering Information Questions (sample responses)

a. Married couples in the United States generally live apart from their relatives.

b. In most societies, marriage strengthens the main family line by bringing new daughters-in-law into the main family.

c. The members of an ideal Indian family include the parents, the oldest son, and his wife and children.

d. The Roys are afraid Romesh might choose his own wife.

e. Before the wedding, Romesh and his bride's family will exchange gifts.

f. Romesh's wife will choose a bride for her son when he is grown.

III. THE READING PROCESS

Paraphrasing

(1) a and d   (2) b and c   (3) c and d   (4) b and d   (5) a and c

IV. VOCABULARY

1. New Words

a. *CHOOSING SYNONYMS*

1. conquer = c
2. personal = f
3. strengthen = i
4. suitable = a

5. reputation = h
6. arrangement = m
7. benefit = d
8. loyalty = j

9. cooperation = k
10. gradually = b
11. romantic = e

b. *USING VOCABULARY*

(1) grow old/become proficient in English/learn to walk
(2) strong/strongly/strength
(3) c
(4) variety of schools/museums/public transportation/job opportunities/personal freedom
(5) playing tennis/eating proper foods/taking dance lessons
(6) a, d

2. Word Families

a. management, development, government, agreement

    b. unkindness, unhappiness

    c. loneliness, neatness

    d. honesty, possibility

    e. minority

    f. leadership, citizenship, membership

    g. Intelligent, independence

V. LANGUAGE FOCUS

Simple Present Tense Conditionals

1. Sentence Completion (sample responses)

    a. she will be happy.

    b. she will be obedient.

    c. they may not get their homework done.

    d. you should try to guess it from the context of the sentence.

    e. I will take him to the Empire State Building.

    f. they will need a baby-sitter.

2. Sentence Building Answers will vary.

3. Sentence Composing Answers will vary.

Expressing Conditions Contrary to Fact

1. Sentence Completion

a. (2)	c. (2)	e. (2)	g. (2)	i. (3)
b. (3)	d. (1)	f. (1)	h. (1)	j. (2)

2. Sentence Composing Answers will vary.

3. Sentence Completion Answers will vary.

VI. THE COMPOSING PROCESS

1. Sentence Combining to Form a Paragraph (sample response)

    The dowry is a common kind of marriage gift in Greece. Dowries began in ancient times, many centuries ago. The dowry was a gift of money or land from the bride's parents to their son-in-law. At that time a wife didn't work outside the home. But she was expected to add to her husband's wealth. She was also expected to take care of her home and her children. But the current government of Greece wants to do away with dowries. The government says that dowries aren't necessary because some women work outside the home and earn as much as men do. Also, poor families can't afford to give dowries to all their daughters. Finally, to some women dowries are like buying a husband. A man may marry a woman because she has money, not because he loves her. Dowries present an interesting and difficult question in parts of Europe and Asia.

2. Developing a Paragraph

G / G / S / S / S / S / G / S / G / S / G / G

3. Developing a General Idea with Specific Details

a. (1) It gives a reason.

(2) It contradicts.

(3) however

(4) It gives an example.

(5) They give specific details.

(6) It gives a general reason for the main idea.

The pattern of this paragraph might be stated as follows:

Sentences 1 and 2 are introductory. Sentence 3 states an overall main idea or assertion. Sentence 4 states the first subtopic, or main idea of this paragraph. Sentences 5 and 6 give specific details of the subtopic.

VII. ADDITIONAL READING

Reading Comprehension

1. Understanding the Text

1. a. (1)	e. (2)	i. (2)
b. (2)	f. (2)	j. (3)
c. (2)	g. (1)	k. (2)
d. (1)	h. (1)	

2. Paraphrasing

(1) a, b   (2) b, c   (3) b, d   (4) b, c   (5) b, d

Vocabulary

2. Using Vocabulary

(1) typical   (7) pressure

(2) involve   (8) leisure

(3) promotion   (9) influenced

(4) responsibilities   (10) goals

(5) economic   (11) industry

(6) occupations

Chapter Nine: Reaching Out

I. PREREADING

Vocabulary in Context

1. b	4. a	7. b	10. a
2. a	5. b	8. c	11. c
3. a	6. c	9. b	12. a

II. READING

Plot Summary (sample responses)

(1) elderly (unmarried) sisters

(2) a teenager and his family

(3) much money

(4) do chores

(5) they are stingy

(6) taking in foster children

(7) her home

(8) to the poorhouse

(9) for Love

(10) deliver the newspaper to her

(11) he is taking a job out-of-town

(12) a letter

(13) to visit her in the poorhouse

(14) a lock of hair

(15) to keep it in his drawer

Reading Comprehension

1. Understanding the Text

a. (2)

b. (3)

c. (2)

d. (1)

e. (3)

f. (1)

g. "I suppose they can't afford better."

h. (1)

i. (3)

j. (2)

k. (2)

l. (3)

m. (2) delivers the newspaper to her every day

(3) wonders if she got the paper, wanted it, and what she thought

(4) goes to visit her in the poorhouse; accepts her gift

(5) keeps her lock of hair

n. (2)

o. (1) and (2)

2. Answering Information Questions (sample responses)

a. There was not enough to eat. The towels were small and worn, the soap was tiny, and there was never enough hot water. Also, there was only gaslight to read by, and the chairs were uncomfortable.

b. He was surprised because Love never left her house except to go to a funeral.

c. He stopped waving to Love because he was worried about what people might think of a teenager waving to an old woman in the poorhouse.

d. He was disappointed because he thought the letter would be from his former girlfriend.

e. The room was very small. There was no rug, no curtain, just a faded window shade, an iron bed, and a small table.

f. The boy suddenly realized that Love was lame or feeble and that she was old.

III. THE READING PROCESS

Descriptive Language

b. Gray signifies something colorless; it means old or unhealthy looking.

c. She was expressing disapproval at his remark.

d. This apple is worthless. It's rotten—not good to eat.

e. Biting the lip expresses difficulty in answering the question; it may also express worry.

f. His mouth dropped open in an expression of surprise.

g. Shrugging the shoulders means not knowing the answer to a question or hesitation in expressing an answer.

h. Her glittering, flashing eyes show either her excitement and joy at seeing the boy, or her sadness about her situation—her tears.

i. She was trembling from nervousness and excitement at facing the boy and wanting to give him something. Perhaps she was afraid he would reject her gift. Perhaps it was a sign of infirmity in old age.

IV. VOCABULARY

1. New Words

a. *EXPANDING VOCABULARY*

(1) with feeling; in a compassionate way; with understanding

(2) laughable; absurd; silly

(3) awkward; ill at ease

(4) understand fully; comprehend; know well

(5) slowly; at an unhurried pace; taking my time

(6) admitted; acknowledged; owned up to

(7) a sudden desire; an abrupt urge; a wish

(8) suited; competent; capable

(9) acceptance; approval; attention

b. *USING VOCABULARY* Answers will vary.

2. Word Families

a. one

b. monotonous

c. bicycle; tricycle

d. quadruped; biped; a hundred-legged insect (really a many-legged insect)

e. A mother with five children would be too busy at home to have a career.

f. five others; a duet

g. 1/4; cent

h. March

i. 10; 100; 1,000; 200; centennial

j. eight; four; three

V. LANGUAGE FOCUS

Complex Sentences with *Before* and *After*

1. Sentence Combining

b. We were living near my aunt's house before we moved next door to my grandparents.

c. My grandmother used to read me a story every night before I went to sleep.

d. After my grandfather retired from his job, he took up gardening.

e. Many older people don't like living alone after their spouses die.

f. Some couples sell their house after their children are out on their own.

g. We were living in our house a while before we made new friends among our neighbors.

h. The house next door was empty a long time after our neighbor moved away.

i. Before a new family bought the house, my children used to play in the empty yard.

j. After my older daughter finishes her homework, she will baby-sit for the neighbors' children.

2. Sentence Building Answers will vary.

3. Sentence Composing Answers will vary.

Adverbs of Manner

1. Sentence Rewriting

b. modestly

c. independently

d. fearfully

e. comfortably

f. respectfully

g. easily

h. cooperatively

2. Sentence Expansion

b. worked hard

c. speak English and Spanish fluently

d. danced awkwardly

e. does his chores cheerfully

f. plays well

g. stopped suddenly

h. enjoy walking leisurely

Punctuation: Quotations

1. Proofreading

I stood still and my mouth dropped open. "You mean Miss Love came out of her house?"

My mother nodded.

"Came over here?"

"Yes," said my mother.

What a surprise! We had never known Miss Love to go out alone except once in a while for a funeral, and never alone.

"After all," said my mother, "her sister was dying."

I thought it over. "What'll she do now?" I said.

My mother shrugged sadly. "Live on there alone, I guess."

VI. THE COMPOSING PROCESS

1. Sentence Combining to Form a Paragraph

Some high school students are enrolled in special courses in the Health Services program. These courses are preparing the students for work with the elderly. These students study biology, sociology, and psychology in regard to aging. These subjects are important because they help the students understand the physical, social, and mental problems of the elderly. Their studies include fieldwork in hospitals and nursing homes. They visit the elderly to talk to them, to listen to them, to read to them, and to do whatever they can to make their lives more pleasant. The patients greatly appreciate having ties with the young students because they are often alone in the world or their families may live far away. For the students, too, it is a satisfying relationship. When someone asked a student in the program about her feelings, she replied sympathetically, "When I see an elderly woman, I see my grandmother." The student continued, "These people need me, and I need them too."

2. Developing a Paragraph

c.

VII. ADDITIONAL READING

Reading Comprehension

1. Understanding the Text

a. (3)

b. (3)

c. (2)

d. (3)

e. (1)

f. (1) T   (2) F   (3) F   (4) T   (5) F   (6) T   (7) F

g. (3)

h. The main idea is that men and women handle conflict differently.

i. (2)

j. (1)

k. (2)

l. Ms. Tannen wrote her book to help men and women learn to communicate better.

2. Signal Expressions

(1) e	(4) d	(7) e	(10) h	(13) c	(16) a
(2) c	(5) a	(8) a	(11) a	(14) g	(17) g
(3) f	(6) b	(9) a	(12) g	(15) b	

A P P E N D I X   A

BASIC TERMINOLOGY FOR ENGLISH-LANGUAGE STUDY

1.   Parts of Speech

Noun: A word that names a person, place, thing, quality, idea, or action.

Peter Rodriguez, girl, country, chair, attention, democracy

Pronoun: A word used in place of or as a substitute for a noun. (See Language Focus in Chapter 2.)

The instructor gave the exam to the students at 9:00 A.M.
He asked *them* to stop writing at 9:35.

Verb: A word that expresses a state of being, feeling, or appearance.

You *seem* ill today.
I *am* nervous about my exam.

A word that expresses physical or mental action.

I *thought* about you yesterday.
My friends *play* soccer very well.

Adjective: A word that describes a noun. Articles (*a, an, the*) and numbers are adjectives.

Many students find English *a difficult* subject.

Adverb: A word that tells how often or in what way verb action is done. (See Language Focus in Chapter 1 for more examples.)

Young people *often* have part-time jobs.
New Yorkers speak *rapidly.*

A word that tells us the degree to which an adjective is true. (See Language Focus in Chapter 9 for more discussion of adverbs.)

My cat is *very* healthy.

Preposition: A word that generally has some meaning of place, direction, time, or connection with a noun. (See Language Focus in Chapter 1 for a list of common prepositions and their use.)

Please put the book *for* John *on* the table *in* the hall.

Conjunction: A word that joins related words, phrases, or clauses of similar form.

And, but, or may connect independent clauses or other kinds of parallel expressions.

Many women work outside the home, *but* they still have household responsibilities.

If, because, when, while, before, after, although begin dependent clauses. These clauses must be connected to independent clauses.

Because you speak French, you may learn Spanish easily.

2.   Phrases

A group of two or more words forming a unit of thought.
Prepositional Phrase: A phrase that begins with a preposition.

The United Nations is located *in New York City.*

Infinitive Phrase: A phrase that begins with *to* and is followed by the basic form of a verb.

Archeologists like *to explore* ancient cities.

3.   Clauses

A group of words with a subject and a complete main verb.
Independent Clause: A group of words that can stand by itself as a complete sentence.

Last week he saw a white tiger at the zoo.

Dependent Clause: A clause that cannot stand by itself as a complete sentence because it begins with such words as *if, because, when, while, before, after, who, which,* or *that.*

It is difficult to live on the moon *because there is no water.* Professor Jones knows *which students will pass the course.*

4.   Punctuation

Period: Closes off a finished thought that can stand by itself as a complete sentence.

I enjoy this class.

Comma: Separates parallel items in a series.

Many words from German, Latin, and French are found in English. Computer science is a new, interesting, and important field of study.

Follows a dependent clause that begins a sentence.

When you have finished your exam, leave your paper on the desk.

Marks off signal words and expressions.

Some languages do not use a Latin alphabet. Russian, for example, uses the Cyrillic alphabet.

Precedes *but, and,* and *or* in a compound sentence.

Weight lifting used to be a sport only for men, but today many women are lifting weights.

Quotation Marks: Surrounds direct speech, that is, the exact words spoken by someone.

> At 12:00 the professor said, "The exam will begin."

5.   Pronoun Chart

	Subject	Object (of verb or preposition)	Possessive	Possessive Adjective (+ noun)	Reflexive
Singular	I	me	mine	my (tradition)	myself
	you	you	yours	your (tradition)	yourself
	he	him	his	his (tradition)	himself
	she	her	hers	her (tradition)	herself
	it	it	—	its (tradition)	itself
Plural	we	us	ours	our (traditions)	ourselves
	you	you	yours	your (traditions)	yourselves
	they	them	theirs	their (traditions)	themselves

6.   Verb Summary

Basic Form: Simple verb, no endings for person or tense.

> *hold   study   speak   write*

Infinitive: to + basic form of verb.

> The movie is going ***to begin*** at noon.

Simple Present: Basic form of verb, except for third person singular, which adds *s*. For habitual or general action.

> Every summer Jean ***visits*** his family in Haiti.
> Both girls and boys ***need*** physical exercise.

Present Continuous: am, is, or *are + ing* form of main verb. For actions that are taking place right now.

Two people *are waiting* to use the telephone.

For actions that suggest continuous activity.

When *I'm studying*, I like peace and quiet.

Simple Past: Basic form of verb + *ed*, or irregular form. For actions that were completed in the past.

Yesterday I *finished* my work by dinner time.
Traffic *was* slow because a car *broke* down in the middle of the highway.

Past Continuous: was or *were* + *ing* form of main verb. For continuous action in the past.

The class *was practicing* verb forms all last week.

For interrupted past actions, usually with another clause in the simple past.

Our team *was playing* well until our best batter injured his arm.

7.   **Modals + Basic Form of Verbs.**   A modal is a helping part of a verb. Modals tell about certain conditions related to the main verb and are used to express ability, possibility, probability, or advisability. The main verb following a modal is always in the basic form. (See Language Focus in Chapter 6 for a detailed discussion of modals.)
     Study the following explanations and examples of some common modals.

To show present ability or possibility.

We *can* go to the library after class.

To show past ability or possibility less certain than *can*.

We *could* go to the library after class if we eat lunch now.

To show present or future possibility and permission.

Students *may* take Monday off as a holiday.

To show possibility less certain than *may.*

Stanford University *might* expand its Asian history classes.

To show necessity or strong probability.

He *must* attend the lecture today to take notes.

To show obligation, advisability, or expectation.

Both teachers and students *should* come to class prepared.

To show future certainty or probability.

I *will* pass the test.
If you went to class, you *would* know about the quiz.

8. Useful Signal Expressions

Thought Relationship	Signals Marking Independent Clauses	Signals Marking Dependent Clauses
Time	now later then next afterward	before after when while
Sequence	first second . . . finally	
Addition of items	in addition moreover also too and (connector)	
Addition of description (adjective clause)		who which/that
Contrast	however nevertheless in contrast on the other hand but (connector)	though though
Reason		because since
Result	therefore as a result thus consequently so (connector)	
Condition		if
Example	for example for instance such as (to introduce noun examples)	

Commonly Used Irregular Verbs

Basic Form	Simple Past	Past Participle	Basic Form	Simple Past	Past Participle
arise	arose	arisen	forget	forgot	forgotten
awake	awoke	awoken	freeze	froze	frozen
be	was	been	get	got	gotten
beat	beat	beaten	give	gave	given
become	became	become	go	went	gone
begin	began	begun	grow	grew	grown
bend	bent	bent	have	had	had
bet	bet	bet	hear	heard	heard
bite	bit	bitten	hide	hid	hidden
bleed	bled	bled	hit	hit	hit
blow	blew	blown	hold	held	held
break	broke	broken	hurt	hurt	hurt
bring	brought	brought	keep	kept	kept
build	built	built	kneel	knelt, kneeled	knelt
burst	burst	burst			
buy	bought	bought	know	knew	known
cast	cast	cast	lay	laid	laid
catch	caught	caught	lead	led	led
choose	chose	chosen	leap	leaped, leapt	leapt
come	came	come			
cost	cost	cost	leave	left	left
deal	dealt	dealt	lend	lent	lent
dig	dug	dug	let	let	let
do	did	done	lie		
draw	drew	drawn	(to recline)	lay	lain
dream	dreamed	dreamt	(to tell a	lied	lied
drink	drank	drunk	falsehood)		
drive	drove	driven	light	lit, lighted	lit
eat	ate	eaten	lose	lost	lost
fall	fell	fallen	make	made	made
feed	fed	fed	mean	meant	meant
feel	felt	felt	met	met	met
fight	fought	fought	pay	paid	paid
find	found	found	put	put	put
flee	fled	fled	quit	quit	quit
fly	flew	flown	read	read	read
forbid	forbade	forbidden		(pronounced "red")	

Basic Form	Simple Past	Past Participle	Basic Form	Simple Past	Past Participle
ride	rode	ridden	stand	stood	stood
ring	rang	rung	steal	stole	stolen
rise	rose	risen	stick	stuck	stuck
run	ran	run	sting	stung	stung
say	said	said	stink	stank	stunk
see	saw	seen	strike	struck	struck
seek	sought	sought	swear	swore	sworn
sell	sold	sold	sweep	swept	swept
send	sent	sent	swim	swam	swum
set	set	set	swing	swung	swung
shake	shook	shaken	take	took	taken
shoot	shot	shot	teach	taught	taught
shrink	shrank, shrunk	shrunk	tear	tore	torn
			tell	told	told
shut	shut	shut	think	thought	thought
sing	sang	sung	throw	threw	thrown
sink	sank, sunk	sunk	understand	understood	understood
sit	sat	sat	wake	woke, waked	woken
sleep	slept	slept	wear	wore	worn
slide	slid	slid	weave	wove	woven
speak	spoke	spoken	weep	wept	wept
speed	sped	sped	win	won	won
spend	spent	spent	wind	wound	wound
spin	spun	spun	withdraw	withdrew	withdrawn
spit	spit, spat	spat	write	wrote	written
split	split	split			

PARAGRAPH CORRECTION SYMBOLS

ap.	apostrophe error (*Tony's parents are going to the Far East.*)
cap.	capitalization (*A visit to the brooklyn botanical gardens is a delightful experience.*)
caret ∧	something left out (*My neighbor was walking ∧ dog last night at 10:00.*)
frag.	fragment; incomplete sentence; dependent clause used as a sentence (*For example.; Many college students holding part-time jobs.; Although I like my neighborhood.*)
omit ℓ	(*I received the ℓ good instruction in English at the University of California.*)
⌷	paragraph; begin new paragraph for a new topic.
pl.	plural error; disagreement in number between plural nouns and related words (*There are many good reason for continuing your education.; Many students at our college want to become accountant.*)
punct.	punctuation error: comma or semicolon incorrectly used (*Because, I have to work part-time, I can't study too much.; Although it's raining; the game will go on.*)
RO	run-on sentences: two independent clauses incorrectly joined by a comma (*I only watch the news on TV, everything else is junk.*)
sp.	spelling (*Do your two children have seperete rooms?*)
s-v	subject-verb disagreement (*The world of older people have changed a lot.*)
VF	verb form or tense wrong (*I was lived in Hawaii for two years.*)
WF	wrong form or word: noun-adjective-adverb confusion (*Not having a car is very inconvenience for me.*)
WW	wrong word (*There are many attentive [for attractive] restaurants in most large cities.*)

Ocean

land

Estonia
ia
Byelarus
Czech Republic
Slovakia
Ukraine Moldova
ary Romania
Bosnia
Yugoslavia
Bulgaria
Greece Macedonia
a Turkey

Russia

Kazakhstan

Mongolia

North
Korea

Japan

South
Korea

Georgia
Armenia Uzbekistan
Azerbaijan Turkmenistan

Afghanistan

China

Syria
Lebanon Iraq Iran
Israel Kuwait
Jordan

Pakistan

Nepal Bhutan

Taiwan

Pacific Ocean

Egypt

Saudi Qatar
Arabia
United Arab
Emirates

India

Bangladesh

Myanmar

Laos

Oman

Philippines

Eritrea Yemen
Sudan
Djibouti

Thailand Vietnam
Cambodia

Ethiopia
Somalia
Uganda
Kenya
Rwanda
Burundi
Tanzania

Sri Lanka

Brunei
Malaysia

Indonesia

Papua
New Guinea

Malawi
ambia
Zimbabwe Madagascar
swana Mozambique

Indian Ocean

Australia

Swaziland
Africa Lesotho

New Zealand